To Sarah and Gael.
To Ely, Max, Jacob, and Danny.
To Jeffrey, Jordan, and Matthew.

Contents

PART III THINKING ABOUT LEGAL RESEARCH

PART IV PAPER LEGAL RESEARCH RESOURCES

PART V COMPUTER-ASSISTED LEGAL RESEARCH

Preface

The traditional method of teaching legal research centres on familiarizing students with the sources of research—primary sources (cases, statutes, and regulations) and secondary sources (encylopedias, abridgements, citators, and digests), whether in print or electronic format. The first edition of *Legal Research: Step by Step* (1998) took an innovative approach to teaching research. It explained not only how to use sources, but also how to think about a research problem and solve it by making proper use of the sources. After all, a researcher can know everything there is to know about how to use a statute citator to update the case of *Smith v. Jones*, but be totally flummoxed when asked whether *Smith v. Jones* actually applies to a client's fact situation, and, if it doesn't, to find a case and/or statute that does.

The first edition worked well for teaching legal research, and was enthusiastically received by both instructors and students. However, although thinking through a problem has not changed in the past seven years, the format, extent, and availability of sources has. Computerized sources, both primary and secondary, are now much more widely available and important—and also easier to use—than in 1998. This second edition has been revised to keep pace with research sources (both print and electronic), and to give considerably more information about computerized legal research. The section on legal writing has also been expanded in response to requests from instructors. Apart from being even better, the second edition of *Legal Research* is the same great book as the first edition was.

PART I

Introduction to Legal Research

Don't let anyone tell you that legal research is easy. But, if you enjoy problem solving, legal research can be interesting—even fun.

Legal research often is taught as a series of exercises in using resources— for example, the *Canadian Abridgment* or Quicklaw. However, there's not much point in working with resources if you don't know how to read and understand the basic sources to which the Abridgment or Quicklaw direct you—statutes, regulations, and cases. Nor is there any point in working with resources if you don't know how to identify the issues you have to research.

The purpose of this book is to take you through the research process step by step so that you can

- identify an issue after hearing the story of a client's problem;
- identify and use the right research tools, in both paper and computerized format, to find information about that issue;
- read and understand the basic sources to which the research tools point you; and
- apply the law you find so that you can solve the client's problem.

CHAPTER 1

The Basics of Legal Research

Research is something that lawyers and law clerks are always doing, whether it's strictly "legal" research—that is, finding out the law from statutes and cases—or various other kinds of research, such as

- finding out the name of a person or company your law firm wants to sue;
- finding out whether there are executions against the vendor of real property that your client is purchasing;
- finding out whether there's a security lien under the *Personal Property Security Act* on a chattel your client is purchasing;
- finding out the legal description of real property;
- finding out in what municipality a town or city is located;
- finding an expert witness;
- finding an ordinary witness to an accident or incident; or
- finding out exactly what happened to a client so you know what you have to do to get a remedy for that client.

As a result, the ability to find things out—in other words, to research—is an essential skill for a lawyer or law clerk.

We live in an information age. Information is all around us—in books, magazines, and newspapers and on television and the Internet. The information containing the answers to a lawyer's questions is available somewhere, but you have to know where and how to find it and be able to understand, evaluate, and apply it.

In this chapter, we look at the basics of legal research:

- the purpose and basic steps of legal research;
- categories of law;
- sources of law;
- primary sources versus secondary sources;
- paper sources versus computerized (electronic) sources; and
- what it takes to be a good legal researcher.

THE PURPOSE AND BASIC STEPS OF LEGAL RESEARCH

All research, legal or otherwise, has the same purpose—either to find out something that you don't already know, or to confirm the accuracy of something you know, but about which you are unsure. All research, legal or otherwise, involves the same basic steps whether you are using traditional paper sources or electronic sources:

- identifying the issue to be researched in order to solve a specific problem;
- identifying and using the right research tools to find information about that issue;
- reading and understanding the sources to which the research tools point you; and
- applying the information you find to solve the problem.

In legal research, the something you don't know is the law; therefore, the research steps are a bit more complicated because

- you must be able to identify a *legal issue* after hearing the story of a *client's* problem;
- you must be familiar with and be able to work with specialized *legal research tools and sources*; and
- you must be able to apply the *law* you find so that you can solve the *client's* problem.

A lawyer or law clerk will engage in legal research to learn about the law in order to take action or advise a client how to proceed in a given situation. For example:

- A commercial lawyer researches case law to advise a client whether a contract she entered into is valid and the other party can be forced to carry it out.
- A family lawyer researches statute law to advise a client whether the divorce he got in Mexico is valid so that he can marry again without accidentally committing bigamy.
- A tax lawyer researches statute law and regulations to find out if a client's business expense is deductible for tax purposes.
- A litigation lawyer researches case law to prepare for legal argument in a motion, trial, or appeal.

CATEGORIES OF LAW

substantive law
defines legal rights and obligations; legal rights may be enforced by way of legal proceedings, to which substantive law sets out the defences

procedural law
sets out the procedure that a party must follow to enforce his or her rights in a court proceeding or to defend a proceeding

No lawyer knows all the law all the time. Instead, lawyers know enough law to fit a client's problem into the proper category of law, so that they know where to look to find the answers to their clients' problems. In order to navigate your way through the vast amount of legal information out there, it is important to have some understanding of the categories of law.

Law is categorized among substantive law, procedural law, and the law of evidence. **Substantive law** defines legal rights and obligations. Legal rights may be enforced by way of legal proceedings; substantive law also sets out the defences to such proceedings. **Procedural law** sets out the procedure that a party must follow to enforce his or her rights in a court proceeding or to defend a proceeding. The

law of evidence sets out the manner in which facts are proved in a trial or a proceeding.

Substantive law may be divided between public law and private law. **Public law** governs the relationship between persons (individuals and corporations) and the state, and includes such areas of law as

- municipal law,
- immigration and refugee law,
- environmental law,
- constitutional law,
- criminal law, and
- tax law.

Private law governs the relationship between persons, and includes such areas as

- contracts,
- family law,
- property law,
- real estate,
- torts, and
- wills and estates.

SOURCES OF LAW

Canadian law is made up of a combination of

- statutes passed by either the federal Parliament or provincial legislatures;
- regulations made by the federal or a provincial government pursuant to statutes; and
- decisions made by judges in court proceedings (case law).

The law in all the categories in the previous section is derived from these sources.

PRIMARY VERSUS SECONDARY SOURCES

In legal research we make a distinction between primary sources and secondary sources. **Primary sources** are the actual statutes, regulations, and case decisions that create the law. **Secondary sources** are sources that summarize, discuss, or explain primary sources and include

- legal encyclopedias,
- digests of cases,
- indexes to statutes,
- textbooks, and
- articles.

When you perform legal research, you cannot rely on secondary sources alone. Secondary sources are tools that help you gain an understanding of the law and that, as finding tools, direct you to the primary sources that actually create the law. You must then examine the primary sources you have been referred to—that is, read them and understand what they say.

law of evidence
sets out the manner in which facts are proved in a trial or a proceeding

public law
governs the relationship between persons (individuals and corporations) and the state, and includes such areas of law as municipal law, immigration and refugee law, environmental law, constitutional law, criminal law, and tax law

private law
governs the relationship between persons, and includes such areas as contracts, family law, property law, real estate, torts, and wills and estates

primary sources
the actual statutes, regulations, and case decisions that create the law

secondary sources
sources that summarize, discuss, or explain primary sources, and include legal encyclopedias, digests of cases, indexes to statutes, textbooks, and articles

PAPER VERSUS COMPUTERIZED SOURCES

Until recently, all primary and secondary legal sources came in paper format only. Over the last few years, more and more legal information has become available in computerized format as well. It is now possible to do everything with computerized sources that was previously done using only paper sources.

Computerized legal sources take a variety of forms:

- CD-ROM and online versions of secondary sources such as legal encyclopedias, digests of cases, and indexes to statutes; *Index*
- online versions of primary sources—statutes, regulations, and cases—available on free Internet sites or through subscription services; and
- online services such as Quicklaw and Westlaw*e*CARSWELL that combine the finding features of a secondary source with access to the primary source, such as the text of statutes and case reports.

Paper legal research sources are discussed in part IV of this book; computerized legal research sources are discussed in part V.

WHAT IT TAKES TO BE A GOOD LEGAL RESEARCHER

The legal research you perform will be relied on to take legal action or to give legal advice to a client. Your legal research must therefore be:

- Accurate: You must find *all* the relevant statutes, regulations, and case decisions; you must understand the meaning of the statutes, regulations, and cases that you find; and you must summarize or copy them accurately.
- Reliable: Your information must come from the most reliable sources—in other words, primary sources.
- Current: You must make sure that the statutes and regulations you find have not been amended or repealed; that the cases you find have not been overturned on appeal; and that the legal principles in statutes, regulations, or cases have not been changed by subsequent statutes, regulations, or cases.

KEY TERMS

law of evidence
primary sources
private law
procedural law
public law
secondary sources
substantive law

RESEARCH EXERCISE

This exercise will introduce you to the basic steps of research and allow you to develop some basic research skills using both paper and electronic sources.

Read the following fact situation. Answer the questions that follow, *twice*. The first time, use only a local telephone book. The second time, use the Internet. Use your creativity and powers of deduction. You are not being asked to consider questions of legal jurisdiction, procedure, or substantive law.

Fact Situation

Angelina Jolly was visiting Niagara Falls, Ontario. While she was driving near the falls, her car was struck by a car driven by Jennifer Annistone. Brad Pitts, a driver in another car, witnessed the incident; he gave his name and telephone number to Angelina before Angelina was taken by air ambulance to Toronto Slicendice Hospital. While Angelina was recuperating at the hospital, a nurse entered her room in the middle of the night and stole her watch, a gift she received from her brother, valued at $3,000.

After her release from the hospital, Angelina approaches your firm to represent her in two separate actions: a Superior Court action against Jennifer Annistone for damages for her injuries and the damage to her car, and a Small Claims Court action against the Slicendice Hospital for the theft of her watch.

After meeting with Angelina, the firm asks you to find the answers to some preliminary inquiries:

1. What is the filing fee for a claim in the local Small Claims Court? How can you find that out?

2. Angelina has already filed a statement of claim relating to the car accident at the local Superior Court office. You have to contact the court office to find out whether a statement of defence has been filed. How can you find the location and telephone number of the court to contact?

3. You need to contact the witness, Brad Pitts. Unfortunately, Angelina lost his telephone number, but remembers that he lives in Los Angeles, California. How can you find Brad's telephone number?

4. You're going to telephone Mr. Pitts long distance. You want to know the cost of the telephone call so that the firm can bill Angelina for all disbursements at the end of this month. The telephone bill won't come in until after the billing date. How can you find out the cost of the call right away?

5. Angelina is claiming that she suffered neurological injuries in the accident. If the action goes to trial, your firm will need an expert witness in the field of neurology to testify about the effects of Angelina's injuries on her ability to work. Where can you find an up-to-date list of all neurologists registered in your province?

6. It turns out that Angelina's watch was bought in the United States and Angelina has an insurance certificate valuing it at U.S.$3,000. Because the legal proceedings will be brought in Canada, you need to know the Canadian dollar equivalent of the U.S. dollar amount at today's exchange rate. Where can you find this information?

7. Another lawyer who used to practise in the city represented a client in a similar car accident case (the well-known case of *Holmes v. Kidman*). This lawyer is no longer listed in the city telephone book, but someone mentioned that she had moved to a small town, either to the north or the east, to set up a new practice. How can you find the lawyer's address and/or telephone number?

8. A Small Claims Court summons has to be served on Angelina's roommate, who was in the next bed at Slicendice when the nurse made off with Angelina's watch. Angelina happens to know the roommate's home telephone number, but not her street address. It doesn't seem like a good idea to alert the roommate to the summons by calling her. How can you use the roommate's telephone number to find out her address so that she can be personally served?

9. In an unrelated commercial matter, you need to send a package to the Banff Springs Hotel in Banff, Alberta, but the courier service won't accept the package without a postal code. You don't want to call the hotel directly because then you'll have to pay long distance charges. How can you find the postal code?

10. In another unrelated matter, you need to write to a Member of
     Parliament on behalf of a client. How can you find out the name and
     address of your client's MP, the member for the Rosedale riding in
     Toronto?

PART II

Sources of Canadian Law

The basic sources of legal research are statutes, regulations, and case law. Statutes are created by Parliament and the provincial legislatures, regulations are created by government departments, and case law is created by judges to explain their reasons for making a decision after hearing a case. A client who needs legal advice may be affected by one, two, or all three of these kinds of law. The purpose of legal research is to solve a client's problem. When you know what law governs the problem, you know what can be done and you can give the client choices on how to proceed.

CHAPTER 2

Statutes

Statutes are one of the three primary sources of law in Canada mentioned in chapter 1. Lawyers and law clerks need to know how to read and understand a statute. This chapter discusses

- why we read statutes,
- how to read a statute, and
- how to read a statutory provision.

WHY READ A STATUTE?

Statutes lay down the law. They set out approved methods of doing things that are required or permitted. They may require people to do things in certain circumstances; they may require people *not* to do things in other circumstances; or they may permit people to do things. Statutes create penalties for not doing what is required, or for doing what is prohibited. A client who seeks legal advice needs to know what statutes apply to him or her and how he or she is affected.

statute
law created by
Parliament or a
provincial legislature

HOW TO READ A STATUTE

Most statutes are organized as follows:

1. Statutes are headed by the *chapter number* of the statute, and, when first enacted, by the statute's **long title** (the full name of the statute, beginning with "An Act respecting"). Either at the end or at the beginning of the statute there may be a section that sets out the **short title** of the statute (beginning with "This Act may be cited as"). If a statute has a short title, use this in citing it. When statutes are subsequently amended they use the short title only. An amended statute will also list the amendments that have been made. Lengthy statutes may include a table of contents setting out all the parts and sections of the statute.

long title
full, unabbreviated title
of a statute

short title
abbreviated title
of a statute

preamble
part of a statute that
outlines its purpose and
main principles

2. Statutes may begin with a **preamble**, which sets out the purpose and main principles of the statute. The preamble usually begins with "Whereas."

3. Statutes are usually subdivided as follows:

   I Part

      I. Section

         (1) Subsection

            (a) Subsection

               (i) Subsection

   Brief notes in the margins may indicate what the sections (and sometimes subsections) are about.

4. Statutes have introductory sections that set out

   a. the *scope* of the statute (what the statute applies to),
   b. the definitions of words used in the statute,
   c. the officials who are to administer the statute, and
   d. other details about how the statute is to be administered.

5. The law itself is contained in the *body* of the statute. In some statutes, the body concludes with sections that create offences for disobeying the law and penalties.

housekeeping provisions
sections that cover
the details of statutes,
such as the date of
coming into force

6. Statutes end with **housekeeping provisions**, which can include the date when the statute will come into force and the right of officials who administer the statute to make regulations under the statute.

The organization of a statute is illustrated in figure 2.1, which reproduces some provisions from the *Family Law Act* (as first enacted). Note the following:

- The long title of the original statute is *An Act to Amend the Family Law Reform Act*.
- The Act is quite lengthy—77 sections—and is divided into six parts.
- Definitions are found in s. 1.
- A housekeeping provision—the power to make regulations—is found in s. 69.
- The short title of the Act is set out in s. 77.

In later versions of the statute, only the short title is used. Figure 2.2 shows the first page of the 1990 version of the same statute. Note that the statute is now entitled the *Family Law Act*.

HOW TO READ A STATUTORY PROVISION   Reading

You are more likely to read a **provision** (a section or subsection) in a statute than to read a whole statute.

provision
section or subsection

When you quote a statute for research, never paraphrase. Quote the statute exactly, or you'll change its meaning. For example, "any individual may apply" does not mean the same as a researcher's own words "any person may apply" ("individual" excludes corporations, but "person" usually includes corporations).

FIGURE 2.1   Selections from the Family Law Act, 1986

CHAPTER 4

An Act to revise the Family Law Reform Act

Assented to January 17th, 1986

TABLE OF CONTENTS

FIGURE 2.1   Continued

Chap. 4   FAMILY LAW   1986

Preamble   Whereas it is desirable to encourage and strengthen the role
                of the family; and whereas for that purpose it is necessary to
                recognize the equal position of spouses as individuals within
                marriage and to recognize marriage as a form of partnership;
                and whereas in support of such recognition it is necessary to
                provide in law for the orderly and equitable settlement of the
                affairs of the spouses upon the breakdown of the partnership,
                and to provide for other mutual obligations in family relation-
                ships, including the equitable sharing by parents of responsi-
                bility for their children;

                Therefore, Her Majesty, by and with the advice and con-
                sent of the Legislative Assembly of the Province of Ontario,
                enacts as follows:

Definitions   **1.**—(1) In this Act,

"enfant"   "child" includes a person whom a parent has demonstrated a
                settled intention to treat as a child of his or her family,
                except under an arrangement where the child is placed for
                valuable consideration in a foster home by a person having
                lawful custody;

"cohabiter"   "cohabit" means to live together in a conjugal relationship,
                whether within or outside marriage;

"tribunal"   "court" means the Provincial Court (Family Division), the
                Unified Family Court, the District Court or the Supreme
                Court;

"contrat   "domestic contract" means a domestic contract as defined in
familial"   Part IV (Domestic Contracts);

FIGURE 2.1   **Continued**

Chap. 4   FAMILY LAW   1986

"père ou mère"

"parent" includes a person who has demonstrated a settled intention to treat a child as a child of his or her family, except under an arrangement where the child is placed for valuable consideration in a foster home by a person having lawful custody;

"accord de paternité"

"paternity agreement" means a paternity agreement as defined in Part IV (Domestic Contracts);

"conjoint"

"spouse" means either of a man and woman who,

    (a)   are married to each other, or

    (b)   have together entered into a marriage that is voidable or void, in good faith on the part of the person asserting a right under this Act.

Polygamous marriages

(2) In the definition of "spouse", a reference to marriage includes a marriage that is actually or potentially polygamous, if it was celebrated in a jurisdiction whose system of law recognizes it as valid.

Staying application

2.—(1) If, in an application under this Act, it appears to the court that for the appropriate determination of the spouses' affairs it is necessary or desirable to have other matters determined first or simultaneously, the court may stay the application until another proceeding is brought or determined as the court considers appropriate.

All proceedings in one court

(2) Except as this Act provides otherwise, no person who is a party to an application under this Act shall make another application under this Act to another court, but the court may order that the proceeding be transferred to a court having other jurisdiction where, in the first court's opinion, the other court is more appropriate to determine the matters in issue that should be determined at the same time.

Applications in Supreme or District Court

(3) In the Supreme or District Court, an application under this Act may be made by action or application.

Statement re removal of barriers to remarriage

(4) A party to an application under section 7 (net family property), 10 (questions of title between spouses), 33 (support), 34 (powers of court) or 37 (variation) may serve on the other party and file with the court a statement, verified by oath or statutory declaration, indicating that,

    (a)   the author of the statement has removed all barriers that are within his or her control and that would prevent the other spouse's remarriage within that spouse's faith; and

FIGURE 2.1   **Continued**

Chap. 4   FAMILY LAW   1986

GENERAL

Regulations

69. The Lieutenant Governor in Council may make regulations respecting any matter referred to as prescribed by the regulations.

Application
of ss. 5-8

70.—(1) Sections 5 to 8 apply unless,

R.S.O. 1980,
c. 152

(a)   an application under section 4 of the *Family Law Reform Act* was adjudicated or settled before the 4th day of June, 1985; or

(b)   the first spouse's death occurs before the day this Act comes into force.

Extension of
limitation
period

(2) The limitation period set out in clause 7 (3) (b) does not expire until six months after this Act comes into force.

Application
of Part II

(3) Part II (Matrimonial Home) applies unless a proceeding under Part III of the *Family Law Reform Act* to determine the rights between spouses in respect of the property concerned was adjudicated or settled before the 4th day of June, 1985.

Interpretation
of existing
contracts

(4) A separation agreement or marriage contract that is validly made before the day this Act comes into force and that excludes a spouse's property from the application of sections 4 and 8 of the *Family Law Reform Act*,

(a)   shall be deemed to exclude that property from the application of section 5 of this Act; and

(b)   shall be read with necessary modifications.

71.—(1) The *Family Law Reform Act*, being chapter 152 of the Revised Statutes of Ontario, 1980, except the title, subsection 27 (1) and sections 69, 70 and 71, is repealed.

(2) Subsection 27 (1) of the *Family Law Reform Act* is repealed.

(3) Section 3 of the *Children's Law Reform Amendment Act, 1982*, being chapter 20, section 179 of the *Courts of Justice Act, 1984*, being chapter 11, section 10 of the *Courts of Justice Amendment Act, 1984*, being chapter 64 and section 18 of the *Land Registration Reform Act, 1984*, being chapter 32, are repealed.

FIGURE 2.1   **Concluded**

Chap. 4   FAMILY LAW   1986

(4) The title to the *Family Law Reform Act* is repealed and the following substituted therefor:

DOWER AND MISCELLANEOUS ABOLITION ACT

72. Subsection 12 (2) of the *Ontario Municipal Employees Retirement System Act*, being chapter 348 of the Revised Statutes of Ontario, 1980, is repealed and the following substituted therefor:

Application
of subs. (1)

(2) Notwithstanding subsection (1), payment to a person out of the Fund is subject to execution, seizure or attachment in satisfaction of an order for support or maintenance enforceable in Ontario.

73. Subsection 27 (3) of the *Pension Benefits Act*, being chapter 373 of the Revised Statutes of Ontario, 1980, as enacted by the Statutes of Ontario, 1983, chapter 2, section 5, is repealed.

74. Subsection 34 (4) of the *Public Service Superannuation Act*, being chapter 419 of the Revised Statutes of Ontario, 1980, as enacted by the Statutes of Ontario, 1984, chapter 22, section 15, is repealed.

75. Subsection 43 (3) of the *Teachers' Superannuation Act, 1983*, being chapter 84, is repealed.

Commence-
ment

76. This Act comes into force on a day to be named by proclamation of the Lieutenant Governor.

Short title

77. The short title of this Act is the *Family Law Act, 1986*.

FIGURE 2.2   **First Page of the 1990 Family Law Act**

CHAPTER F.3

Family Law Act

CONTENTS

1. Definitions
2. General
3. Mediation

PART I
FAMILY PROPERTY

4. Definitions
5. Equalization of net family properties
6. Estates
7. Applications to court
8. Statement of property
9. Powers of court
10. Questions of title
11. Business or farm
12. Preservation orders
13. Security
14. Presumptions
15. Conflict of laws
16. Application of Part

PART II
MATRIMONIAL HOME

17. Definitions
18. Matrimonial home
19. Spouse's right of possession
20. Designation of matrimonial home
21. Alienation of matrimonial home
22. Right of redemption and to notice
23. Powers of court
24. Orders for possession
25. Variation of order
26. Title to matrimonial home
27. Registration
28. Application of Part

PART III
SUPPORT OBLIGATIONS

29. Definitions
30. Obligation of spouses for support
31. Obligation of parent to support child
32. Obligation of child to support parent
33. Order for support
34. Powers of court
35. Filing of domestic contracts
36. Effect of divorce proceeding
37. Variation
38. Indexation of existing order
39. Existing orders
40. Restraining orders
41. Financial statement
42. Access to information
43. Arrest of absconding debtor
44. Provisional orders
45. Credit for necessities of life

CHAPITRE F.3

Loi sur le droit de la famille

TABLE DES MATIÈRES

1. Définitions
2. Dispositions générales
3. Médiateur

PARTIE I
BIENS FAMILIAUX

4. Définitions
5. Égalisation des biens familiaux nets
6. Successions
7. Requêtes
8. Déclaration des biens
9. Pouvoirs du tribunal
10. Questions relatives à la propriété
11. Commerce ou ferme
12. Ordonnance pour conserver les biens
13. Sûreté
14. Présomptions
15. Conflit des lois
16. Champ d'application

PARTIE II
FOYER CONJUGAL

17. Définitions
18. Foyer conjugal
19. Droit de possession du conjoint
20. Désignation du foyer conjugal
21. Aliénation du foyer conjugal
22. Droit de rachat et de recevoir des avis
23. Pouvoirs du tribunal
24. Ordonnances relatives à la possession
25. Modification de l'ordonnance
26. Titre du foyer conjugal
27. Enregistrement
28. Champ d'application

PARTIE III
OBLIGATIONS ALIMENTAIRES

29. Définitions
30. Obligation alimentaire des conjoints
31. Obligation alimentaire du père et de la mère
32. Obligation alimentaire de l'enfant
33. Ordonnance alimentaire
34. Pouvoirs du tribunal
35. Dépôt du contrat familial
36. Effet de l'action en divorce
37. Modification
38. Indexation
39. Ordonnances existantes
40. Ordonnances de ne pas faire
41. État financier
42. Accès aux renseignements
43. Arrestation du débiteur en fuite
44. Ordonnances conditionnelles
45. Crédit pour les objets de première nécessité

In order to understand a statutory provision, begin by asking the following questions:

1. With what matters in general does the statute deal?
2. With what matters does this particular provision of the statute deal?
3. To whom is the particular section directed—for example, the general public, a corporation, a real estate agent, or a spouse?
4. Does the provision
   a. order,
   b. prohibit, or
   c. permit
   something to be done? What? In what circumstances?
5. If there is an order or prohibition, how is it enforced?

These questions give you a general idea about the provision.

In order to understand a provision more particularly, break it down into its elements. Once you understand these, you will be able to identify all the important information in the provision.

Example

Section 265(1)(b) of the *Criminal Code*, R.S.C. 1985, c. C-46 defines a particular form of assault. As written in the statute, it looks like this:

265(1) A person commits an assault when …

(b) he attempts or threatens, by an act or gesture, to apply force to another person, if he has, or causes that other person to believe upon reasonable grounds that he has, present ability to effect his purpose.

Broken down into its separate elements, it looks like this:

A person
commits an assault when

(ONE OF THE FOLLOWING)

1. he attempts
   by an act
   or a gesture
   to apply force
   to another person

2. he threatens
   by an act
   or a gesture
   to apply force
   to another person

(PLUS ONE OF THE FOLLOWING)

1. if he has
   present ability
   to effect his purpose

2. if he causes
   that other person
   to believe on reasonable grounds
   that he has
   present ability
   to effect his purpose

If you break down a provision into its elements, you can use the breakdown as a checklist to compare with your client's fact situation. Each element must be accounted for in the facts of your client's situation if the statutory provision is to be applicable. For example, if your client (who has been charged with assault under

s. 265(1)(b)) yelled at and raised his fist to a ticket seller who was safely inside a locked Plexiglas booth, then he threatened by a gesture to apply force to the ticket seller. But he had no present ability to effect his purpose, and the ticket seller had no reasonable grounds to believe that he had present ability. Therefore, your client has not committed assault as defined by s. 265(1)(b).

Sometimes you will have to research further to find out what each element of a statutory provision means. For example, what exactly is "present ability"? Would your client have present ability to apply force to the ticket seller if your client were standing outside the locked booth with a tire iron in his hand? Or what are "reasonable grounds" for believing that the accused has present ability? Would the ticket seller have reasonable grounds to believe that your client could get into the booth using only his bare hands? To answer these, you might have to look at another section of the statute for a definition, or you might have to look for cases that discuss these issues.

As well as breaking down a statutory provision into its elements, you may have to build up the elements by referring to other provisions. You may have to look in the definition section of the statute in order to understand the legal meaning of a word. For example, the *Change of Name Act*, R.S.O. 1990, c. C.7, s. 4(3) says:

> 4(3) An application by a child requires the written consent of every person who has lawful custody of the child.

In order to know exactly who is a "child," you must look at s. 1 of the Act, which contains definitions. There, "child" is defined as "a person under the age of eighteen years."

Building up a statutory provision can be more complex than that, however. Instead of adding the definition of a word, you may have to add other entire provisions. For example, s. 108(1) of the *Canada Business Corporations Act*, R.S.C. 1985, c. C-44 reads:

> 108(1) A director of a corporation ceases to hold office when,
>   (a) he dies or resigns;
>   (b) he is removed in accordance with section 109; or
>   (c) he becomes disqualified under subsection 105(1).

So, in order to find out what s. 108(1) *really* means, you have to refer to these other sections. Section 109(1) says:

> 109(1) Subject to paragraph 107(g), the shareholders of a corporation may by ordinary resolution at a special meeting remove any director or directors from office.

Section 105(1) says:

> 105(1) The following persons are disqualified from being a director of a corporation:
>   (a) anyone who is less than eighteen years of age;
>   (b) anyone who is of unsound mind and has been so found by a court in Canada or elsewhere;
>   (c) a person who is not an individual; or
>   (d) a person who has the status of bankrupt.

The sections referred to have to be incorporated into s. 108 to understand it. For example, s. 108(1)(c) would have to be read like this:

> 108(1) A director of a corporation ceases to hold office when, ...
>
> (c) he becomes disqualified under subsection 105(1).
>
> 105(1) The following persons are disqualified from being a director of a corporation: ...
>
> (b) anyone who is of unsound mind and has been so found by a court in Canada or elsewhere; ...
>
> (d) a person who has the status of bankrupt.

Once you have built up a statutory provision by adding all the references, you have to break down your new creation into its elements in order to understand it properly. A built-up, broken-down s. 108(1)(c) will look like this:

> 108(1) A director of a corporation
>   ceases to hold office
>   when ...
>
> (c)   he becomes disqualified
>   under subsection 105(1).
>
> 105(1) The following persons
>   are disqualified from being
>   a director of a corporation: ...
>
> (b)   anyone who is of unsound mind
>   and has been so found by a court
>   in Canada or elsewhere; ...
>
> (d)   a person who has the status of bankrupt.

KEY TERMS

housekeeping provisions
long title
preamble
provision
short title
statute

EXERCISES

1. Break down the following statutory provisions into their separate elements.

   a. The *Criminal Code*, R.S.C. 1985, c. C-46, s. 265 provides, in part, as follows:

   > 265(1) Any person commits an assault when ...
   >   (c) while openly wearing or carrying a weapon or an imitation thereof, he accosts or impedes another person or begs.

   b. The *Criminal Code*, R.S.C. 1985, c. C-46, s. 265 provides, in part, as follows:

   > 265(1) Any person commits an assault when
   >   (a) without the consent of another person he applies force intentionally to that other person directly or indirectly; ...

   > 265(3) For the purposes of this section, no consent is obtained where the complainant submits or does not resist by reason of
   >   (a) the application of force to the complainant or to a person other than the complainant;
   >   (b) threats or fear of the application of force to the complainant or to a person other than the complainant;
   >   (c) fraud; or
   >   (d) the exercise of authority.

c. The *Land Titles Act*, R.S.O. 1990, c. L.5, s. 93, prior to its amendment in 1998, provided, in part, as follows:

> 93(2) A charge that secures payment of money shall contain the amount of the principal sum that the charge secures, the rate of interest, and the periods of payment including the due date.

d. The *Canada Evidence Act*, R.S.C. 1985, c. C-5, s. 4 provides, in part, as follows:

> 4(3) No husband is compellable to disclose any communication made to him by his wife during their marriage, and no wife is compellable to disclose any communication made to her by her husband during their marriage.

2. Read the following fact situations and answer the questions, using the applicable statutory provision from question 1.

   a. A mortgage (charge) made in Ontario in 1997 contains the following payment clauses. Does it meet the statutory requirements then in effect?

      > The amount of principal secured by this Charge/Mortgage of Land is Thirty Thousand ($30,000) dollars and the rate of interest chargeable thereon is Ten (10%) per cent per annum calculated quarter-yearly not in advance.
      >
      > Provided this Charge/Mortgage to be void on payment of Thirty Thousand ($30,000) dollars of lawful money of Canada with interest at Ten (10%) per cent per annum as follows:
      >
      > > Five hundred ($500) dollars on account of the principal sum shall be payable on the 8th days of each of the months of May, August, and November in the year 1998 and the 8th days of each of the months of February, May, August, and November in the year 1999. The first payment of interest is to be computed from the 8th day of February 1998 upon the whole amount of principal hereby secured, to become payable on the 8th day of May 1998.

b. Richie and Maya lived together for years. During that time, he robbed several banks and told her the details of each robbery. Eventually, Richie and Maya decided to get married and had the ceremony performed at the city hall. Unfortunately, as they were leaving the building, a police officer who had been called to the scene of one of the robberies, bumped into them and recognized Richie. Two days later, Richie was in jail, charged with armed robbery. Should he worry that Maya will be forced to testify against him at his trial?

c. Is it assault?

   i. Lisa and her husband, David, were having an argument. To emphasize a point, David threw a vase at the wall. He expected it to shatter, but the vase bounced off the wall and hit Lisa.

ii. When their next-door neighbour dropped by to show off the karate moves she had just learned, Lisa's husband told the neighbour that she had his permission to demonstrate on Lisa. The neighbour whacked Lisa across the arm.

iii. Lisa went to her doctor to set her broken arm. It was excruciatingly painful, far worse than she expected. The only reason she went through with it and didn't run screaming from the doctor's office was that she was afraid of ending up with a deformed arm.

iv. Lisa later found out that the doctor who had set her arm was not licensed to practise medicine.

CHAPTER 3

Regulations

Regulations are the second primary source of law in Canada, and lawyers and law clerks must know how to read and understand a regulation. This chapter discusses

- why we read regulations, and
- how to read a regulation.

WHY READ A REGULATION?

Regulations, also called subordinate legislation, are rules made under the authority of a statute. They are not created by Parliament or a legislature, but by department or ministry officials to whom the statute gives the power to make regulations.

Regulations are as important as statutes. In the case of **framework legislation**—legislation that creates a general framework and leaves the details to be worked out in the regulations—the regulations may be more important than the statute. Regulations are also important to those working in civil or criminal litigation because the rules of court are regulations made under the authority of the statute that creates the court system.

As with statutes, regulations require, prohibit, or permit certain actions and set out a method of doing what is required or permitted. They also create penalties for not doing what is required, or for doing what is prohibited.

regulations
rules made under the authority of a statute

framework legislation
legislation for which the details are worked out in the regulations

HOW TO READ A REGULATION

The text of a regulation is much like the text of a statute, except that it may be more detailed. You read a regulatory provision the same way that you read a statutory provision. In order to understand the law fully, it may be necessary to read a regulation together with one or more provisions of the statute under which it was made.

KEY TERMS

framework legislation
regulations

EXERCISES

Read the following regulations and answer the questions below.

A provision from SOR/97-390, made under the *Canada Shipping Act*, states:

18.(1) The complement of every passenger ship certified to carry 12 passengers or fewer and every cargo ship shall be sufficient in number to carry out simultaneously the following activities:

(a) to man and employ the fire extinguishing equipment required by the *Fire Detection and Extinguishing Equipment Regulations* to fight a fire at any one location on the ship;

(b) to operate the ship's pumping and emergency power system; and

(c) to prepare for launching the survival craft carried in accordance with the *Life Saving Equipment Regulations*.

(2) The complement of every passenger ship certified to carry more than 12 passengers shall be sufficient in number to carry out simultaneously the following activities:

(a) to man and employ the fire extinguishing equipment required by the *Fire Detection and Extinguishing Equipment Regulations* to fight a fire at any one location on the ship;

(b) to operate the ship's pumping and emergency power system; and

(c) to prepare for launching the survival craft carried in accordance with the *Life Saving Equipment Regulations*;

(d) to direct and control the passengers who are on board in an emergency; and

(e) to provide communication between the person in immediate charge of the ship and the persons directing and controlling the passengers who are on board.

Liquor Licence Act, R.S.O. 1990, c. L.19, ss. 30(1), (13)(a), and 31(1) and (2) state:

30.(1) No person shall knowingly sell or supply liquor to a person under nineteen years of age. ...

(13) This section does not apply,

(a) to the supplying of liquor to a person under nineteen years of age in a residence as defined in section 31 or in a private place as defined in the regulations by a parent of the person or a person having lawful custody of the person. ...

31.(1) In this section, "residence" means a place that is actually occupied and used as a dwelling, whether or not in common with other persons, including all premises used in conjunction with the place to which the general public is not invited or permitted access, and, if the place occupied and used as a dwelling is a tent, includes the land immediately adjacent to and used in conjunction with the tent.

(2) No person shall have or consume liquor in any place other than,

(a) a residence;

(b) premises in respect of which a licence or permit is issued; or

(c) a private place as defined in the regulations.

Revised Regulations of Ontario, Reg. 718, ss. 3(1), (2), and (3), made under the *Liquor Licence Act*, state:

> 3.(1) For the purposes of clauses 30(13)(a) and 31(2)(c) of the Act, "private place" means a place, vehicle or boat described in this section.
>
> (2) An indoor place to which the public is not ordinarily invited or permitted is considered to be a private place except at the times when the public is invited or permitted access to it.
>
> (3) Despite subsection (2), an indoor place that is available for rental by members of the public for occasional use is not a private place.

Criminal Appeal Rules (Ontario), SI/93-169, rules 14(1)(a-k), made under the authority of the *Criminal Code*, state:

> APPEAL BOOKS
> Contents of Appeal Book
>
> 14.(1) Except in an inmate appeal, the appeal book shall contain, in consecutively numbered pages arranged in the following order, a copy of,
>
> (a) a table of contents describing each document, including each exhibit, by its nature and date, and, in the case of an exhibit, identified by exhibit number or letter;
>
> (b) the notice of appeal and any supplementary notice of appeal;
>
> (c) the order granting the leave to appeal, if any, and any order or direction made with reference to the appeal;
>
> (d) the information or indictment, including all endorsements;
>
> (e) the formal order or decision appealed from, if any, as signed and entered;
>
> (f) the reasons for judgment, if not included in the transcript of the trial or hearing, together with a further typed or printed copy if the reasons are handwritten;
>
> (g) any order for release from custody pending appeal and any other order suspending the operation of the sentence;
>
> (h) all documentary exhibits filed at the trial arranged in order by date, or, where there are documents having common characteristics, arranged in separate groups in order by date;
>
> (i) all maps, plans, photographs, drawings and charts that were before the trial judge and are capable of reproduction;
>
> (j) the agreed statement of facts, if any;
>
> (k) where there is an appeal as to sentence, the pre-sentence report, the criminal record of the convicted person and any exhibits filed on the sentencing proceedings.

Questions

1. Your client, Northern Resources Ltd., is a Canadian company that has just bought a freighter to handle transportation of materials used in its operations. Although the freighter's main purpose will be to ship cargo, the client wants to take advantage of the travel market—many freighters now carry a few paying passengers, as well as cargo. This particular freighter can carry up to 15 passengers. The client wants to know whether

it is required by law to have a specified minimum number of crew on the freighter because of the passengers.

a. Make a list of the technical terms in the regulation that you need to define (by looking in the definition section at the beginning of the regulation) before you go any further.

b. Make a list of other sources that you need to see before you can tell the client the exact minimum number of crew required by law on this freighter.

2. You have been put in charge of preparing the appeal book for client Ava Bump's appeal. She is appealing the sentence imposed on her after her conviction for criminal negligence causing death (she is not appealing the conviction). She is at present free, pending the outcome of the appeal.

   a. Make a list of the documents that must be created by your law firm.

   b. Make a list of court documents that may have to be included in the appeal book.

   c. Make a list of documents from the trial that may have to be included in the appeal book.

d. Make a list of any legal terms you do not understand but need to understand in order to prepare the appeal book.

3. Your client J.W. Hart, president and CEO of Hart Industries Inc., is having a party to which both adults and children will be invited. The client intends to serve champagne and would like to serve the older children (the 17- and 18-year-olds) as well, with their parents' permission. The legal drinking age in Ontario is 19. The client wouldn't ask if the party were being held in his own home, but he's concerned because the party is being held in a big tent on the grounds of a well-known public garden. A large area around the tent will be roped off to keep out uninvited people.

Can the client legally serve wine to anyone under 19 at the party? Explain, quoting the relevant statute and regulation.

CHAPTER 4

Cases

Cases are the third primary source of Canadian law. Just as with statutes and regulations, lawyers and law clerks have to know how to read and understand a case. This chapter discusses

- what a case is,
- why we read a case, and
- how to read a case.

WHAT IS A CASE?

A case is the written record of a judge's reasons for deciding a legal dispute. Before a case gets into a report series or a legal database, it is known as the **reasons for decision** in a legal action.

reasons for decision
term for a case before it is included in a report series or legal database

WHY READ A CASE?

Case law research can tell you many things—for example, whether a client has a cause of action, how much a client could expect to be awarded in damages, and what evidence has to be presented at trial for the client's action to succeed.

All cases contain law, but that law is only useful to your particular client if

- the issues in the case and in the client's situation are similar,
- the facts in the case and in the client's situation are similar, and
- the case is binding or at least persuasive in your jurisdiction (see chapter 6 under the headings "What Is Binding Law?" and "Case Law: What Decisions Bind Which Courts?").

If the issues and the facts are similar, and the case is at least a persuasive authority, the law in the case can be applied to your client's situation.

HOW TO READ A CASE

If you haven't read many cases, any case looks like just a mass of words; but all cases, however long or short, share the same structure. Once you learn how to identify the different parts of a case that make up its structure, you will be able to use the case in research. Cases or reasons for decision contain these structural elements: purpose, facts, issues, law, *ratio decidendi* (Latin for "reason for deciding"), decision, and disposition. If there are several decision makers, such as in a Court of Appeal, the Supreme Court of Canada, or the House of Lords in England, there may be several separate reasons for decision in the same case—sometimes very different from each other.

headnote
editor's explanation of
the case before the
body

If the reasons for decision have been edited for a report series or database, a short **headnote** at the beginning will explain the case. For example, a headnote might read "Children—Custody and access—Factors governing award of custody— Best interest of child." A brief summary of the facts, *ratio decidendi*, and decision usually follow. The headnote and summary are useful in several ways. They let you know before you read the case whether the subject matter is relevant to your problem. They usually identify the issues and this helps to understand the case. Finally, if you do use the case, they will remind you what the case is about, so that you don't have to reread it too often as you prepare a memo of law. A word of warning about headnotes and summaries, however: they are not always correct, and they rarely quote the judge word for word. Never rely on the headnote and summary alone. Read the case yourself, and quote that rather than the headnote or summary.

Purpose

purpose
the nature of the
proceedings

Before the judge's reasons, there usually will be a short reference to the **purpose**, or nature of the proceedings, which has been provided by the editor of the report series—for example, "Action for damages for negligence," "Motion for summary judgment," and "Appeal from a decision of the General Division." If no such reference appears to give you a hint, you'll find that judges usually begin their reasons with a brief mention of why the case is before them.

Facts

Although most judges set out the facts at the beginning of their reasons, they often do not include *all* the facts in that section and instead scatter them throughout their reasons, usually putting facts in with the issue to which they are relevant.

The facts can fall into these categories:

1. The events leading up to the moment when the cause of action comes into existence. Note that important facts may exist before the plaintiff even comes into the picture.
2. The theory of the plaintiff and the theory of the defendant. A party's theory (or **theory of the case**) consists of the cause of action or the defence, plus the evidence that supports that cause of action or defence.
3. The decision at trial and the grounds of appeal (if the case is a decision on appeal).

theory of the case
the cause of action or
the defence, and the
evidence that supports
that cause of action or
defence — also known
as "the theory"

Look for the facts that are relevant to the issues decided. You will have to examine the issues and the law before you can decide which facts are relevant. Many written decisions—especially at the trial level—are long and contain much information that is not necessarily essential in understanding the issues. With practice, you can learn to identify the facts that were used to reach the actual decision on an issue.

Issues

The **issues** are the specific problems that the judge must solve in order to reach a decision. Often, they are set out in question form or introduced by the word "whether."

Once the judge has identified an issue, he or she must consider all the elements that make up that issue. The judge does this by

- looking at the law concerning the issue to find out what the elements involved are, and then
- looking at the relevant facts in that particular situation to see whether the legal test set out by the law has been met.

For example, if the issue is "whether the defendant committed battery on the plaintiff," the judge has to examine the law to see what the legal test for battery is (what elements make up the tort of battery). Then the judge has to examine the facts to see whether the defendant's actions meet that test.

Students often find that identifying issues is the hardest part of legal research. It takes practice to identify issues either in a case or your own client's fact situation. For help, see chapter 5 under the heading "Identify the Issues on a Preliminary Basis."

issues
specific problems that the judge must solve to reach a decision

Law

After the judge sets out the issues, there is usually a discussion of the existing law on each issue. Statutes, other cases, and texts may be quoted, cited, and relied on as authorities. Sometimes the judge simply will make a general statement of the law without referring to any authority, if the law is well known—for example, "A plaintiff must prove his or her case on the balance of probabilities." At other times, a judge will not set out a statement of law for every issue addressed.

Because the two sides in a case usually cite different **lines of authority** to persuade the judge to decide the case in each side's favour, the judge may cite two or more cases, statutes, or texts that give very different views of the law on a single issue. The judge must choose which line of authority to follow before applying the law to the facts of the case and reaching a decision. If the judge has examined more than one line of authority on a single issue, note which one he or she has chosen to follow before proceeding to the *ratio* for that issue.

The law that the judge chooses to follow is law for which you can cite the case for research. Again, do not paraphrase because that will change its meaning. Quote it exactly from the case.

lines of authority
statement of existing law found in statutes, cases, and texts

Ratio Decidendi and Decision

The *ratio decidendi* is the pre-existing principle of law on which the judge based the decision on an issue, applied to the facts of the particular case. The *ratio* is frequently introduced by words such as "here," "in this case," or "in my view," and is often short—a sentence or a brief paragraph. The *ratio decidendi* of a case is law for which you can cite the case when you are using it for research. Do not paraphrase because that will change its meaning. Quote it exactly from the case.

ratio decidendi
Latin for "reasons for deciding"

A decision is made on each issue that the judge addresses. The decision itself—for example, "The action in negligence must fail," or "The plaintiff has made out a good case in battery"—usually appears either at the beginning or the end of the *ratio*.

If there is more than one issue, there probably will be more than one *ratio* and more than one decision.

Disposition

disposition
judge's orders set out at
the end of a case

At the end of the case, the judge's **disposition** or orders about the entire case are set out—for example, "Judgment for the Plaintiff," "Judgment for the Plaintiff in the amount of $30,000," "Motion for summary judgment granted," or "Appeal dismissed." The disposition usually includes an award of costs to one party and also may include administrative directions to the parties, such as an order that documents be filed by a certain date or a referral of the matter to another judicial official for an accounting or an assessment of damages.

KEY TERMS
disposition
headnote
issues
lines of authority
purpose
ratio decidendi
reasons for decision
theory of the case

EXERCISES

1. Read the following cases. In each one, identify the purpose, facts, issues, law, *ratio decidendi*, decision, and disposition.

Cyrenne v. Moar

(1986), 2 R.F.L. (3d) 414

Manitoba Court of Appeal,

Monnin C.J.M., Huband, and Twaddle JJ.A.

M.J. Bennett, for appellant.

C.N. Guberman, for respondent.

(No. 193/86)

16th June 1986. The judgment of the court was delivered by

MONNIN C.J.M. (orally):—This is an appeal from a decision of Helper J. who dismissed the mother's application to strike out the access privileges granted to Mr. Cyrenne by a prior order of Simonsen J.

We are of the view that it is not in the best interest of the child, Sonya Rose Moar, that access be given to Mr. Cyrenne. The original order most probably would not have been made if all the facts had been disclosed.

We strike out the access rights granted to Mr. Cyrenne and will give more detailed reasons in due course.

The matter of costs is reserved and will be dealt with in our extended reasons.

20th June 1986. Written reasons for judgment. The judgment of the court was delivered by

HUBAND J.A.:—This court has decided that the visiting privileges accorded to John Cyrenne should end. What follows are my reasons for allowing the appeal of Annette Moar on 16th June 1986.

John Cyrenne is not the father of the child, Sonya, in whom he has taken such keen interest. John Cyrenne met Annette Moar in 1979 and had some form of relationship with her extending through to 1982. During part of 1981 and 1982 they maintained adjoining suites in the same dwelling house, and during that period of time the relationship seemed to have been at its closest.

Annette Moar was already the mother of a son who was born in 1974. The daughter, Sonya, was born on 19th June 1981. Initially John Cyrenne believed that he had fathered the child, but subsequent blood tests have confirmed that he is not the father of the child.

Believing the child to be his, John Cyrenne participated to some degree in the care of the baby, although he made no significant financial contribution. No doubt he developed a genuine fondness for the child.

In June 1982 John Cyrenne was sentenced to jail for six months, and the somewhat tenuous relationship between himself and Annette Moar began to crumble. When he was released from prison two months later, Annette Moar had moved to different accommodation. She began a new relationship with another man in the fall of 1982—a relationship which has persisted through to the present date. In October 1982 she told John Cyrenne that he was not the father of the child, Sonya, but John Cyrenne did not accept her statement at that time.

During 1983 John Cyrenne continued to visit the child from time to time, but with growing reluctance on the part of the mother and her new companion.

By the beginning of 1984 Annette Moar made it clear that she wanted John Cyrenne's visits with her daughter to end. His response was to seek custody or access by way of proceedings in court. On 22nd February 1984 he applied in the Provincial Court, Family Division, for custody of, or access to, the child. Annette Moar caused an answer to be filed asserting that John Cyrenne was not the father of the child, and on 27th February his application for custody or access was withdrawn.

A fresh application seeking custody or access was filed in the same court on 21st March 1984. This application also sought a declaration of parentage. The parties submitted to blood tests, and the results of those tests demonstrated that John Cyrenne was not the father of the child. Ultimately, this second application was discontinued on 6th December 1984.

But once again, a fresh action was commenced a few weeks later. This time a petition was filed in the Court of Queen's Bench on 17th December 1984, seeking access only, and relying upon s. 1.5 of the *Child Welfare Act* of Manitoba.

Annette Moar did not contest this petition. Later on she was to explain that she wilted under the bombardment of continuing applications and the constant harassment of John Cyrenne to gain access to the child. In any event, on 18th February 1985 John Cyrenne obtained an order from Simonsen J. in the Court of Queen's Bench granting him access to the child each Sunday from 10:00 a.m. to 7:00 p.m. While the order was made without opposition from Annette Moar, it would appear that given the unusual nature of the order allowing access in favour of a person who is not a blood relation, Simonsen J. insisted upon some evidence before making the order. John Cyrenne testified and, since the petition was not opposed, the order was made.

Problems with respect to the access arose almost immediately. About one month after the order was made, Annette Moar was seeking legal aid in order to move to set aside the access order, and within a further month John Cyrenne had instituted criminal contempt proceedings against Annette Moar for her disobedience of the access order. Attendances at Annette Moar's residence to exercise rights became confrontations. In June 1985 Annette Moar brought a motion in the Court of Queen's Bench seeking an order to vary the order of Simonsen J. by deleting the access privileges. John Cyrenne countered with a motion for an order of contempt against Annette Moar, and an order to vary the terms of the access order of Simonsen J. by "increasing the times of access." These two motions came before Schwartz J. of the Court of Queen's Bench in July 1985. In order to defuse the confrontations between the protagonists, Schwartz J. ordered an immediate variation to provide that some third party, other than John Cyrenne, attend to pick up the child. As to the merits of the motion and counter-motion, Schwartz J. ordered that they be dealt with by way of a trial in the fall of 1985.

The trial commenced before Helper J. in November 1985. After two days of testimony the learned trial judge decided to order an assessment report from a family conciliation counsellor, and the testimony of the author of that report was heard on 26th April 1986. Helper J. delivered judgment on that same date. Helper J. did not vary the access as ordered by Simonsen J. approximately a year earlier.

The learned trial judge seemed to believe that there must be proof of changed circumstances to justify a variation in the previous order of Simonsen J. She asked the rhetorical question, "What circumstances have changed since the pronouncement of the order to warrant any change in the existing order?" The learned trial judge went on to observe that animosity between John Cyrenne and Annette Moar both preceded and followed the order of Simonsen J. Helper J. found no significant change in circumstances to justify a variation.

With respect, I do not think that proof of changed circumstances is essential. The order of Simonsen J. was made pursuant to s. 1.5 of the *Child Welfare Act*, S.M. 1974, c. C80. Section 1.5 was added by way of an amendment to the Act in 1983, and the provision reads as follows:

> 1.5. In exceptional circumstances, a court may make an order granting any person who has had or ought to have the opportunity to visit a child, the right to visit the child at such times and on such conditions as the court considers appropriate.

The basis for varying an access order made under the *Child Welfare Act* is to be found in s. 21 of the *Family Maintenance Act*, C.C.S.M. c. F20, which reads as follows:

> 21. An order made under this Act or under [t]he *Wives' and Children's Maintenance Act* or under the *Family Maintenance Act*, being chapter 47 of the *Statutes of Manitoba*, 1977, or an order made under [t]he *Child Welfare Act* granting custody of, access to or maintenance for a child, may upon an application therefor be varied from time to time or discharged by the court making the order, if the court thinks it fit and just to do so, but no variation or discharge granted under this section shall be effective before the date on which the application therefor is made.

The test for a variation or discharge would seem to be what is "fit and just" and unlike a variation to an order made under the *Divorce Act* of Canada, the variation or discharge does not hinge upon proof of changed circumstances.

However, there is no need to dwell upon this difference between provincial and federal legislation, because using either test the appeal must be allowed. There were in fact changed circumstances between the granting of the access order by Simonsen J. and the trial before Helper J. The conflict between Annette Moar and John Cyrenne had escalated in intensity.

Of greater significance, the passive toleration of access on the part of the mother had become firm and resolute opposition.

This was not a case where Annette Moar had consented to access on a basis approaching an agreement. Non-opposition is not the same thing as active consent. As mother and guardian of the child, Annette Moar is entitled to say that she has changed her mind, and that John Cyrenne's visits with her child are no longer welcome. In a case of this kind, where the statute requires exceptional circumstances before the court may make an order of access, the opposition of the mother is enormously significant. She has the responsibility of rearing the child, and the child has the right to be reared by her. Her opinion as to who should visit with the child and under what circumstances deserves very great consideration. When non-opposition turns to defiant hostility, the circumstances have clearly altered.

Further, I think it is "fit and just" that access be denied. The case of *Lapp v. Dupuis* (1985), 45 R.F.L. (2d) 28, 31 Man. R. (2d) 261, was a decision by this court dealing with similar circumstances. The petitioner had a brief romantic interest in the mother of the child, which was not reciprocated. The petitioner became good friends with the mother, however, and from that relationship he developed an interest in her 5-month-old child. That interest continued over a period of a few years, and for approximately a year and one half the petitioner served as principal babysitter for the child. As time went by, the mother entered into a relationship with another man. There was animosity between the petitioner and the mother's new friend. When the mother insisted that the petitioner's visits cease, the petitioner applied for access, and the application was firmly opposed by the mother of the child. This court decided that an association emerging out of a babysitting arrangement, albeit over a lengthy period of time, was insufficient to establish the "exceptional circumstances" required under s. 1.5 of the *Child Welfare Act*. In that case, as in the present case, the petitioner had a genuine interest in the child, and his visits were not disagreeable from the standpoint of the child. But the court concluded that an access order in favour of someone who is not a blood relation should be set aside in face of the opposition of the mother who wished to exercise responsible control over the destiny of her child and herself. As in the *Lapp v. Dupuis* case, a fit and just disposition is to cancel the access privileges.

In my opinion, it was appropriate for the learned trial judge to vary the order of Simonsen J. and, given the evidence presented before her, she should have done so by deleting access.

I am mindful of the argument on behalf of John Cyrenne that the paramount consideration is the best interests of the child. The very wording of s. 1.5 of the *Child Welfare Act*, however, suggests that it will only be under rare circumstances that court-ordered visits of a non-relative will be considered to be in the child's best interests, at least where there is opposition by the parent or parents. As noted in the case of *Lapp v. Dupuis*, the parents' attitude is not to be relegated to a parity with all other surrounding circumstances in determining what is best for the child. While not determinative, the parents' position is of prime importance in making the determination of best interests. I have no hesitation in this case in concluding that the access awarded to John Cyrenne is not in the child's best interests.

For some period of time leading up to the date of the appeal hearing, Annette Moar was defiant of the order for access in favour of John Cyrenne. Under the circumstances, while her appeal is allowed, it is allowed without costs.

Appeal allowed;
access terminated.

Purpose

Facts

Issues

Law

Ratio Decidendi

Decision

Disposition

Bell v. St. Thomas University

(1992), 97 D.L.R. (4th) 370

New Brunswick Court of Queen's Bench, Russell J.

Grant M. Ogilvie, for plaintiff.

J. William Cabel, for defendant.

RUSSELL J.:—In 1987, the plaintiff was in the final year of a four-year program at the defendant institution leading to a Bachelor of Social Work (hereafter called a B.S.W.) degree. One of the requirements to complete that degree was the successful completion of a field practice course entitled Social Work 410. The plaintiff took that course from May to July, 1987. He failed the course and has not yet received a B.S.W.

That failing grade and the defendant's following actions have led to this litigation.

The action is framed in negligent misrepresentation and breach of contract. Paragraphs 21 and 22 of the statement of claim as amended say:

> 21. As a result of the plaintiff's protracted efforts to either change his final grade mark or be accepted to repeat SW 410 which have not been successful, the plaintiff asserts that the defendant is in breach of a contract between the plaintiff and the defendant and more particularly that the defendant:
>
>> (i) contracted to provide a course of studies leading to a BSW degree when completed and has failed to allow the plaintiff to complete the BSW program …
>
> 22. The plaintiff asserts that the defendant has negligently misrepresented to him the failing grade the plaintiff was to receive upon completion of SW 410 and that during the course of the field placement the defendant through its employees:
>
>> (i) neglected to properly warn the plaintiff that he was going to fail …

The university calendar (ex. P-1) describes Social Work 410 as follows:

410. Field Instruction II

This course is a continuation of Field Instruction 1(b), and also provides practical experience in the field, in an approved setting, under faculty supervision. Students are expected to develop knowledge and skills in the field sufficient for initial professional practice with various client constituencies. Two days per week. Two semesters. Prerequisite: Field Instruction I. Available to B.S.W. students only.

Field placements were normally made at various institutions and sites around the Fredericton area such as the Dr. Everett Chalmers Hospital and the Mental Health Clinic. These are only representative examples of the institutions that accepted placements.

The plaintiff was accepted by the Fredericton Police Department and carried out his field practicum at the so-called Devon storefront which I infer is a form of community policing service established by the

Fredericton Police Department. Mr. Bell was under the direct supervision of Constable Peggy Blackmore of the Fredericton Police Department and his academic supervisors were Sandra DeVink and Gaynell Cloney both of the Faculty of Social Work.

His assignments at the Devon storefront are described in ex. P-10 as follows:

> This group experience was to involve consultation and shared leadership with Ms. Gaynell Cloney.
>
> Mike had joint responsibility with another student to design and implement a needs assessment questionnaire in order to determine the perception of and needs of a segment of the community with respect to the Storefront. Although the adolescent and young adult population was the largest group for Mike's work, he also had involvement with the adult population, primarily single-parent mothers, who attend the Storefront on a daily basis. Mike became very involved in a few cases where he took on the various roles of client advocate, educator and counsellor. He had opportunities to liaise with other agencies and consult with resource people on behalf of his clients. Finally Mike participated in some of the on-going activities at the Storefront, community meetings and attended two of the women's support group meetings, as well as a Self-Help Conference resource fair.

His supervisors were not satisfied with his performance. His mid-term assessment (ex. P-9) completed on July 2, 1987, and completed by Sandra DeVink contains the following paragraphs:

> In order to pass this field placement, Mike needs to demonstrate that he has satisfactory assessment and intervention skills and satisfactory skills in the areas requiring improvement.
>
> In the event that Mike has not been able to learn these skills to a satisfactory degree, we will consider extending this field placement and or selecting another field placement which may be more appropriate in teaching the skills required.

They were particularly concerned about several aspects of his performance. One example will suffice to indicate the nature of the supervisors' concerns.

At one point during the plaintiff's placement the Fredericton police decided to enforce a 10 p.m. curfew for children under 17 years of age who lived in the neighbourhood of the storefront operation. The plaintiff had considerable contact with the adolescents of the affected age group and his response to this effort on the police's part was somewhat outlandish. His journal (ex. P-8) kept for assessment purposes contains the following:

> Mike: The curfew law is an abuse of power and a form of state control. You cannot tell a 14 or 15 year old to be in at 10.00 p.m. It represents age discrimination, it's unconstitutional.

. . .

Mike: What do—think this is the Soviet Union, a totalitarian state, this is in a free country and that law restricts freedom. That's bizzare [*sic*] to keep a kid in the house when it's 90° outside.

The above statements were made by the plaintiff at a meeting of neighbourhood residents to discuss the curfew issue.

Naturally his sponsor—the Fredericton Police Department—was concerned about this attitude and his on-site supervisor, Constable Blackmore wrote (ex. P-12) in her final assessment:

Mike has a tendency to want to buck the system. For instance when the children on Doone St. started to get out of hand, the police and New Brunswick Housing decided to enforce the curfew by-law. This caused an uproar amongst the children and Mike got on the band wagon and advised the kids to fight the laws of the land and start protesting what the establishment stood for. He told them laws like this were made for Russia and that it was against their charter of rights to be told when they should be in the house etc. This caused a great deal of concern amongst the parents who were already having disciplinary problems with their children. On [the] one hand they were telling their children to be in by 10 p.m. and on the other here is this professional telling them to fight the law that states they must be in by 10 p.m. My other concern was that I was hired as a police officer to uphold the laws that are written and here I am employing a guy who is telling everyone not to follow these laws.

Mike and I as well as several of the mothers of the community had a long discussion about the consequences of this action he was planning, and I think after he thought about it he realized that if he had followed through with his plan of action he may have started an all out war amongst the children, their parents and the police department.

In the end Professor DeVink, in a reasoned and responsible fashion gave the plaintiff a failing grade in Social Work 410. Although not strictly necessary for me to say so in order to reach a decision on the issues it is evident that the plaintiff at the best displayed considerable immaturity and lack of judgment during the practicum and at the worst the practicum demonstrated that he had made an unfortunate career choice. These qualities were further emphasized by his behaviour toward Professor DeVink during the appeal process and his conduct during a November, 1987 Provincial Court matter as described by Laurel Lewey, at the time an employee of the Fredericton Police Department. It is not necessary to detail these incidents except to say I accept Professor DeVink's and Ms. Lewey's testimony as being factual.

The final assessment (ex. P-11) of Professor DeVink says in part:

After careful consideration of all the facts as I know them and after having consulted with both Cst. Peggy Blackmore and Gaynell Cloney, I am recommending that Mike Bell fail this field placement.

As Coordinator of Field Instruction it is my decision that any future training plans will be discussed with Mike after I have consulted with the faculty on available options.

For your information, the first level of appeal of this decision is with the Chairperson of the Department of Social Work and the second level of appeal is with the Student Academic Grievance Committee.

The plaintiff then followed two approaches to alleviate the situation. He appealed the failing grade and he tried to retake the course.

He followed the appeal approach through various levels finally reaching the university senate. At each level his appeal was rejected. The university senate said in a letter to the plaintiff of February 1, 1989 (ex. P-45):

The University senate met on January 19, 1989 and considered the report from the senate committee on your appeal of your final grade in SW 410. Senate accepted the recommendation of the committee, viz. "That there be no change in the final grade in SW 410 awarded Mr. Michael Bell."

During the time the appeal was wending its way through the university bureaucracy the faculty decided to re-admit the plaintiff to S.W. 410 on certain terms. On September 28, 1987, Ms. Marilyn McKay wrote the plaintiff (ex. P-20) in part as follows:

At this point I want to formally let you know that in consultation with the faculty of the Department of Social Work I have decided to allow you to repeat SW 410, if you chose [*sic*] to do so, and if you are able to demonstrate that you are ready and willing to fully involve yourself in the learning process.

What I mean by "involving yourself in the learning process" is that you must be willing to:

(1) reflect on and evaluate your own professional behaviour in light of its impact on the practice situation,
(2) identify your own strengths and weaknesses and to set goals for development,
(3) take initiative in identifying and seeking out opportunities for learning and development,
(4) seek out and make use of feedback as a guide in your learning and practice,
(5) work at clearly articulating what you are learning from your practice experience. ...

In order to demonstrate your readiness to re-enter SW 410, you must submit the following documentation:

1. A detailed account of your learnings from the placement which you did in May, June and July, 1987.
2. An evaluation of your strengths and weakness by filling out the skills evaluation sheet (attached) and drawing up a written report summarizing the results.

3. A detailed outline of your needs in relation to the learning process (i.e. the conditions under which you learn best, the kind of assistance you need from others, etc.)

4. A detailed account of how you see your responsibility in the learning process.

5. A list of learning objectives for the placement.

Pending your response to these five questions and depending on the quality of your response, plans will then be made with you to repeat SW 410.

The plaintiff made three attempts to comply with the department's demands.

The first submission which was undated, unsigned and handwritten on paper torn from a notebook met with the following response (ex. P-25) from Professer McKay:

3. Your statement regarding how you see your role and responsibility as a learner is unacceptable in the sense that being "subservient" does not suggest a willingness to take responsibility for your learning. In fact I felt your response was flippant and reflective of a lack of respect for yourself and for the social work faculty.

In summary, then, your submission is not convincing of your readiness to engage in the learning process or to undertake another fourth year field placement. We will consider another submission from you but would suggest that you take the time you need to reflect carefully on what is being asked of you in this submission and to be sure in your own mind that you are ready to do a field placement. I will expect to hear something from you by the end of the academic year (April 29, 1988) regarding your plans (i.e. either another request to redo the course or some indication of when you would be ready to do so).

Please be advised that your status in this program is in jeopardy and I would advise you to think carefully before making another inappropriate and inadequate submission or request.

The plaintiff tried again on two further occasions and each time his submissions were rejected. The university rejected his last submission as follows:

The Department has reviewed your recent application to repeat SW 410 Field Instruction II and is in unanimous agreement not to accept you for enrollment in this course.

Your written submission, once again, was not convincing that the problems which persisted in your previous field placement have been satisfactorily resolved by you—particularly in terms of your ability to accept responsibility for your own actions, and to work in collaboration with field supervisors.

This action was started in April, 1989.

The plaintiff as already mentioned has pleaded negligent misrepresentation and breach of contract.

The plaintiff's counsel in argument said the defendant negligently misrepresented in the mid-term assessment that the plaintiff could retake the course or that a different field placement would be considered (see: ex. P-9) and the plaintiff relied on this statement.

Although not specifically mentioned in the pre-trial brief or in argument I conclude the plaintiff's counsel is referring to tort liability on the basis of the *Hedley Byrne* principle when he mentioned negligent misrepresentation.

For tort liability to attach on the basis of the judgment in *Hedley Byrne & Co. v. Heller & Partners, Ltd.*, [1963] 2 All E.R. 575 (H.L.), it is generally considered there must be, inter alia, a false statement negligently made, reasonable reliance on the statement by the recipient and a loss resulting from that reliance: see *V.K. Mason Construction Ltd. v. Bank of Nova Scotia* (1985), 16 D.L.R. (4th) 598, [1987] 1 S.C.R. 271, 35 R.P.R. 118.

At the time the mid-term evaluation was written the plaintiff had not yet failed the course. He was cautioned by his faculty advisor that he stood in danger of failing the course but that, of course, was somewhat conjectural at that time and the result was largely in the plaintiff's hands.

The following statement was made on the mid-term evaluation:

> In the event that Mike has not been able to learn these skills to a satisfactory degree, we will consider extending this field placement and or selecting another field placement which may be more appropriate in teaching the skills required.

I cannot see how it can be said that it was a false statement or that the plaintiff relied on it. Perhaps after the plaintiff failed the course the faculty did "consider" extending the field placement or selecting another placement and rejected both in favour of the action they did select. Further, when the statement was written the plaintiff had not yet failed the course. He could not at that time and there is not evidence that he did rely on the statement to his detriment.

The plaintiff's action on the basis of negligent misrepresentation fails.

I turn now to the plaintiff's claim that the defendant breached the contract between them by not allowing him to retake Social Work 410.

There is no dispute that there was a contractual relationship between the plaintiff and defendant. The calendar formed an essential part of that contract in setting out the terms of the relationship: see *Acadia University v. Sutcliffe* (1978), 30 N.S.R. (2d) 423 (C.A.), and *Doane v. Mount Saint Vincent University* (1977), 74 D.L.R. (3d) 297, 24 N.S.R. (2d) 298 (T.D.).

The calendar (ex. P-1) says with reference to retaking a course:

Repeating Courses

Students may, without special permission, register for a course already taken in order to meet a prerequisite or other degree requirement or in order to improve their grade in the course. Students should note that the final grades of repeated courses will be counted in the annual gps's but the course credit will be counted only once towards the minimum number of credits required for a degree.

In his pre-trial brief counsel for the defendant argues that the "peculiarities of the situation make it reasonable to infer other terms of the relationship, specifically the right to impose reasonable conditions on the repeat of the SW 410 course."

Counsel was unable to direct me to any material which would indicate a modification or variation of the clear wording contained in the calendar.

Professors McKay and DeVink testified conditions were imposed on the plaintiff because of S.W. 410's peculiar nature. Students, while taking the practicum, come face to face with individuals who might have severe personal and social problems and there is substantial potential for damage to individuals other than the student. Such is not the case with the normal academic university course. Accordingly, the faculty imposed conditions on the plaintiff's re-entry to the course.

The faculty may well have had ample reason for imposing conditions on the plaintiff; however, those conditions, in my view, violated the terms of the contract between the plaintiff and the university. The contract should have allowed him to re-enter the course without condition or, in the words of the calendar "without special permission," and the defendant is in breach of its contractual obligations in not permitting the plaintiff to do so.

Mr. Bell seeks damages in the following terms:

> As a result of the breach of contract and negligent misrepresentation asserted above the plaintiff has been damaged in that he is unable to work as a Social Worker, his reputation has been impugned, he has suffered mental anguish and he has suffered a loss of income and the plaintiff claims damages from the defendant as follows:
>
> i. Special damages:
>
> (a) Costs of registering and attending St. Thomas University; $11,550.00
> (b) Loss of income of $8,750.00 per year over 20 years; $175,000.00.
>
> ii. General damages;
> iii. Exemplary damages;
> iv. Costs of this action;
> v. Any other remedy this Honourable Court deems just.

There was no evidence adduced with respect to either exemplary or general damages. Exemplary damages are of a preventative [*sic*] character and I do not see how the defendant's conduct warrants such damages inasmuch as its actions were, in my view, taken in good faith. General damages are not available in an action of this type: see *McBeth v. Governors of Dalhousie College & University* (1986), 26 D.L.R. (4th) 321, 10 C.P.C. (2d) 69, 72 N.S.R. (2d) 224 (C.A.).

The object of awarding damages for breach of contract is to place the aggrieved party in the same situation as if the contract had been carried through. It may be the breach has, in exceptional cases, not caused a loss. Here the breach has simply prevented the plaintiff from retaking the course.

He had already incurred substantial expenses in attending university to that point and has claimed the cost of registering and attending the defendant institution amounting to $11,500. Has he lost these expenses as a result of the defendant's actions? There was evidence the plaintiff has returned to St. Thomas and taken courses which, when coupled with the courses taken before the practicum have given him sufficient credits to obtain a Bachelor of Arts degree. In my view, the plaintiff has not established the value of the money expended by him at St. Thomas has been diminished by the defendants' action.

The plaintiff further claims a loss of income of $8,750 per year over 20 years amounting to $175,000. The plaintiff's pre-trial brief says:

> Had the Plaintiff been able to fufill [sic] the requirements for the bachelor of Social Work degree, which he was entitled to do, he would probably have obtained gainfull employment as a Social Worker. The program boasts a 90 per cent employment placement rate. It is reasonable to expect that the Plaintiff would have been employed. There is, therefore, serious claim for loss of income. This would commence in the fall of 1987, when he should have received his bachelor of Social Work degree, or at least as of January, 1988 at which time he would have had all the necessary degree requirements for his degree. This would amount to loss of more than four and a half years.

The only evidence about social workers' salaries and their employment placement rate came from the plaintiff. Such evidence at the best can only be called anecdotal and not conclusive.

As well, should the plaintiff retake the course he may well fail it again. It is too remote to say that he has lost income as a social worker at this juncture.

It has been said the plaintiff has the burden of proving both the fact and the amount of damage before he can recover substantial damages: see *McGregor on Damages*, 15th ed. (London: Sweet and Maxwell, 1988), p. 1134, para. 1779, cited with approval in *Mason v. Royal Insurance Canada*; Court of Appeal of New Brunswick, June 9, 1992 [summarized 33 A.C.W.S. (3d) 1181].

I am not satisfied the plaintiff has established an entitlement to damages under this head.

The plaintiff has not established that any damages have flowed from the defendant's breach of contract. The plaintiff's action therefore fails. As I have mentioned, the question of the plaintiff's entitlement to an order compelling the defendant to re-admit him to the course is not before me. Had it been, the result might well have been different.

The plaintiff has established the defendant has breached the contract but he has not established any damages. Accordingly, each party will bear their own costs.

Action dismissed.

Purpose

Facts

Issues

Law

Ratio Decidendi

Decision

Disposition

Banyasz v. K-Mart Canada Ltd.

(1986), 33 D.L.R. (4th) 474
Ontario High Court of Justice, Divisional Court,
Callaghan A.C.J.H.C.

S. Pasternak, for appellant.

G. Will, for respondent.

CALLAGHAN A.C.J.H.C. (orally):—This is an appeal by the plaintiff from the judgment of the Provincial Court (Civil Division) of North York, Ontario, dated February 12, 1985, wherein the plaintiff's claim for damages for false imprisonment was dismissed.

The plaintiff was suspected of shoplifting and was taken into custody by the security personnel employed by the defendant store. It was suspected that the plaintiff had stolen a battery for a walkie-talkie and had left the store without paying for the same. Upon investigation it became immediately apparent that the cashier had made a mistake in ringing up the amount chargeable to the plaintiff. Notwithstanding the admitted mistake, the security personnel continued to hold the plaintiff for a short period of time thereafter.

The learned trial judge considered the pertinent elements of the cause of action and concluded on the evidence that the plaintiff in fact was detained by the security personnel and that there was a constructive imprisonment (transcript, p. 24, line 2). As there was evidence to support such a finding this court will not interfere therewith on this appeal. The trial judge further concluded that while the plaintiff left the store with a battery he had not paid for there was no evidence of any intent on the plaintiff's part to commit theft or fraud (*ibid.* p. 76, line 15). The aforesaid conclusion was consistent with the finding that the mistake was that of the cashier in failing to charge the plaintiff the cost of the battery which was not included in the walkie-talkie. The effect of the trial judge's finding was that a criminal offence in the circumstances of this case had not been committed.

In considering a disposition of the matter, the trial judge stated the applicable test as follows:

> If there is reasonable and probable grounds. If the defendant objectively had reasonable and probable grounds for believing that fraud had been committed, then the actions of the defendant were justified.

(*Ibid.* p. 75, line 29).

The trial judge concluded that in the circumstances the security personnel had reasonable and probable grounds for believing that theft had been committed and accordingly dismissed the plaintiff's action. In so doing he erred.

At the outset it must be noted that "security personnel" employed to guard against theft of merchandise have no higher rights of arrest than those conferred on citizens generally: *Dendekker v. F.W. Woolworth Co.,* [1975] 3 W.W.R. 429. The appropriate rule is that established in the case of *Williams v. Laing* (1923), 55 O.L.R. 26 at p. 28, wherein Mr. Justice Hodgins stated:

The law is quite clear that in order to succeed in establishing this defence the appellants must prove first that the crime they suspected had actually been committed, not necessarily by the person detained, but by some one, and that they had reasonable ground for suspecting the person detained.

Mere suspicion that an offence has been committed is not sufficient when arrest is effected by a citizen. The person alleging justification for arrest must be prepared to establish that the crime was in fact committed: see also *McKenzie v. Gibson* (1852), 8 U.C.Q.B. 100 at p. 101-2, *per* Sir John Robinson C.J.

Under s. 449 of the *Criminal Code* a citizen can make an arrest where he or she finds another committing an indictable offence. Where the defendant is unable to prove that the person arrested has committed an indictable offence, the defendant cannot arrest merely on reasonable and probable grounds: see *Hayward v. F.W. Woolworth Co. Ltd. et al.* (1979), 98 D.L.R. (3d) 345, 23 Nfld. & P.E.I.R. 17, 8 C.C.L.T. 157; *Kendall et al. v. Gambles Canada Ltd. et al.*, [1981] 4 W.W.R. 718, 11 Sask. R. 361.

The defendant/respondent herein relied on the judgment in *Karogiannis v. Poulus et al.* (1976), 72 D.L.R. (3d) 253, [1976] 6 W.W.R. 197. In that case it was held that it was not necessary that the defendant show that the plaintiff had actually committed theft but only that he had reasonable grounds for believing and did believe that a theft had been committed. The court therein held that s. 449(1)(a) of the *Criminal Code* is to be read as if it included the word "apparently" so that it would read "whom he finds (apparently) committing an indictable offence" and thereby affords justification for a defendant who arrested a person who in fact did not commit an offence. With respect, I cannot agree with that decision. I am in agreement with the reasoning of Mr. Justice Goodridge in *Hayward v. F.W. Woolworth Co. Ltd.*, *supra*, and Mr. Justice Cameron in *Kendall et al. v. Gambles Canada Ltd.*, *supra*, wherein that interpretation of s. 449 is rejected.

The problem of shoplifting is a serious one for storekeepers notwithstanding that the law of tort favours the interest in individual freedom over that of protection of property. While there may be a developing privilege of temporary detention for investigation in favour of a property owner (see Prosser, *Handbook of the Law of Torts*, 4th ed. (1971), p. 121), this is not a case where such a privilege should prevail. The continued detention after the cashier admitted her mistake negatives any consideration of such a privilege in this case.

In result, therefore, the appeal must be allowed, a verdict entered for the plaintiff, and the matter referred back to the trial judge for an assessment of damages. The plaintiff will have its costs of this appeal and the costs of the first trial in the court below. The costs of this assessment will be reserved to the trial judge.

Appeal allowed.

Note that a case may interpret or explain a statutory provision. In *Banyasz*, the court had to interpret s. 449 (now s. 494) of the *Criminal Code*.

449.(1) Any one may arrest without warrant

(a) a person whom he finds committing an indictable offence; or

(b) a person who, on reasonable grounds, he believes

(i) has committed a criminal offence, and

(ii) is escaping from and freshly pursued by persons who have lawful authority to arrest that person.

Section 449 should be read together with s. 450. Section 449 establishes the right of a citizen to make an arrest, while s. 450 establishes the right of a peace (police) officer to make an arrest.

450. [now s. 495] (1) A peace officer may arrest without warrant

(a) a person who has committed an indictable offence or who, on reasonable grounds, he believes has committed or is about to commit an indictable offence,

(b) a person whom he finds committing a criminal offence.

Purpose

Facts

Issues

Law

Ratio Decidendi

Decision

Disposition

2. Read the following fact situations. Using the case law you examined in question 1, answer the question following each fact situation.

a. A babysitter in Manitoba became very fond of the little girl she looked after, and the child adored the babysitter. The parents decided to hire a live-in nanny and let the babysitter go, but the babysitter still came each afternoon to visit the child. After a while it became clear that these visits were making it difficult for the nanny to establish a good relationship with the child. The parents told the babysitter that she could no longer visit the child. The babysitter has come to you for advice. She would like to apply to the court for access.

Would the babysitter's application for access be likely to succeed? Explain, quoting the relevant law.

b. Natalie Davies is a student in the law clerk program at Maple Leaf
    College in your province. When she enrolled, she was given a copy of
    the student calendar, which stated in part:

    > Withdrawal before the third scheduled class of a subject with seven
    > or more scheduled classes will delete any reference in the student
    > academic record. Full tuition fees less an administrative charge will
    > be refunded.

    > Natalie registered in four courses, one of which was corporate law.
    > It had 28 scheduled classes over a 14-week period. At the end of the
    > second scheduled class, Natalie went to the registrar's office to
    > withdraw from the course. There, she was told that no reference to
    > corporate law would appear in her academic record, but that she
    > would not receive a refund because too many people were registering
    > in courses and then dropping them after one or two classes, and the
    > college wanted to discourage students from doing that. Natalie has
    > come to your law firm for advice.

    i. What legal action can Natalie take?

    ii. What is your authority for saying so? (Be specific; quote the
        relevant law.)

    iii. In your province, does the *Bell* case have binding authority or persuasive authority? Explain. (In order to answer this question, you'll first have to read chapter 6, pages 81-83 on binding law.)

c. In each of the following fact situations, can Mrs. McGillicuddy win an action for false imprisonment? Explain, quoting the relevant law. (In order to answer this question, you will first have to read chapter 6, pages 81-83 on binding law.)

    i. Mrs. Lucy McGillicuddy was shopping in Zellers for children's clothing. When she shops, she always carries a large straw bag for her purchases. She picked up a dress and examined it closely and then put it back on the rack. When she was leaving the store, a sales clerk followed her and said, "Excuse me, ma'am, just a minute." The clerk then signalled to a police officer who was walking past the entrance. The officer came in and the clerk said to her, "Please arrest this woman, she shoplifted something and it's in her bag." The officer took Mrs. McGillicuddy by the arm and asked her to come with her to a back room. She would not allow Mrs. McGillicuddy to leave while she searched her bag. The officer found nothing and told Mrs. McGillicuddy she was free to go. Mrs. McGillicuddy then left.

ii. Mrs. Lucy McGillicuddy was shopping in Zellers for children's clothing. When she found a little dress she liked, she dropped it into the large straw bag she always carries when she shops. After looking at various other items in the store, she went to the exit. A sales clerk stopped her just outside the store and said, "Will you please come with me. I was watching you on the security monitor and you have stolen something." The sales clerk then asked her to come with him to a back room, where he and a store manager searched her bag and found the dress. Mrs. McGillicuddy was locked in the small, windowless room for half an hour until a police officer came to arrest her and took her to the police station.

Thinking About Legal Research

Many of the exercises in this workbook can be done in the classroom. However, eventually you will have to go to a law library or have access to a computer to find and use the legal research resources. The exercises relating to working in a law library and working with computerized sources are necessarily general in this book. Your instructor should have exercises that will require you to find out what the law actually is during the time that you are doing the exercises, because one of the purposes of this research is to update the law as much as possible.

Sometimes legal research merely means having to find and photocopy a particular statute, regulation, or case. Analysis may not be necessary.

Other times, however, you must perform legal research involving a stated fact situation. When this happens, going to the library or turning on the computer to look for cases and statutes is *not* the first thing to do. The first thing is to analyze the given facts in order to identify which relevant issues and tools you'll need to do the research.

CHAPTER 5

How To Analyze a Fact Situation

When researching a given fact situation, you will

- identify the issues on a preliminary basis,
- formulate the issues, and
- identify the need for further information.

IDENTIFY THE ISSUES ON A PRELIMINARY BASIS

Identifying issues is not easy. Issues are the specific problems that must be solved in order to provide a solution to the entire fact situation. The following questions may help you to decide what issues arise out of a given set of facts.

What Is the Question Being Asked?

The question may be direct—for example, "Please find a case that says that an unborn child has no legal status in Canadian courts."

The question may be indirect—that is, in the form of a statement of what the client wants. The client may want to be financially compensated for an injury, to avoid having to pay damages for breach of contract in an action that has been brought against him or her, or to protect an interest in real or personal property.

What Is the Area of Law?

First,

- Identify the problem by general area—for example, criminal law, tort, contracts, family law, or real property. (If you are unsure, try this: identify key words in the fact situation and find them in the key word index of the *Canadian Encyclopedic Digest* (CED), discussed in chapter 8.

For example, in a fact situation involving a loan at a high rate of interest, the key word "interest" will lead you to the CED's "Debtor and Creditor" title.)

Then,

- Identify the problem by specific area: if the general area is contract law, is the specific area breach of contract or assignment of a contract? If the general area is family law, is the specific area divorce or custody?

Narrow the area of law further. If the specific area is custody, is the narrower area the child's best interests or the jurisdiction of a court to hear the matter? The more specific the area of law that you investigate, the more quickly and easily you will find answers.

What Is Needed? Develop a Theory of the Case

A theory of the case is a strategy for winning. What is needed to win may be different from what is being asked for. Clients may *want* things that are not legally possible or that do not provide the best solution to the problem. The issue—the problem to be solved—may not be the one that the client has identified.

You may have to identify possible causes of action for a plaintiff or defences for a defendant, or, to be more general, the best legal means by which the client can reach the best solution. Once you have identified a cause of action or defence, examine it element by element to make sure that the requirements of that action or defence can be made out. To do this, you must review the evidence that is available in support of the action or defence. You are now developing a theory of the case.

Are There Any Hidden Issues?

The obvious issues can be hard enough to find, but you have to keep in mind that some issues, such as the following, are hidden:

- Are there any special procedural requirements—for example, is there a limitation period that may expire shortly? Are there any statutes or regulations governing procedure in the court or tribunal? Is the correct jurisdiction federal or provincial?
- Who, in law, are the parties involved? Issues may arise out of the parties' legal status. For example, are they natural persons, corporations, adults, minors, spouses, mentally incompetent persons, the Crown, or an agent?

FORMULATE THE ISSUES

Write down the issues you have identified, starting with the word "whether."

Examples
- whether a person who is not a parent of a child may apply for custody of that child;
- whether the limitation period for medical malpractice begins to run from the date of the medical procedure;
- whether a defence of consent may exist in an action for assault.

IDENTIFY THE NEED FOR FURTHER INFORMATION

After you have made a preliminary identification of the issues as set out above under the heading, "Identify the Issues on a Preliminary Basis," you may realize that you need more information before you can do your research. For example, you may need more facts to decide whether a cause of action has arisen, or you may need to know the legal status of all parties involved in the problem.

EXERCISES

Analyze the following fact situations. You need a basic understanding of tort and contract law to do this exercise; you also need to refer to statute law, covered in chapter 2.

1. The client is an imposing man. He is 2 metres tall, weighs 100 kilograms, has a beard and several tattoos, dresses in biker clothing, and wears a small knife dangling from one ear as an earring. Two days ago, the client attended a business meeting downtown. He parked his motorcycle at a meter and inserted money. The meeting took longer than he expected and he excused himself to put more money in the meter. When he reached his motorcycle, he found that he only had a loonie and pennies, and the meter would take only quarters, nickels, and dimes. He noticed a meter officer issuing tickets four vehicles away from his. He then spoke to a woman who was passing by with a child in a stroller. He said, "Excuse me, madam, do you have any change?" The woman screamed, said "Please don't hurt my baby," and ran. The client then spoke to a man and asked him if he had change for a dollar. The man said that he did not, but that he had a quarter and the client could have it. The client accepted the quarter with thanks and was about to put it into the meter when a police officer approached him. The officer asked to see the client's identification and wrote down his name and address. The client has come into the law office on another matter, but mentioned this incident because of his concern about being charged with a crime.

    a. What is the question being asked?

b. What is the area of law?
    i. General area

    ii. Specific area

    iii. What key words helped you identify the area?

c. What is needed? Develop a theory of the case (for a defence).

d. Formulate the issues
        Whether …

e. Are there any hidden issues?

f. Do you need any further information?

2. Your client, a Canadian charity called the World United Fund, has come to you with a problem. It recently ran a $1 million campaign to get donations to build a school in a poor country. Mrs. Euphemia Welsher promised to give $25,000; when the Fund had the entire $1 million in hand except for Mrs. Welsher's donation, it publicly declared the campaign successfully ended. Mrs. Welsher then told the Fund that she was going to give the money to a home for cats in New York City, where she lives (except for the two months in the summer when she comes to Canada). Your client wants to know if it can sue Mrs. Welsher and get the money she promised to pay.

   a. What is the question being asked?

b. What is the area of law?

    i. General area

    ii. Specific area

    iii. What key words helped you identify the area?

    c. What is needed? Develop a theory of the case.

    d. Formulate the issues
          Whether …

    e. Are there any hidden issues?

f.   Do you need any further information?

3. A client has instructed your firm to bring an action for malicious prosecution against the local police. One night last week, he was celebrating his 21st birthday with friends at a suburban strip club. The friends didn't have a lot to drink, but when they became quite lively in the club they were asked to leave. In the parking lot, they talked to each other for a while and then left in their own cars. The client was the last to leave.

As he was getting into his car, a man suddenly appeared and told him to step away from the car. The client asked the man who he was. The man, who was wearing jeans and a T-shirt, told him that he was a police officer, showed him a police badge, and asked him to accompany him to his car—not a marked police car—which was close by. The man told the client to sit in the back seat while he checked out the client's driver's licence and vehicle licence. He did so using a cell phone.

The client says that at one point the man said something such as, "A bunch of us are just out here having a good time with Stan. Yeah, he's retiring, and we have to deal with some gang." At another point, the man said, "It's my day off, can't you hurry it up?" The client says he and his friends have never been in trouble with the law, and that he was just getting picked on because he's young, not because he was doing anything wrong. The client was forced to sit in the man's car for about 10 minutes before he was told he could go.

a.   What is the question being asked?

b. What is the area of law identified by the client?
    i. General area

    ii. Specific area

    iii. What key words helped you identify the area?

c. Why would you discourage the client from bringing this action?

d. What different (and more promising) cause of action have you identified?

e. Formulate the issues
Whether …

f. Are there any hidden issues?

g. Do you need any further information?

h. From a practical point of view, would you advise the client to go ahead with the action you have identified? Why or why not?

CHAPTER 6

How To Research a Subject

After you have analyzed the given fact situation, you will be ready to proceed with your research to find out the law that applies to your client's fact situation.

This chapter discusses the following topics:

- binding law and persuasive law,
- which secondary and primary sources may be useful, and
- performing the research.

BINDING LAW AND PERSUASIVE LAW

When you research, you are looking first for **binding law** in favour of your client, and next for **persuasive law** in favour of your client. You also want to know about binding law and persuasive law that go against your client, so that you understand what opposition you face. Unfavourable case law may be "distinguished" in argument—that is, a lawyer may persuade a judge that the facts in *this* case are so different from those in existing case law that the case law is not applicable.

What Is Binding Law?

Binding law is law that must be followed by a court and includes statute law, regulatory law, and case law.

1. Federally enacted statute law and regulations bind the courts in all provinces; provincially enacted statute law and regulations bind the courts in the province of enactment. Both federal and provincial legislation must meet the requirements of the Canadian constitution (the

binding law
law that must be followed by a court

persuasive law
law that a court is not required to follow, but may follow if it wishes (usually case law)

British North America Act, 1867, and the *Constitution Act, 1982,* including the *Charter of Rights and Freedoms*).

2. A **binding decision** is an existing decision in a case that a judge must follow if the facts in that case and in the case before the court are sufficiently similar. The principle that similar cases should be decided in a similar fashion is known as ***stare decisis*** (Latin for "to stand by those things that have been decided"). Note that the only part of a binding decision that is actually binding is the *ratio decidendi*.

3. ***Obiter dicta*** (Latin for "words by the way"—in the singular, *obiter dictum*; whether singular or plural, often referred to simply as "*obiter*") are opinions expressed by a judge in his or her reasons for a decision that did not directly concern the legal issue(s) that had to be decided in the case. *Obiter* is not binding. Note, though, that *obiter* of the Supreme Court of Canada is often treated with great respect and, according to at least one case, may be binding on lower courts.

4. In a case on appeal where there is a majority opinion and a **dissent** (a different decision by a minority of the appeal judges), only the majority *ratio* is binding. (If there is more than one majority opinion, of course there will be more than one *ratio*.) Dissenting opinions have no judicial value, although they sometimes have persuasive value and lead the way for a change in the law, especially when expressed by judges on the Supreme Court of Canada.

binding decision
existing decision that a judge must follow if the facts in that case and in the case before the court are sufficiently similar

stare decisis
Latin for "to stand by those things that have been decided"

obiter dicta
Latin for "words by the way"

dissent
different decision by a minority of appeal judges

Case Law: What Decisions Bind Which Courts?

The theory underlying *stare decisis* is that it is pointless for a judge not to follow a decision of a higher court, because if the judge's decision is appealed, it will be reversed on appeal in accordance with the higher court's existing decision. Obviously, this theory does not apply unless the courts are in the same chain of appeal.

A decision of the *Supreme Court of Canada* binds every court in Canada, but it does not bind the Supreme Court itself. However, the court will not depart from its previous decisions without strong reasons.

Until 1949, a decision of the Supreme Court of Canada could be appealed to the *Privy Council* (P.C.) in Britain. The Privy Council was the House of Lords hearing an appeal from a British colony or former colony, and its decisions bound the Supreme Court of Canada and all Canadian courts below.

A decision of a *provincial Court of Appeal* binds every court and tribunal in that province, but does not bind the Court of Appeal itself, although the Court of Appeal will follow it unless there are good reasons not to. Where there are conflicting Court of Appeal decisions on an issue, lower courts should follow the most recent decision. A Court of Appeal decision is only persuasive outside the court's province.

A decision of the *Federal Court of Appeal* is binding on the Federal Court Trial Division, but is limited to the same persuasive value on courts of the provinces as a Court of Appeal decision made by a court outside the province.

A decision of the *Federal Court Trial Division* is binding on the Tax Court of Canada and may be persuasive to other judges of the Federal Court and of the provinces.

A decision of the *superior court of a province* may be considered binding on the inferior courts (the provincial courts and the small claims courts) of the province.

It is not binding on other judges of the superior court but ought to be followed by them in the absence of a compelling reason to the contrary. A superior court decision may be persuasive to judges in other provinces. These are the superior courts of the provinces:

Alberta	Court of Queen's Bench
British Columbia	Supreme Court of British Columbia
Manitoba	Court of Queen's Bench
New Brunswick	Court of Queen's Bench
Newfoundland	Supreme Court (Trial Division)
Nova Scotia	Supreme Court
Ontario	Ontario Superior Court of Justice
	In Ontario, until 1984, the superior court was called the Supreme Court of Ontario and its trial division was called the High Court of Justice. From 1984 until 1999, the superior court was called the Ontario Court of Justice (General Division). Cases from the High Court or the Ontario Court of Justice (General Division) have the same binding or persuasive effect as cases from the Ontario Superior Court of Justice.
Saskatchewan	Court of Queen's Bench
Northwest Territories	Supreme Court for the Northwest Territories
Nunavut	Nunavut Court of Justice
Yukon	Supreme Court

Until recently, there was another court level in many provinces, below the superior court, called the *County Court* or the *District Court*. County or District Court decisions may be considered persuasive in a province's superior court.

Masters are judge-like officers who decide certain procedural matters in the superior court of some provinces. A decision of a master is not binding on judges of any court but is persuasive to other masters.

A decision of the *Provincial Court of a province* is not binding on, but is persuasive to, other judges of the Provincial Court.

Decisions from jurisdictions outside Canada, such as the United Kingdom and the United States, are not binding on Canadian courts. Whether they are persuasive depends on the similarity of the law of the foreign jurisdiction to the law in the particular Canadian jurisdiction. Be careful about using modern English cases: some of what is still "common law" in Canada is now statute law in England, and English case law in those areas will not be useful in Canadian courts.

master
judge-like officer who decides certain procedural matters in the superior courts of some provinces

WHICH SECONDARY AND PRIMARY SOURCES MAY BE USEFUL?

Whether you are looking for statute law or case law, it is usually wise to begin your research with a secondary source (either in paper or computerized form). Specific primary and secondary sources are discussed in detail in the chapters that follow.

To begin, look at the following secondary sources:

- a legal encyclopedia;
- a text;
- a looseleaf service (a text that is updated on a continuing basis);
- articles, including conference and seminar materials;
- a digest of cases; or
- an index to statutes or cases;

or speak to a person who is knowledgeable about the particular area of law. Two reasons for taking this approach are: (1) a good legal researcher always lets someone else do the work if possible—you may find that the author of a text has considered the issue and lined up the answer for you already, together with citations of statutes and cases (all you will need to do is update); and (2) a good legal researcher does not focus on the pre-identified issue as quickly as possible, but scans the law in the area generally to check whether the issue has in fact been correctly identified, or if there is another way of looking at the problem to be solved.

PERFORMING THE RESEARCH

Performing the research can be time-consuming and require a lot of concentration. You don't want to do the research more than once if you can avoid it. Follow these guidelines:

Take Notes

As you look through primary and secondary sources, take notes. You should have notes on the following:

1. *Information that seems relevant or interesting*—for example, the citation of a case and a short description of what is useful about the case.

   A sense of *déjà vu* as you look for new information indicates that you have exhausted the topic. Then you must *update* the information. Check for

   a. amendments to a statute or regulation,
   b. interpretation of a statute or regulation in case law,
   c. whether a case was appealed, and
   d. whether a case has been considered by judges in more recent cases and, if so, whether it has been followed or ignored.

2. *The sources you have looked through*—make careful note of the edition or latest date of publication.

   After you have spent an hour or two on a particular text, statute, statute citator, or website, you may think you never will forget that you looked at that source, when you looked at it, or how much of it you looked at. But you will. If you return to research on a subject after two or three weeks, you will not remember exactly which sources you already have covered thoroughly. Noting carefully what you have done and on what date will help you to avoid doing the same research twice.

Review Your Analysis of the Fact Situation

Once you have looked at the law, you may find that the issues you identified on a preliminary basis are not right; you may also find that you need more information from the client or that you have discovered unexpected procedural problems.

If Necessary, Research the Subject Again

If your preliminary identification of the issues was faulty or if you receive new information to add to the fact situation, you may need to re-research the subject.

KEY TERMS

binding decision
binding law
dissent
master
obiter dicta
persuasive law
stare decisis

PART IV

Paper Legal Research Resources

The first question you are likely to have about the part of the book that follows is why is there so much of it? Why do you have to know so many different ways of finding one thing?

It's certainly true that there are usually several ways to find the same answer when you are doing legal research. However, unless you're in a well-equipped law library, such as a library at a big law school or a courthouse library in a large city, you won't have to worry about choosing one among many resources. Law books are expensive, and in many law libraries—in a community college, law firm, or a small courthouse—there is only one tool for finding statutes, one for regulations, and one for cases. That one tool could be any of the possibilities discussed below. So you don't need to know about all of them—just about the ones that are in the law library you use. But since you won't know what resources a law library has until you get there, you need to have an idea about when and how to use all the resources.

CHAPTER 7

An Overview of Paper Sources

The purpose of legal research is to find binding law that is relevant to a legal problem you need to solve. The law that you are looking for will be found in the form of statutes, regulations, and/or cases. These primary sources are not at all user-friendly, and, as we said in chapter 6, it is usually wise to start your research with secondary sources, using them to gain an understanding of the law and as "finding tools" to direct you to the primary sources that actually create the law.

This chapter begins to examine the process of finding law that is binding, using paper primary and secondary sources. We will start to look at the various legal research sources, according to the purpose they serve or the job that they do, and will discuss the following topics:

- finding tools,
- primary sources,
- updating tools, and
- working with paper sources.

The various sources are discussed more fully chapters 8, 9, 10, and 11.

FINDING TOOLS

Generally speaking, you will start your legal research using secondary sources that we call *finding tools*. These tools can be used to help you find

- a general statement of the law,
- specific statutes,
- specific regulations, and
- specific cases.

General Statement of the Law

It is best to start your research by finding a general statement of the law as it applies to the problem to be solved. Secondary sources that provide a general statement of the law include

- legal encyclopedias such as the *Canadian Encyclopedic Digest*,
- textbooks on a particular subject, and
- journal articles on a particular subject.

These sources will not only provide you with a summary of the law, but will refer you to the relevant statutes, regulations, and cases from which the principles of law are derived.

Finding a general statement of the law is discussed in more detail in chapter 8.

Specific Statutes

There are more specialized sources that are designed specifically to help you find statutes on a particular subject or area of law. These finding tools include:

- table of statutes or table of public statutes, and
- Mary McLean's *Index to Federal and Ontario Statutes*.

Finding statutes is discussed in more detail in chapter 9.

Specific Regulations

There are also more specialized sources that are designed specifically to help you find regulations on a particular subject or area of law. These finding tools include

- Carswell's *Canada Regulations Index*, and
- Carswell's *Ontario Regulation Service*.

Finding regulations is discussed in more detail in chapter 10.

Specific Cases

Legal encyclopedias, textbooks, and articles will refer you to only the leading cases on a particular subject. If you want to find additional cases, there are specialized sources designed specifically to help you do so. These finding tools include

- *Canadian Abridgment Case Digests* for cases dealing with specific subjects;
- *Canadian Statute Citations* (*Canadian Abridgment*) or statute citators for cases that interpret sections of statutes;
- *Words and Phrases Judicially Defined in Canadian Courts and Tribunals* (also part of the *Canadian Abridgment*) for cases considering a word or phrase;
- *Consolidated Table of Cases* or the *Canadian Case Citation* (also part of the *Canadian Abridgment*) if you are treasure hunting (in other words, trying to find a case using a partial or incorrect citation); and
- Digest services and legal newspapers for unreported cases.

Finding cases is discussed in more detail in chapter 11.

PRIMARY SOURCES

The finding tools will give you the names of the relevant statutes, regulations, and cases, and sometimes a summary of their provisions. As mentioned in chapter 1, you cannot rely on secondary sources alone. You may use them to gain an understanding of the law and as finding tools to direct you to the primary sources that actually create the law. You must then look at the primary sources they refer you to, read them, and understand what they say.

Finding the text of statutes is discussed in chapter 9; finding the text of regulations is discussed in chapter 10; and finding the text of cases is discussed in chapter 11.

UPDATING TOOLS

Once you find relevant statutes, regulations, and/or cases, you must make sure that the statutes and regulations you have found have not been amended or repealed and that the cases you have found have not been overturned on appeal nor the legal principles in them been changed by subsequent cases. You do this using secondary sources that we call *updating tools.*

The following sources will help you update statutes:

- statute citators;
- *Canadian Current Law: Legislation* (part of Carswell's *Canadian Abridgment*); and
- table of public statutes.

These updating tools are discussed more fully in chapter 9.

The following sources will help you update regulations:

- Ontario Regulation Service or *Canadian Current Law: Legislation* under "Regulations" (Ontario) for Ontario regulations; and
- Canada Regulations Index or *Canadian Current Law: Legislation* under "Regulations" for federal regulations.

These updating tools are discussed more fully in chapter 10.

The following sources will help you update cases:

- *Consolidated Table of Cases* (part of the *Canadian Abridgment*); and
- *Canadian Case Citations* (part of the *Canadian Abridgment*).

These updating tools are discussed more fully in chapter 11.

WORKING WITH PAPER SOURCES

As you can see, there are many paper legal research sources available. Before you begin to work with a particular source, you should take some time to become familiar with it. Every source takes a little time to understand. Useful tools for understanding include

- user's guide,
- table of contents, and
- index.

User's Guide

Most research sources include a **user's guide** or at least some information about how to use the source. In a single-volume source, the user's guide is usually found at the beginning of the volume. In a multiple-volume source, the user's guide may be found in the first volume of the source or in a separate volume. If you have not used a particular source before, it's a good idea to read the user's guide before you start.

Table of Contents

Most research sources contain a **table of contents**, which is a listing of the chapters or article titles in the source in the order in which they appear in the source, along with the page numbers where each chapter or article starts. The table of contents of a single-volume source is usually found at the beginning of the volume, after the title page. Each volume of a multi-volume source, such as an encyclopedia, usually contains a table of contents. In addition, there may be a table of contents for the entire multi-volume source.

A table of contents provides a quick overview of the content and organization of the source. Some tables of contents are quite detailed and provide not only chapter names, but a breakdown of the subjects covered in each chapter, in the order in which they are covered. Reading a detailed table of contents will therefore give you a sense of the major areas of importance in a particular subject and how they fit together.

Index

Most research sources also contain an **index**, which is a detailed list of the names, places, and subjects discussed in the source and the pages on which each subject appears, in alphabetical order. The index of a single-volume source is usually found at the end of the volume. Each volume of a multi-volume source, such as an encyclopedia, usually contains an index. In addition, there may be an index for the entire multi-volume source.

An index provides more detailed information about the contents of the source than the table of contents does. It is designed to help the reader quickly find information about a specific topic or concept in all of its locations throughout the source, not to give the reader an overview of what the source contains.

Table of Contents or Index?

If you are looking for information on a particular subject, start by looking at the table of contents. If there is a chapter dealing with your subject, turn to it. If the subject you are looking for is not listed in the table of contents, then look for the subject in the index. Even if the subject you are looking for is in the table of contents, you should also use the index if you are looking for specific, detailed information on a subject.

Working with Multi-volume Sources

If you are working with a multi-volume source, such as an encyclopedia, take some time to see how the volumes are organized. Generally, topics will be dealt with alphabetically across the entire source, with each volume dealing with topics starting with a particular letter (or letters) of the alphabet.

KEY TERMS

index
table of contents
user's guide

CHAPTER 8

Finding a General Statement of the Law: The Canadian Encyclopedic Digest

It is usually wise to start your research with secondary sources, using them to gain an understanding of the law and as finding tools to direct you to the primary sources that actually create the law. It is best to start your research by finding a general statement of the law as it applies to the legal problem you need to solve. Secondary sources that provide a general statement of the law include

- legal encyclopedias,
- textbooks on a particular subject, and
- journal articles on a particular subject.

These sources will not only provide you with a summary of the law, but will refer you to the relevant statutes, regulations, and cases from which the principles of law are derived.

This chapter deals with the only Canadian legal encyclopedia—the *Canadian Encyclopedic Digest* or CED. The CED is available in both print and computerized versions. This chapter focuses on the print version only. The computerized version of the CED is discussed in chapter 14.

WHAT IS THE CED?

The CED is one of the most comprehensive secondary sources dealing with Canadian law. It is a loose-leaf multi-volume legal encyclopedia that provides a very general overview of most areas of law. The CED is an excellent place to begin when you know very little about the area of law that you are researching. In the print version, there are two editions of the CED. The Ontario edition focuses on Ontario and federal laws. The western edition focuses on the law in the four western provinces—Manitoba, Saskatchewan, Alberta, and British Columbia.

THE CED VOLUMES

The CED is made up of over 150 subject titles contained in approximately 40 loose-leaf binders. The subject titles are broad topics of information or general areas of law, such as animals, contracts, evidence, or income tax. The spine of each CED volume sets out the volume number and the alphabetical range of subject titles contained in that volume. Each binder is given a volume number and is organized alphabetically by subject title.

Each subject title contains parts, sections, subsections, and sub-subsections, breaking the title down into increasingly more topic-specific areas of information. By narrowing down your research problem within the relevant subject title, you can find the general statement of law dealing with your particular topic.

At the beginning of each subject title there is a table of contents to help you find the specific topic within that subject that you would like to research. There is also a subject index at the end of each title that refers you to relevant paragraph numbers within that subject title.

Each subject title is given a name and a title number. Each subject title is then divided into parts that are given both a number (in uppercase roman numerals) and a name. Each part is divided into sections that are given both a number and a name. Each section may be further divided into headings (subtopics) that are given a letter and a name. Each heading may be further divided into subheadings that are given a number (lowercase roman numerals) and a name. Each section is divided into numbered paragraphs (not named) that provide the summary of the law, together with references to relevant cases and statutes.

The CED is updated regularly with supplemental sheets, found at the front of each subject title (printed on yellow or grey-edged paper). The supplemental sheets update case and statute references as well as other significant developments that have occurred since the publication date of the subject title. The paragraph numbers in the supplement correspond to the paragraph numbers in the main body of the text.

FINDING TOOLS

There are two separate finding tools to help you look for information in the CED:

- the Research Guide and Key, and
- the Index Key.

Research Guide and Key

The Research Guide and Key helps you find information in all the titles. It is found in a separate binder and contains three keys:

- the Contents Key,
- the Statutes Key, and
- the Rules and Regulations Key.

Contents Key

The **Contents Key** provides a list, in alphabetical order, of all the subject titles in the CED. It gives both the title number of the subject title and the volume number in which the subject title can be found.

Statutes Key

The **Statutes Key** provides a list, in alphabetical order, of all current federal and provincial statutes referred to in the various subject titles of the CED. It also provides the volume number, title number, and paragraph numbers where specific provisions of the statute are discussed or referred to.

Rules and Regulations Key

The **Rules and Regulations Key** provides a list, in alphabetical order, of the rules of court (rules of civil procedure) and regulations referred to in the CED's subject titles. It also provides a reference to the relevant volume and paragraph numbers.

Index Key

The **Index Key** is a separate binder containing an alphabetical list of keywords, together with extensive cross-references within and among subject titles. It combines the individual indexes from all the titles.

The Index Key is the best place to start when you do not know what subject title your research topic falls under. By looking up keywords dealing with your research problem, you can easily find the relevant subject title. By looking under specific topics within the relevant subject title, you will be referred to the volume, title, and paragraph number that provides a general statement of law on your specific topic.

As we mentioned above, there is also a table of contents at the beginning of each subject title, as well as a subject index at the end of each subject title. Both provide yet another way to find increasingly more specific information on your research topic.

How To Use the CED

The approach you take with the CED will depend on whether you know the area of law that deals with the problem to be solved.

If you know your area of law:

1. Choose the volume that contains the appropriate subject title.
2. Look at the table of contents at the beginning of the title, or look at the index at the end of the title. Either will refer you to a paragraph number.
3. Find the useful paragraphs and read about your topic. It's usually a good idea to at least skim the entire section.

Contents Key
alphabetical list of all the subject titles in the CED

Statutes Key
alphabetical list of all current federal and provincial statutes referred to in the various subject titles in the CED

Rules and Regulations Key
alphabetical list of the rules of court and regulations referred to in the subject titles in the CED

Index Key
separate binder combining the individual indexes from all titles and containing an alphabetical list of keywords, together with extensive cross-references within and among subject titles in the CED

4. Write down what the law is and note which cases or statutes are referred to.

5. Update each relevant paragraph by looking at the supplemental sheets at the front of the title.

If you don't know the area of law, use the Index Key, which combines the individual subject indexes from all the titles. This general index will refer you to a volume number, title number, and paragraph number.

Below we go into more detail about using the CED when you do and when you don't know your area of law.

AN EXAMPLE

The best way to learn how to use the CED is to work through an example. Assume that you have received a memo from a lawyer in your law firm that reads as follows:

> Our client in Toronto, Ontario has a cocker spaniel that barks constantly. One day last month, her neighbour went to her apartment to complain. When our client opened the door, the dog rushed out to attack the neighbour, who fell backwards and broke his leg. The neighbour is now suing your client for the injuries caused by the dog. Can our client be held legally responsible?

In order to advise your client, you will need to find a general statement of the law dealing with the issue whether a dog owner is responsible for the injuries caused by his or her dog.

Finding Your Topic When You Don't Know the Area of Law

If you do not know which area of law to look in, go to the Index Key. Find the relevant subject title by looking up keywords dealing with your problem. For example, if you look up the word DOG, you will be referred to the relevant subject title: ANIMALS. See figure 8.1, which reproduces the relevant page of the Index Key.

Next, look in the Index Key for the heading ANIMALS; then look for your specific topic, in this case "injuries by dogs (Ontario)." The entry refers you to the volume number, title number, and paragraph numbers for the specific topics under this general heading. See figure 8.2, which reproduces the relevant page of the Index Key dealing with ANIMALS. Note that for "general" information you are referred to 1A-6§373, 374. These numbers tell you that the summary or general statement of the law on your research topic can be found in volume 1A of the CED, under subject title number 6 in paragraph numbers 373 and 374.

Finding Your Topic When You Know the Area of Law

If you already know something about this area of law, including the relevant subject title, you can start your research by looking at the Contents Key (in the Research Guide and Key) to find the relevant volume number and subject title for your specific topic. The relevant page of the Contents Key is reproduced in figure 8.3. The Contents Key tells you that ANIMALS is subject title number 6 and can be found in volume 1A of the CED.

FIGURE 8.1   CED Index Key Showing Subject Title "Dogs"

INDEX

DIVORCE AND NULLITY – *cont.*

inflation 9-49§§444, 445, 445.1
   (Supp.)
interim orders 9-49§428
jurisdiction (general) 9-49§§414.2
   (Supp.), 414.3 (Supp.), 420.1
   (Supp.)
jurisdiction (Supreme Court)
   9-49§§415-17
jurisdiction (to increase) 9-49§422.2
   (Supp.)
limited term awards 9-49§§450
   (Supp.), 450.1 (Supp.)
lump sum awards 9-49§§451-53
material change 9-49§§410.1
   (Supp.)-10.3 (Supp.), 413.5 (Supp.),
   430.4 (Supp.), 430.5 (Supp.)
notice of objection 9-49§429
occupation, change 9-49§434.2
   (Supp.)
onus 9-49§424
parens patriae jurisdiction 9-49§428
   (Supp.)
payee's windfall 9-49§436
payor's arrears 9-49§§432, 433
payor's contempt 9-49§432
permanent 9-49§260
practice generally 9-49§§423, 423.1
   (Supp.)
principles governing court's discretion
   9-49§§430, 430.1 (Supp.), 430.2
   (Supp.)
provincial jurisdiction 9-49§§415,
   416, 418, 418.3 (Supp.)
provisional order 9-49§418.3 (Supp.)
reconciliation, effect of 9-49§422.1
   (Supp.)
remarriage/cohabitation 9-49§§437,
   437.1 (Supp.), 438, 438.1 (Supp.),
   439-43
report of referee 9-49§429
res judicata doctrine of 9-49§§420.2
   (Supp.), 424.1 (Supp.)
retirement of payor 9-49§434.1
   (Supp.)
scope of examination for discovery
   9-49§425
secured awards 9-49§454
severability of entitlement and quan-
   tum 9-49§427
submissions 9-49§418.2 (Supp.)
trilogy cases, principles 9-49§§410.3
   (Supp.), 421.2 (Supp.)

DOCKS. *See* SHIPPING.

DOCTORS. *See* HOSPITALS AND
   HEALTH CARE; NEGLIGENCE.

DOCUMENTS. *See* CONTRACTS; DEEDS
   AND DOCUMENTS; DISCOVERY; EVI-
   DENCE; REAL PROPERTY; SALE OF
   LAND; WILLS.

DOGS. *See* AGRICULTURE; ANIMALS;   ◄
   MUNICIPAL CORPORATIONS.

DOMESTIC CONTRACTS. *See* FAMILY
   LAW.

DOMICILE. *See* CONFLICT OF LAWS;
   CORPORATIONS; DIVORCE AND
   NULLITY; EXECUTORS AND AD-
   MINISTRATORS; INFANTS AND
   CHILDREN.

DOMINANT TENEMENT. *See* EASE-
   MENTS.

DONATIO MORTIS CAUSA. *See* GIFTS.

DOUBLE ACTIONABILITY. *See* CON-
   FLICT OF LAWS.

DOUBLE CRIMINALITY. *See* EXTRADI-
   TION.

DOWER. *See* DEVOLUTION OF ESTATES;
   EQUITY; FAMILY LAW; OIL AND
   GAS; REAL PROPERTY.

DRAFTS. *See* BANKING; BILLS OF EX-
   CHANGE.

DRAINAGE. *See also* AGRICULTURE;
   EASEMENTS; ENVIRONMENTAL
   LAW; HIGHWAYS AND STREETS;
   MUNICIPAL AND SCHOOL TAXES;
   MUNICIPAL CORPORATIONS;
   NEGLIGENCE; NUISANCE; PROFES-
   SIONS AND OCCUPATIONS; PUBLIC
   UTILITIES; RAILWAYS; REFERENCES
   AND INQUIRIES; TRESPASS; WATERS
   AND WATERCOURSES.
   assessment
      allowances 9-50§49-53
      appeal 9-50§§77, 78, 83
      area 9-50§54
      benefit 9-50§§46-48
      branch drains 9-50§54
      by-law 9-50§72

V-375   April 2005

FIGURE 8.2   CED Index Key Showing Topic "Injuries by Dogs (Ontario)"

THE KEY TO C.E.D.

ANIMALS – *cont.*

injuries by dogs (negligence)
   Alberta 1A-6§§355, 365
   British Columbia 1A-6§§357-60
   causation 1A-6§341
   collisions with persons 1A-6§§343, 358
   contributory negligence 1A-6§346
   dogs on highways/streets 1A-6§§347-50
   foreseeability 1A-6§341
   general 1A-6§§339-46, 351
   municipal by-law, effect of breach of 1A-6§§342, 359
   occupiers' liability (Alberta) 1A-6§356
   police dogs 1A-6§344
   trespassing cattle, driving off 1A-6§345
   volenti non fit injuria 1A-6§346
injuries by dogs (Ontario)
   control orders 1A-6§§377, 378
   damages, measure of 1A-6§374
   destruction orders 1A-6§§377, 378
►   general 1A-6§§373, 374
   "harbouring" 1A-6§375
   livestock/poultry 1A-6§§380-82
   occupiers' liability 1A-6§376
   offence 1A-6§§373, 379
   "owner" 1A-6§375
   proceedings re 1A-6§377
injuries by dogs (parties liable)
   1A-6§330
injuries by dogs (Saskatchewan)
   fine not barring action 1A-6§369
   general 1A-6§§367, 368, 371
   offence 1A-6§370
   police dogs 1A-6§372
   "protected animal" 1A-6§367
injuries by dogs (scienter)
   Alberta 1A-6§§355, 356
   British Columbia 1A-6§357
   barking at horses 1A-6§335
   elements of scienter 1A-6§331
   evidence of ferocious/savage nature 1A-6§332
   Manitoba 1A-6§361
   nuisance/negligence, effect of 1A-6§338

   running at large 1A-6§336
   sufficiency of precautions 1A-6§334
   volenti 1A-6§§333, 334
   warning to strangers, sufficiency 1A-6§333
injuries by dogs (statutory remedies)
   British Columbia 1A-6§360
   Manitoba 1A-6§§339, 36 1A-66
   Ontario 1A-6§§340, 373-82
   Saskatchewan 1A-6§§367-72
injuries by dogs (trespassers)
   1A-6§§473, 474
injuries to animals. *See also* **offences; prevention of cruelty.**
   apportionment of liability 1A-6§§435, 437
   bailment situations 1A-6§§28-44
   carriage of animals 1A-6§§61-63
   damages 1A-6§§408, 409
   defences 1A-6§430
   dogs 1A-6§§43, 44, 287, 425, 435, 437
   highways, on or near 1A-6§§457-59
   horses 1A-6§§28-42, 61, 62
   livestock/poultry (Ontario) 1A-6§§380-82
   negligence by 1A-6§§28, 32-34, 62, 457
   noise 1A-6§406
   overdriving 1A-6§35
   Saskatchewan 1A-6§§367-72
   statutory compensation 1A-6§360
   trespassing animals 1A-6§§345, 426-28, 430
   wrongful killing 1A-6§§12, 394
inspections. *See* **diseased animals; sale of animals.**
insurance 1A-6§§25, 26, 26.1 (Supp.), 350
kennels. *See also* **dogs.**
   Alberta 1A-6§284
   British Columbia 1A-6§285
   licensing of 1A-6§281
   Manitoba 1A-6§§288-99
   Ontario 1A-6§302
   Saskatchewan 1A-6§300
liability. *See* **agistment; bailment; highways/streets; injuries by animals; injuries by dogs; injuries to animals; nuisance; wild animals; wrongful killing.**

V-46

FIGURE 8.3   **CED Contents Key Showing Title "Animals"**

CONTENTS KEY
LIST OF TITLES

The following is a list of the subject titles in C.E.D. (Ont. 3rd), showing the volumes in which they appear and their respective title numbers.

Subject Title		Volume
1.	Absentees	1
1.1	Access to Information and Protection of Privacy	1
2.	Actions	1
3.	Administrative Law	1
4.	Agency	1
5.	Agriculture	1A
6.	Animals	1A
7.	Annuities	1A
8.	Arbitration	1A
9.	Armed Forces	1A
10.	Associations and Non-Profit Corporations	1A
11.	Auctions	1A
12.	Aviation and Air Law	1A
13.	Bailment	2
14.	Banking	2
15.	Bankruptcy and Insolvency	2
16.	Barristers and Solicitors	3
17.	Bills of Exchange	3
18.	Bills of Sale	3
19.	Boundaries and Surveys	3
20.	Building Contracts	3
21.	Bulk Sales	3
22.	Burial and Cremation	3
23.	Carriers	4
24.	Charities	4
26.	Churches and Religious Institutions	4
27.1.	Condominiums	4A
28.	Conflict of Laws	4A
29.	Conspiracy	4A
30.	Constitutional Law	4A
30.1.	Construction Liens	4A
31.	Contempt of Court	5
32.	Contracts	5
33.1.	Co-operatives	5
34.	Copyright	5
35.	Coroners and Medical Examiners	5

II-1   April 2005

Alternatively, you can simply refer to the spine of the CED volumes to find the volume that contains your subject title. Each volume provides the volume number and the alphabetical range of subject titles contained in that volume. Once you find the right volume, you can simply refer to the tab that has your subject title name on it. To find more specific information within the title, use the table of contents found at the beginning of the subject title or the subject index found at the end of the title.

The table of contents breaks down the subject title into increasingly more topic-specific information, by dividing the title first into parts that are given both a number (uppercase roman numerals) and a name, and then into sections that are given both a number and a name. Sections may be further divided into headings (subtopics) that are given a letter (a, b, c) and a name, which may be further divided into subheadings that are given a number (lowercase roman numerals) and a name. Each section is divided into numbered paragraphs (not named) that provide the summary of the law. Figure 8.4 reproduces part of the table of contents for the subject title ANIMALS.

The following table illustrates how the research topic in this problem is broken down within the subject title ANIMALS.

	Number	Name
Subject title	6	ANIMALS
Part	IX	Dogs
Section	5	Liability for injuries inflicted by dogs
Heading	(j)	Ontario
Subheading	(i)	Dog owners' liability
Paragraph	§373	

The subject index at the end of the title breaks down general topics into more specific topics using keywords and phrases, and refers you to the relevant paragraph numbers within the title that contain the general statement of law on your research topic. Figure 8.5 reproduces part of the subject index for the title ANIMALS. Note that the subject index directs you to paragraphs 373 and 374 for general information about "injuries by dogs (Ontario)."

Finding and Reading the Text

Once you have identified your specific topic using one of the finding tools discussed above, read the relevant paragraph(s). In our example, we have been directed to paragraphs 373 and 374 of subject title 6 (ANIMALS) in volume 1A of the CED. Those paragraphs are reproduced in figure 8.6.

Note how the paragraphs themselves contain a statement of the law. Paragraph 373 also contains footnotes referring to the *Dog Owners' Liability Act*, the statute from which the statement of the law in that paragraph is drawn. Paragraph 374 also contains footnotes referring to cases from which the statement of the law in that paragraph is drawn.

FIGURE 8.4   CED Table of Contents for Subject Title "Animals"

ANIMALS

      (g) Change,   §185
      (h) Assignment,   §186
      (i) Cancellation,   §190
      (j) Game production animals,   §192
  6. Saskatchewan,   §195
      (a) Definitions,   §195
      (b) Registration and licensing,   §200
      (c) Evidence of ownership,   §210
      (d) Cancellation of registration,   §212
      (e) Errors,   §213
      (f) Other matters,   §214
      (g) Domestic game farm animals,   §215
  7. Ontario,   §221
  8. Offences,   §230

VII   Diseases of Animals,   §231

  1. General,   §231
  2. Inspection and reporting,   §232
  3. Identification of animals,   §238
      (a) Canada,   §238
      (b) British Columbia,   §242
  4. Infected places and control areas,   §243
  5. Forfeiture and removal,   §245
  6. Disposal of animals,   §247
  7. Compensation,   §251
  8. Offences and civil liability,   §258
      (a) General,   §258
      (b) Sale of diseased animals,   §264
      (c) Unlawful importation,   §268
      (d) Other offences,   §269
      (e) Liability in tort or contract,   §270

VIII   Wild Birds,   §275

► **IX   Dogs,   §279**

  1. General,   §279
  2. Regulations of dogs and kennels,   §280
      (a) General,   §280
      (b) Alberta,   §284
      (c) British Columbia,   §285
      (d) Manitoba,   §288

5   January 2000

FIGURE 8.4   Concluded

ANIMALS

(e) Saskatchewan,   §300
(f) Ontario,   §302
3. Police or tracking dogs,   §304
4. Guide dogs,   §315
   (a) Alberta,   §315
   (b) British Columbia,   §320
   (c) Manitoba,   §325
   (d) Saskatchewan,   §327
   (e) Ontario,   §328
▶   5. Liability for injuries inflicted by dogs,   §330
   (a) Responsibility,   §330
   (b) Scienter,   §331
   (c) Negligence,   §339
      (i)   General,   §339
      (ii)   Dogs on highways and streets,   §347
   (d) Cattle-trespass,   §351
   (e) Assault,   §353
   (f) Alberta,   §355
   (g) British Columbia,   §357
   (h) Manitoba,   §361
   (i) Saskatchewan,   §367
▶   (j) Ontario,   §373
▶   (i)   Dog owners' liability,   §373
      (ii)   Protection of livestock and poultry,   §380
6. Killing of dogs,   §383

X   **Liability Regarding Animals,**   §396

1. General,   §396
2. Negligence,   §398
   (a) General,   §398
   (b) Measure of damages,   §407
3. Scienter,   §410
   (a) General,   §410
   (b) Statutory modification,   §417
4. Trespass or running at large,   §418
   (a) Liability at common law,   §418
   (b) Driving away trespassing animals,   §426
   (c) Defences,   §429
   (d) Measure of damages,   §431
   (e) Apportionment of liability,   §434
   (f) Distress damage feasant,   §439

C.E.D. (3rd)   6

FIGURE 8.5   CED Subject Index for Subject Title "Animals"

INDEX TO ANIMALS

injuries by animals (scienter) – *cont.*
    running at large 417
    statutory modifications 417
    trespassing animals 415
    vicious 410
    volenti non fit injuria 416
injuries by animals (statutory remedy – Manitoba) 339, 362-66
injuries by animals (trespassers) 473, 474
injuries by dogs. *See also* **highways/streets (dogs on); injuries by animals; injuries to animals; nuisance; stray animals.**
injuries by dogs (assault) 353, 354
injuries by dogs (cattle-trespass) 338, 351, 352, 425
injuries by dogs (killing perpetrator)
    Alberta 384, 385
    British Columbia 386-88
    common law rule 383, 395
    damages where killing wrongful 394
    Manitoba 389
    offence re 395
    Ontario 391, 392
    order for destruction 393
    Saskatchewan 390
injuries by dogs (Manitoba)
    cattle-trespass, abolition of 352
    damages, measure of 364
    destruction order, effect of 366
    exceptions to liability 362
    general 339, 361, 362
    joint liability 365
    "owner" 363
    scienter, abolition of 361
injuries by dogs (negligence)
    Alberta 355, 365
    British Columbia 357-60
    causation 341
    collisions with persons 343, 358
    contributory negligence 346
    dogs on highways/streets 347-50
    foreseeability 341
    general 339-46, 351
    municipal by-law, effect of breach of 342, 359
    occupiers' liability (Alberta) 356

    police dogs 344
    trespassing cattle, driving off 345
    volenti non fit injuria 346
injuries by dogs (Ontario)
    control orders 377, 378
    damages, measure of 374
    destruction orders 377, 378
    general 373, 374   ◀
    "harbouring" 375
    livestock/poultry 380-82
    occupiers' liability 376
    offence 373, 379
    "owner" 375
    proceedings re 377
injuries by dogs (parties liable) 330
injuries by dogs (Saskatchewan)
    fine not barring action 369
    general 367, 368, 371
    offence 370
    police dogs 372
    "protected animal" 367
injuries by dogs (scienter)
    Alberta 355, 356
    British Columbia 357
    barking at horses 335
    elements of scienter 331
    evidence of ferocious/savage nature 332
    Manitoba 361
    nuisance/negligence, effect of 338
    running at large 336
    sufficiency of precautions 334
    volenti 333, 334
    warning to strangers, sufficiency 333
injuries by dogs (statutory remedies)
    British Columbia 360
    Manitoba 339, 362-66
    Ontario 340, 373-82
    Saskatchewan 367-72
injuries by dogs (trespassers) 473, 474
injuries to animals. *See also* **offences; prevention of cruelty.**
    apportionment of liability 435, 437
    bailment situations 28-44
    carriage of animals 61-63

225

FIGURE 8.6   **CED Volume 1A Showing Subject Title "Animals"**

§371   ANIMALS

that the dog is, or that the owner knew that the dog was, of a dangerous and mischievous nature or is accustomed to doing acts causing injury.[1]

> 1. Urban Municipality Act, 1984, S.S. 1983-84, c. U-11, s. 135.6 [en. 1988-89, c. 61, s. 21]; Rural Municipality Act, 1989, S.S. 1989-90, c. R-26.1, s. 222; *Karras v. Richter*, [1995] 7 W.W.R. 406 (Sask. Q.B.) (defence to action substantive matter conferring vested rights; Rural Municipality Act, s. 222, not applying to actions arising before its enactment); *Gaudry v. Binning* (1996), 149 Sask. R. 250 (Sask. Q.B.) (under Urban Municipality Act, s. 135.6).

§372   A police officer is not negligent in using a police dog to take down a suspect if the level of force used is justified.[1]

> 1. *Arnault v. Prince Albert (City) Police Commissioner* (1995), [1996] 4 W.W.R. 38 (Sask. Q.B.) (officer and dog pursuing suspect from break and enter where gun reported stolen; suspect acting in manner indicative of taking drugs; suspect twice warned to stop but continuing to run; suspect taken down by dog three times before being arrested; officer not negligent considering that theft of firearm reported; level of force used justified).

(j) Ontario

(i) Dog Owners' Liability

§373   A dog owner must exercise reasonable precautions to prevent the dog from biting or attacking a person or domestic animal.[1] Failure to do so is an offence[2] and also exposes the owner to civil liability.[3]

> 1. Dog Owners' Liability Act, R.S.O. 1990, c. D.16, s. 5(1).
>
> 2. Dog Owners' Liability Act, s. 5(2).
>
> 3. Dog Owners' Liability Act, s. 2.

§374   A dog's owner is liable for damages resulting from a bite or attack by the dog on another person or domestic animal.[1] Liability does not depend on knowledge of the propensity of the dog or fault or negligence on the part of the owner.[2] However, the court must reduce the damages awarded in proportion to the degree, if any, to which the plaintiff's fault or negligence caused or contributed to the damages.[3] An owner who is liable to pay damages is entitled to recover contribution and indemnity from any other person in proportion to the degree, if any, to which the other person's fault or negligence caused or contributed to the damages.[4]

> 1. Dog Owners' Liability Act, R.S.O. 1990, c. D.16, s. 2(1); *Strom (Litigation Guardian of) v. White* (1994), 21 O.R. (3d) 205 (Ont. Gen. Div.) (general damages of $22,000 and special damages of $4,968 for scarring near right corner of child's mouth); *Michalik v. Khan* (1995), 80 O.A.C. 353 (Ont. Div. Ct.); leave to appeal refused (May 29, 1995), Doc. CA M15863 (Ont. C.A.) (owner liable for damages resulting from stray dog biting animal control officer); *Wong v. Arnold* (1987), 59 O.R. (2d) 299 (Ont. C.A.); see **also** *Morsilio v. Migliano* (1985), 52 O.R. (2d) 319

C.E.D. (3rd)   150

Updating Your Research

As a final step, you must update your research by checking the relevant paragraph numbers in the supplemental pages found at the front of the subject title you are researching. The supplemental page for paragraph 373 is reproduced in figure 8.7. Note how paragraph 373 refers to a change in the legislation. Paragraph 374 is not mentioned, meaning that there has been no change in the law as set out in that paragraph.

KEY TERMS

Contents Key
Index Key
Rules and Regulations Key
Statutes Key

FIGURE 8.7　CED Supplemental Page for Paragraph 373

ANIMALS §373

§356 note 1

Occupiers' Liability Act, R.S.A. 1980, c. O-3, s. 5: see now R.S.A. 2000, c. O-4, s. 5.

§357 note 1

Levesque v. Miko, 2001 CarswellBC 1042 (B.C. Prov. Ct.) (dog not manifesting propensity to bite or act aggressively and owners not knowing of any such propensity; doctrine of scienter not applying; mere fact that dog being German Sheppard not establishing propensity for aggression or owner's awareness of aggression).

§360 note 1

Municipal Act, R.S.B.C. 1996, c. 323, s. 706: see now Local Government Act [title re-en. 2000, c. 7, s. 1], R.S.B.C. 1996, c. 323, s. 706.

§362 note 1

Animal Liability Act, S.M. 1998, c. 8, C.C.S.M., c. A95, s. 2(3) [am. 2002, c. 24, s. 4(3)].

§367 **[Replacement]** In an action for the recovery of damages for injury done to a protected animal by a dog, it is not necessary for the plaintiff to prove that the defendant knew of the dog's propensity to pursue and injure animals, and the defendant's liability does not depend on any previous knowledge of the dog's propensity.[1] A "protected animal" means, subject to the regulations, any animal that is raised in captivity on a farm for the purpose of producing offspring or animal products, as defined in The Animal Products Act.[2]

1. Animal Protection Act, 1999, S.S. 1999, c. A-21.1, s. 22(2).

2. Animal Products Act, R.S.S. 1978 (Supp.), c. A-20.2; Animal Protection Act, 1999, S.S. 1999, c. A-21.1, s. 19(c).

§369 **[Replacement]** No penalty imposed pursuant to the Act[1] bars an action by the owner or possessor of a protected animal for the recovery of damages for injury done to the protected animal by a dog.[2]

1. Animal Protection Act, 1999, S.S. 1999, c. A-21.1, s. 21.

2. Animal Protection Act, 1999, S.S. 1999, c. A-21.1, s. 22(1).

▶ §373 *In the first line, change* the dog *to* it.

§373 note 1

Dog Owners' Liability Act, R.S.O. 1990, c. D.16, s. 5(1): see now s. 6 [en. 2000, c. 26, Schedule A, s. 6].

27　　　　　　　　　　　　March 2003

CHAPTER 9

Finding and Updating Statutes

When you start to research a legal issue, the first thing you have to do is find out if there is a statute that is relevant to the issue. In chapter 8 we saw that you may be able to find this out by looking in the *Canadian Encyclopedic Digest*, and there are other finding tools that we'll talk about in this chapter. Once you determine that there is a statute relevant to your problem, you also have to be able to locate the text of that statute.

This chapter discusses the following topics:

- how statutes are published,
- finding tools for statutes,
- finding the text of a statute,
- updating statutes, and
- legislative history and concording a statute.

HOW STATUTES ARE PUBLISHED

It is helpful to understand how statutes are published, in order to find the name of a statute that deals with the legal problem you have to solve, and then to find the text of that statute.

Acts passed by Parliament or by the provincial legislatures in any year are collected in a series for that year. They appear in a bound annual volume that is designated by year—for example, S.C. 1992 (*Statutes of Canada, 1992*) contains only statutes passed in 1992. Statutes are given chapter numbers in the volume according to the order in which they were passed in that particular year.

The federal statutes and some provincial statutes are revised every number of years. Producing a set of revised statutes means collecting all the statutes that are in force at the date of the revision and publishing them in a format that incorporates any amendments that have been made to each statute since the previous revision.

The most recent federal revision was in 1985; the one before that was in 1970. Until recently, Ontario statutes were revised every 10 years. However, the most recent revision of Ontario statutes was published in 1990. The current trend is to consolidate statutes (by incorporating subsequent amendments) on a continuing basis rather than to revise them at regular intervals. This has become possible in the last few years because governments are now able to maintain statutes by computer and publish them in computerized format on their websites.

FINDING TOOLS FOR STATUTES

Often the challenge of dealing with statute law is not locating the text of the statute itself, but finding out whether there is a statute on the subject you are researching. There are several different ways of finding whether a relevant statute exists. You can

- ask someone,
- look for a statute directly,
- work from the general to the specific, or
- use a provincial case report series.

Each of these methods is discussed below.

Ask Someone

This is an obvious but frequently overlooked answer. Ask a lawyer who has experience in the subject area, or a law librarian.

Look for a Statute Directly

Revised statute series and consolidated statutes have index volumes, arranged by subject matter, that may be useful; however, note that index volumes are often out of date or have disappeared from the shelf because someone else is using them.

If you cannot locate an index volume, look through the table of statutes or table of public statutes of the revised or consolidated statutes for the name of a statute that looks relevant. If you suspect that you may be dealing with a statute passed since the last revision occurred or before the consolidation has been updated, look through the table of public statutes at the end of the most recent annual volume of statutes. Be very careful when relying on this method alone to find relevant statutes. Often, the names of the statute can be misleading. You may not be able to find a statute that is relevant to your particular problem, or you may find a statute whose name sounds like it is relevant to your particular research topic, but, in fact, is not. For example, if you are researching a residential landlord and tenant problem in Ontario, you will come across a statute called the *Landlord and Tenant Act*. It would be reasonable to assume that this statute deals with your problem—reasonable, but wrong. In fact the *Landlord and Tenant Act* deals only with commercial tenancies and not with residential tenancies. The name of the relevant statute is the *Tenant Protection Act*.

The *Index to Federal and Ontario Statutes*, compiled by Mary McLean, is relevant for research involving federal or Ontario statutes. Although the index gives lists of statutes under general topic headings, it does not break down topics thoroughly or give specific information about what a statute might contain. You may find yourself confronted with several statutes under one heading with no way of telling which one is relevant to your problem. Note that this source was last published in print format in 2001 and is now offered in a computerized version only.

For new statutes, you will need to use an "index to current bills" in order to locate bills that have been enacted recently. For federal and provincial bills, use *Canadian Current Law Legislation*, "Progress of Bills." For federal bills only, you can instead check the *Canada Legislative Index* under the "Titles Index." For Ontario only, look at the *Ontario Legislative Digest Service* under "Acts Affected." You can also find the status of current bills using the statute citators.

Work from the General to the Specific

Instead of starting with statutes, find information on the general subject in which you are interested in

- a text,
- an encyclopedia entry, or
- an article.

If a statute figures prominently in the area, the source you are using almost certainly will mention it. A table of statutes is sometimes all you need and is usually found at the front of the text or encyclopedia entry.

The *Canadian Encyclopedic Digest* (CED, discussed in chapter 8) is an excellent research tool, perhaps the best tool for finding relevant statutes. Once you find the general statement of law dealing with your particular topic, the CED will refer you to the relevant statute governing that area of law, if there is one.

You also can look for articles in the bibliography contained at the front of *some* titles of the CED. They are usually arranged in reverse chronological order—that is, the most recent titles appear first. Conference and seminar materials, which are collections of articles on a single topic, may be more useful to you than an isolated journal article.

NOTE: Do not look for articles until you have looked at a text or an encyclopedia entry. Articles usually have a narrow focus—make sure you know that you want a particular, narrow focus before you spend the time.

Use a Provincial Case Report Series

If you are in a hurry and resources are limited—for example, if you work in a small law office with a meagre library—you might look in the index of your provincial case report series, such as the Ontario Reports, or in the index of the Dominion Law Reports, under the subject that interests you. Look at the case digests under the subject heading; if a statute figures prominently in the area, it likely will be mentioned in a case digest.

FINDING THE TEXT OF A STATUTE

Once you find the name of the statute that deals with your research problem, you will need to find the text of that statute, and, in particular, the section or sections of the statute that apply to your situation. To do this, it is helpful to understand both how statutes are published (see above) and statutory citations.

Statutory Citations

The citation of a statute gives you essential information about the statute, including where to find it. A citation is made up of the following four components:

1. Name of the Statute

The short title of the statute is used, omitting the word "the." (The short title is usually found at the end of the statute and is prefaced by the words "this act may be cited as.") The name of the statute is italicized and is followed by a comma.

2. Volume Title Abbreviation

This tells you the name of the statute series in which the statue appears, including the year of publication. It is followed by a comma. Statutes are published in either an annual volume or a revised series of volumes. Annual volumes are abbreviated as

- S.C. (Statutes of Canada), and
- S.O. (Statutes of Ontario).

Revised volumes are abbreviated as

- R.S.C. (Revised Statutes of Canada), and
- R.S.O. (Revised Statutes of Ontario).

In the citation in the example above, the statute is shown as being published in the Revised Statutes of Ontario, 1990 revision.

The following are some additional examples of volume title abbreviations:

- S.C. 1989 (Statutes of Canada for 1989)
- S.O. 1993 (Statutes of Ontario for 1993)
- R.S.C. 1985 (Revised Statutes of Canada, 1985 revision)
- R.S.O. 1990 (Revised Statutes of Ontario, 1990 revision)

3. Chapter Number

The chapter number tells you the specific number assigned to the statute in the volume. It is followed by a comma. In annual statute volumes, the statutes are put in alphabetical order and then numbered from 1 onward, using numbers only—for example, c. 46. In revised statute volumes, the statutes are put in alphabetical order and then numbered using an alphanumeric—for example, c. A.10, c. B-16, or c. C.32. The uppercase letter in an alphanumeric chapter number is drawn from the title of the statute. So in "c. C.32," the uppercase "C," part of the alphanumeric, means that the statute name begins with the letter "C"; the lowercase "c" just means "chapter number."

In the citation in the example above, the "B" is drawn from the *Business Corporations Act*. Revised Ontario statutes use a period in the alphanumeric (c. A.10). Revised federal statutes use a hyphen in the alphanumeric (c. B-16).

4. Section Number

The section number tells you which section number or numbers in the Act are being referred to. The abbreviation "s." stands for section. The abbreviation "ss." stands for sections.

If a statute has been amended, the citation is slightly different. The original statute is cited first, followed by the words "as am. by," and then the citation of the amending statute. The name of the amending statute is included only if it is different from that of the original statute. For example, *Employment Standards Act*, R.S.O. 1990, c. E.14, as am. by S.O. 1991, c. 16 and S.O. 1991, c. 43, s. 2.

Sometimes a statute is amended to add new sections. Sections that have been added to the statute by amendment and before the statute series has been revised are squeezed into existing sections by adding .1, .2, and so on to the immediately preceding section or subsection number. For example, *Regulated Health Professions Act, 1991*, S.O. 1991, c. 18, as am. by S.O. 1993, c. 37, s. 43.1.

Using the Statutory Citation To Find the Text of the Statute

The statutory citation gives you the information you need to find the text of the statute in the official provincial or federal annual or revised statute volumes.

The volume title abbreviation will direct you to either the revised statute volumes or the annual statute volumes.

If you are directed to the revised statute volumes, remember that all the statutes are organized in alphabetical order and divided into volumes. Look on the spine of the various volumes until you find the volume containing the alphanumeric chapter number of your statute.

If you are directed to the annual volumes, look for the volume or volumes for the year indicated in the volume title abbreviation. The statutes for that year will be organized in alphabetical order. If there is more than one volume for the year, look on the spine of the various volumes until you find the volume containing the numeric chapter number of your statute.

Where Else Can You Find the Text of the Statute?

The statutory citation tells you where to find the statute in the annual volumes or revised volumes. However, there are additional sources for and editions of statutes. These include

- consolidated versions,
- annotated versions, and
- office consolidations.

Choose the one that is most recent to shorten your updating time.

Consolidated versions and annotated versions of important statutes are published by commercial legal publishers, often annually. If you can find the statute edition for the present year, it will shorten the work involved in checking for amendments. These commercial editions of statutes are not the "official" version of the statute (the official text is contained only in the revised statutes or annual statute volumes and, in some cases, the consolidated statutes), but are usually reliable. If you are researching a statute that will be relied on in court, use the revised statutes for the text, plus the annual volumes of statutes for the text of amendments.

Canada and most provinces publish office consolidations of some or all of their statutes. An office consolidation of a statute sets out the text of the statute as amended (that is, with provisions of the statute either changed or "repealed," which means deleted) to the date of printing. An office consolidation is usually not the authoritative version of the statute, although it is useful for research. If you are researching a statute that will be relied on in court, use the revised statutes for the text in addition to the annual volumes of statutes for the text of amendments.

Finding the Text of Bills and Recent Statutes

bills
proposed statutes that
are before Parliament or a
provincial legislature but
have not yet been passed

Proposed statutes that are before Parliament or a provincial legislature but have not yet been passed are called **bills**. The text of federal bills is available through the federal bills subscription service; the text of provincial bills is usually available through the various provincial bills subscription services. You can find federal bills and the bills of your own province in most provincial law libraries; many law firms subscribe to the provincial bills service.

Statutes may have come into existence through receiving royal assent, but may not yet have been bound into an annual volume of statutes. In that case, you'll have to go to another source. Federal statutes are published initially in the *Canada Gazette Part III*. Provincial statutes are initially available in provincial bills subscription services (such as the *Ontario Statute Citator Current Bills Service*), which can be found in most law libraries and in many law firms.

UPDATING STATUTES

Once you've found the text of a statute, you have to update the statute to find out whether any part of it has been amended. If you're dealing with a recently enacted statute, you may also need to find out whether it has actually come into effect— that is, been "proclaimed in force." Some statutes that have received royal assent sit on the books for a while before anyone has to obey them.

Updating Federal Statutes

Start with the most recent version of the statute that you can find—a government-published office consolidation or a privately published consolidated or annotated version of the statute in question. If a consolidated version is not available, start with the *Revised Statutes of Canada, 1985* and supplements, or the annual volumes of the *Statutes of Canada*, depending on the date of the statute. Note that R.S.C. 1985 did not come into force until December 12, 1988; the supplements contain legislation passed between 1985 and 1988. The annual volumes contain legislation passed since 1988.

For amendments, check one of the following sources:

- *Canada Statute Citator*,
- *Canadian Current Law: Legislation*, or
- table of public statutes.

The *Canada Statute Citator* is a loose-leaf service published by Canada Law Book, organized alphabetically by statute short title. It gives the full citations of all statutes in R.S.C. 1985 and later statutes to date, and sets out the text of all amendments to those statutes. Check under the individual statute and in the "Monthly Bulletin" (the green pages at the front).

Canadian Current Law: Legislation is part of Carswell's *Canadian Abridgment*. Check under "Statutes Amended, Repealed or Proclaimed in Force." Note that *Canadian Current Law: Legislation* has been published only since 1989–90, and it does not provide a cumulative overview of amendments. If you are looking for more than the most recent amendments, you will have to go through each annual volume as well as the pamphlets, which are published regularly throughout the year.

If neither of the above is available, look in the table of public statutes in the most recent annual volume of the Statutes of Canada, update with the cumulative table in *Canada Gazette Part III*, and then with individual issues of *Canada Gazette Part III* published since the date of the cumulative table.

A federal statute that has received royal assent, including a statute that amends another statute, has no official authority until it has been proclaimed in force. For proclamation dates of new statutes or amending statutes, check the proposed date of proclamation in force in the statute itself (usually at the end of the statute); the actual date of proclamation in force in *Canadian Current Law: Legislation*, under "Statutes Amended, Repealed or Proclaimed in Force" in the *Canada Statute Citator* under individual statutes; and in the "Monthly Bulletin" (the green pages at the front). You may also look in the latest annual volume of the Statutes of Canada in the "Proclamations of Canada" tables, but this approach will require more work to update.

For proclamations more recent than the date of whichever source you are using, look in the table of proclamations either in *Canada Gazette Part III* or in the quarterly index of *Canada Gazette Part I*. For the most recent information on proclamations, check individual issues of *Canada Gazette Part I*, where they are announced.

Updating Ontario Statutes

Start with the most recent version of the statute that you can find—a government-published office consolidation or a privately published consolidated or annotated version of the statute in question. If a consolidated version is not available, start with the *Revised Statutes of Ontario, 1990*, or the annual volumes of the Statutes of Ontario, depending on the date of the statute.

For amendments, check one of the following sources:

- *Ontario Statute Citator*,
- *Canadian Current Law: Legislation*, or
- table of public statutes.

The *Ontario Statute Citator* is a loose-leaf service published by Canada Law Book organized alphabetically by statute short title. It gives the full citations of all statutes in R.S.O. 1990 and later statutes to date, and sets out the text of all amendments to those statutes. Use the *Ontario Statute Citator* to check for amendments. Note the useful "Consequential Amendments to Acts" heading in the pink "Weekly Bulletin Service."

Canadian Current Law: Legislation is part of Carswell's *Canadian Abridgment*. Check under "Statutes Amended, Repealed or Proclaimed in Force" under Ontario. Note that *Canadian Current Law: Legislation* has been published only since 1989–90 and it does not provide a cumulative overview of amendments. If you are looking for more than the most recent amendments, you will have to go through each annual volume, as well as through the pamphlets.

If you do not have access to *Canadian Current Law: Legislation* or to the *Ontario Statute Citator*, you can look for amendments in the table of public statutes in the most recent annual volume of the Statutes of Ontario. You must then update by checking for new and amending statutes since the date of the annual volume in the *Ontario Statute Citator Current Bills Service*.

A provincial statute has no official authority until it has been proclaimed in force. For proclamation in force dates of new statutes and amendments, look for the proposed date of proclamation in the statute itself, and for the actual date of proclamation in any of the following sources:

- *Canadian Current Law: Legislation* under "Statutes Amended, Repealed or Proclaimed in Force" (Ontario);
- the *CCH Provincial Legislative Record*, under Ontario;
- the *Ontario Legislative Digest*;
- the *Ontario Statute Citator*—the pink "Weekly Bulletin Service" pages at the front of the volume; or
- individual issues of the *Ontario Gazette.*

LEGISLATIVE HISTORY AND CONCORDING A STATUTE

In successive revisions of the statutes of Canada or of a province, the same statute may appear under a different chapter number and the same statutory provision may appear under a different section number. It may be important when reading cases that interpret a provision to compare the provision in different revisions in order to find out if it has been amended. If the wording of the provision is different in the present revision, the case law interpreting an earlier provision may not be useful.

The **legislative history** of a provision is given at the end of each provision in a statute. This history gives the section number of the provision in the previous revision or (if the provision has been amended or newly created between revisions) the year of and the chapter and section in the statute that amended or created the provision. Looking at the legislative history will permit you to find the *previous* section number of a provision for which you know the present section number.

In order to find the *present* section number of a provision if you only know the section number in the previous revision, you will have to consult a **concordance**. A concordance will also show you the previous section number if you know the present section number. Concordances focus on two adjacent revisions of a statute series.

legislative history given at the end of each provision in a statute

concordance a tool for finding corresponding sections in either an earlier or a later version of a statute

Concordance for Statutes of Canada

The *Revised Statutes of Canada, 1985* has a companion volume called *Table of the History and Disposal of Acts* (1995) that concords statutes enacted to December 1, 1988. Look in the "former legislation" column after you have located the statute by name. Similar tables exist for the revisions of 1970 (in the Second Supplement to R.S.C. 1970); 1952 (in the Appendixes volume of R.S.C. 1952); 1927 (in the Appendixes volume of R.S.C. 1927); 1906 (in the Appendixes volume of R.S.C. 1906); and 1886 (in volume 2 of R.S.C. 1886).

Concordance for Statutes of Ontario

Use the *Canadian Encyclopedic Digest (3d)*'s *Ontario Statutes Concordance 1980–1990*; or, in the *Revised Statutes of Ontario, 1990*, volume 12 (Appendix), look at Schedule B, "Table of Disposition."

KEY TERMS
bills
concordance
legislative history

EXERCISES

Where would you look for

1. a federal bill or a bill of your provincial legislature, if you know the bill number;

2. whether the wording of a given statutory provision was different in the previous revision of statutes;

3. the text of a statute of your provincial legislature whose name you know;

4. whether a statute of your province or a federal statute has been amended;

5. the text of a federal statute whose name you know;

6. whether there's a statute of your province or a federal statute on a given subject;

7. whether a statute of your province or federal statute has been proclaimed in force yet?

CHAPTER 10

Finding and Updating Regulations

Regulations are as important as statutes and sometimes may be more important. It is therefore vital to look for regulations after you have found out that there is a statute relevant to the area of law you are researching. Once you determine that there is a regulation relevant to your problem, you must be able to locate the text of the regulation.

Finding and updating regulations using paper sources is difficult, but this chapter sets out how to get through the task with as little pain as possible (which is not to say that there is no pain at all).

This chapter discusses the following topics:

- when regulations come into force,
- finding and updating federal regulations,
- finding and updating Ontario regulations, and
- regulatory citations.

WHEN REGULATIONS COME INTO FORCE

Regulations can come into force upon "filing," "registration," or "publication"; the wording differs in each jurisdiction. Federal regulations come into force on the day specified in the regulation or on the date of registration (recorded at the top of the text of the regulation). You can refer to a province's *Regulation Act* for more information about the coming into force of provincial regulations.

FINDING AND UPDATING FEDERAL REGULATIONS

The last consolidation of federal regulations was made in 1978, so the regulations contained in it are not up to date. You may find the text or amended text of the regulation you are looking for not in the consolidation but in the individual issues of *Canada Gazette Part II*, which is where regulations are published. Federal regulations are included in the general term **statutory instruments**.

statutory instrument
general term that includes federal regulations

1. To find out whether a regulation exists, check the following:
   - *Consolidated Index of Statutory Instruments* (part of *Canada Gazette Part II*). Consolidated semi-annually. Look at Table I for regulations by name of regulation; look at Table II for regulations by name of authorizing statute; look at Table III for statutes whose regulations are exempt from publication. (You guessed it—you will not be able to find regulations for Table III statutes.)
   - Carswell's *Canada Regulations Index*. A monthly consolidated index to all Canadian regulations and statutory instruments currently in force that allows you to find the citation of a specific regulation. You can then use the citation to locate the text of the regulation in the 1978 *Consolidated Regulations of Canada* or subsequent issues of the *Canada Gazette Part II*, depending on the date of the regulation.
2. Update with
   - Carswell's *Canada Regulations Index*,
   - *Canadian Current Law: Legislation* under "Regulations," and
   - *Consolidated Index of Statutory Instruments* (part of *Canada Gazette Part II*). Quarterly cumulation (look at Table I for regulations by name of regulation; look at Table II for regulations by name of authorizing statute; look at Table III for statutes whose regulations are exempt from publication).

AND

3. Update to the present with current issues of *Canada Gazette Part II* published since the date of the source you used.

FINDING AND UPDATING ONTARIO REGULATIONS

You have to first find out whether there are any regulations published under the "enabling" statute—the statute under which the regulation is made—and then locate the text of the regulation.

To find out whether a regulation exists under the enabling statute, look under the name of the statute in

- the *Ontario Gazette Index to Regulations*—published twice a year;
- Carswell's *Ontario Regulation Service*—a monthly subscription service that provides all regulations and amendments published each month, together with an annual consolidated index;
- the table of regulations at the back of each annual volume of the *Statutes of Ontario*.

The text of Ontario regulations is published in the *Revised Regulations of Ontario, 1990*. These regulations have been changed and new regulations have been added in

- the annual supplements to the Revised Regulations (made up of bound issues of the *Ontario Gazette*, and
- the individual issues of the *Ontario Gazette*.

Update by looking in

- Carswell's *Ontario Regulation Service* (updated by the yellow pages), or
- *Canadian Current Law: Legislation* under "Regulations" (Ontario). When you are using *Canadian Current Law: Legislation* to find regulations, remember that (1) it has been published only since 1989–90, and (2) it does not provide a cumulative overview of regulations. If you are looking for more than the most recent regulations, you will have to go through annual volumes as well as the monthly pamphlets.

Update to the present by looking for regulations in the individual volumes of the *Ontario Gazette* published since the date of the source you are using. In some law libraries, check the loose-leaf binder that is kept to update regulations as each *Ontario Gazette* release is received.

REGULATORY CITATIONS

You must be able to read a regulatory citation correctly in order to find the text of the regulation. Regulations are usually cited by year and number—the year in which the regulation was made, and the chronological number of the particular regulation in that year. Regulations of Canada are identified by "SOR," which stands for "Statutory Orders and Regulations." (If you see "SI," it means "Statutory Instrument," which is a broader term than regulation; it may include, for example, rules of court.) Regulations of the provinces are identified by an abbreviated name of the province plus "Reg." for Regulation—for example, B.C. Reg., O. Reg., and Nfld. Reg.

Examples

- SOR/95-18—look in the *Canada Gazette Part II* for 1995 and turn to regulation 18.
- O. Reg. 22/97—look in the *Ontario Gazette* for 1997 and turn to regulation 22.

Regulations of Canada may also appear in the 18-volume *Consolidated Regulations of Canada, 1978*, which includes all regulations in force on December 31, 1977. The citation will look like this:

- SOR Cons./78, Vol. 3, 208—look in volume 3 of the 1978 consolidation at page 208.

Regulations of Ontario are revised when the statutes are revised. If an Ontario regulation appears in the multi-volume *Revised Regulations of Ontario, 1990*, the citation will look like this:

- R.R.O. 1990, Reg. 601—the citation doesn't include the volume, but the spine of each volume shows the numbers it contains.

KEY WORDS

statutory instrument

EXERCISES

1. a. How would you find out whether there are regulations made under your provincial corporations act?

    b. How would you update those regulations?

2. a. How would you find out whether there are regulations made under the federal *Environmental Protection Act*?

    b. How would you update those regulations?

CHAPTER 11

Finding and Updating Cases

After determining whether there are any statutes or regulations relevant to the issue you are researching, you must then find out whether there is any relevant case law. In chapter 8 we saw that you may be able to do this by looking in the *Canadian Encyclopedic Digest*, but there are other finding tools as well. If you determine that there is case law relevant to your problem, you must be able to locate the text of the cases.

This chapter discusses the following topics:

- how cases are published;
- finding tools—are there any relevant cases?;
- looking for cases about a subject—*Canadian Abridgment Case Digests*;
- looking for cases interpreting a statute;
- looking for cases considering a word or a phrase;
- treasure hunting—looking for a case using a partial or incorrect citation;
- looking for unreported cases;
- looking for the text of a case—understanding a case citation; and
- updating cases.

HOW CASES ARE PUBLISHED

It is helpful to understand how cases are published, in order to find the name of a case that deals with your research problem and then to find the text of that case.

As we said in chapter 4, a case is the written record of a judge's reasons for deciding a legal dispute. Judges (and other judicial officers) deal with many matters: motions, trials, and appeals. At the end of the matter, the judge must make a decision. Often the judge's decision is given to the parties and their lawyers orally and then "endorsed on the record" (written on the back of the court documents sent to the judge by the court office). If the reasons for the decision are lengthy or complex, the judge will give his or her decision and reasons in writing. Only some of these written decisions wind up being published, or **reported**, in a law report series—usually the more important ones. Many cases are **unreported**—not published in a law report series.

reported case

judge's decision and reasons about a case published in a law report series

unreported case

case not published in a law report series

There are many different series of law reports. Some are organized by court level, such as the *Supreme Court Reports*, which contain only decisions of the Supreme Court of Canada. Others are organized by region or geographical area, such as the *Ontario Reports*, which contain decisions of the Ontario courts; the *Western Weekly Reports*, which contain decisions from the western provinces; and the *Dominion Law Reports*, which contain decisions from all over Canada. Still others are organized by subject area, such as the *Reports of Family Law* and *Canadian Criminal Cases*.

Some of these law report series are considered official because they are authorized by a particular court or province. The *Ontario Reports* and the *Supreme Court Reports* are official reports; the *Reports of Family Law* is not official. A case may be reported in more than one case report series. For example, an Ontario family law case that goes to the *Supreme Court of Canada* may be reported in the *Ontario Reports*, the *Supreme Court Reports*, and the *Reports of Family Law*.

FINDING TOOLS: ARE THERE ANY RELEVANT CASES?

There are a number of different secondary sources that you can use to find case law on the issue you are researching. The source you use will depend on the reason you are looking for case law. Ask yourself the following questions:

1. Are you looking for case law dealing with a specific subject or legal issue? If so, you should use the *Canadian Abridgment Case Digests*.
2. Are you looking for cases that have interpreted a statute or a section of a statute? If so, you should use *Canadian Statute Citations* (part of the *Canadian Abridgment*) or a Canadian or provincial statute citator.
3. Are you looking for case law considering a word or a phrase? If so, you should use *Words and Phrases Judicially Defined in Canadian Courts and Tribunals* (also part of the *Canadian Abridgment*).
4. Are you treasure hunting—that is, trying to find a case using a partial or incorrect citation? If so, you should use the *Consolidated Table of Cases* or the *Canadian Case Citation* volumes of the *Canadian Abridgment*.
5. Are you looking for an unreported case? If so, you should use a digest service such as *All Canada Weekly Summaries*.

LOOKING FOR CASES ABOUT A SUBJECT: CANADIAN ABRIDGMENT CASE DIGESTS

Many secondary sources will refer you to the leading cases on a subject, such as

- the *Canadian Encyclopedic Digest* (see chapter 8),
- a text on the subject, or
- a loose-leaf service on the subject.

To find a text or loose-leaf service, check in the library catalogue under the subject name. Loose-leaf services are updated on a regular basis and are therefore more likely to cite recent decisions, but they tend to be less organized than texts.

If you want to move beyond the leading cases, the most comprehensive research tool for finding case law on a subject is Carswell's *Canadian Abridgment Case Digests*. The *Case Digests* is a multi-volume publication that collects **case digests**, or summaries of cases from all Canadian courts and many tribunals, and organizes them by subject area. Each digest provides a brief summary of how a legal issue was decided in a particular case, together with a summary of all necessary background facts and the reasons for the decision. Each digest covers only a single legal issue. If a case deals with several legal issues, there is a separate digest for each issue.

case digest
summary of how a legal issue was decided in a particular case

Organization of the Case Digests

The *Case Digests* is currently in transition from its revised second edition to its third edition. During this five-year transition project, which started in 2003, second-edition volumes are being replaced with new third-edition volumes. As of the date of writing, the first 59 volumes of the third edition have been published. The remaining volumes of the *Case Digests* are second-edition volumes.

The second edition of the *Case Digests* contained more than 112 subject titles (being consolidated into 51 subject titles in the third edition). The subject titles are contained in a set of hardcover volumes organized alphabetically by broad subject area. Each volume is numbered. Revised second-edition volumes are black and the volume numbers are preceded by the letter "R." Some of the volumes in the revised second edition have been reissued since their original publication, in which case the volume number is followed by "Reis" for reissued. Third-edition volumes are grey.

In both editions, each hardcover volume is updated by a softcover supplement volume. The supplement volumes are issued annually. Each new annual supplement is "cumulative"—that is, it incorporates the contents of each previous supplement—and replaces the previous supplement. As a result there is only one supplement volume for each hardcover volume. The supplements are further updated by monthly softcover editions of *Canadian Current Law: Case Digests*.

Within the hardcover and supplement volumes, the digests are organized by subject and arranged according to a multi-level classification system, called the **key classification system**. Each digest is classified under one of the *Case Digests'* subject titles. Each subject title is given a name and broken down into increasingly more specific levels. Main topics within the subject title are identified by a roman numeral, subtopics by numbers, and sub-subtopics by letters. For example, PRACTICE is a subject title. PRACTICE III.2.d is:

key classification system
multi-level classification system

PRACTICE
   III. Institution of Proceedings
      2. Writ of Summons
         d. Insurance

Each individual digest has a key classification number and a specific case digest number.

Finding Tools

Two main tools help you to locate all the digested cases on a particular issue in the *Case Digests*: the key and research guide and the general index. Both will direct you to the relevant case digests dealing with your legal issue or topic, but only the key and research guide uses the key classification system.

The **key and research guide** is really an elaborate table of contents. It groups subjects together according to the key classification system. You start by looking up a term that describes your issue. You will be referred to relevant subject titles and their subtitles according to the key classification system. From there you will be referred to the digests falling under those titles and subtitles in the relevant permanent volume and supplement. The key and research guide thus allows you to locate your issue within the classification scheme and then look through all the digests falling under the appropriate title and subtopic. It also provides the classification number to use throughout your search in any part of the *Canadian Abridgment*. In the third edition of the *Case Digests*, some subject titles are so large that they are spread out over more than one volume. When that happens, the classification table indicates the volume number in which each main topic of the subject title appears.

The **general index** arranges terms and key words alphabetically. Each entry is followed by the location of the relevant case digests by reference to the volume number and case digest numbers. The general index does not give you the classification number.

How To Use the Case Digests

Follow these steps when using the *Case Digests*:

1. Look in the general index or key and research guide to find where the relevant case digests are located.
    *   The general index will give you the relevant volume number and digest numbers.
    *   The key and research guide will give you the relevant volume numbers and key classification numbers.
2. Find the hardcover volume that contains your subject title. Look at the digest numbers from the general index or the classification number from the key and research guide.
    *   Scan the digests under the appropriate subject title and classification number, and make a note of the names and citations of important cases.
    *   Within each classification number, the digests are set out in reverse chronological order. The most recent case comes first. Each digest is identified by the key classification number of the subject title, subtitle, and sub-subtitle it belongs to. This number is found in the upper right hand corner of the digest entry. Each digest is also given a digest number, found in the upper left hand corner of the digest entry. The digest entries are numbered consecutively within each volume.
3. Look in the corresponding supplement volume for cases reported after the cut-off date of the hardcover volume. It contains digests from the cut-off date of the main volume to the end of the year shown on the cover of the volume. Find the subject title, and then look at the digests under the key classification number.

4. Consult *Canadian Current Law: Case Digests* to find cases reported after the cut-off date for the supplement.
    • These softcover booklets are published monthly.
    • To find the digests in these booklets, look up your topic in the index found at the back of each monthly issue. The subject titles are set out in alphabetical order.
    • The March, June, September, and December issues contain a cumulative index of all digests that have appeared to that date during the year, so begin your search with the most current volume that contains a cumulative index. Then check each subsequent monthly issue.
    • You can also use the case law update section provided in the general index to direct you. The "scope note" at the start of the case law update section sets out the *Canadian Current Law: Case Digests* issues covered in the update section. Look for the subject title and classification number.

An Example

The best way to learn how to use the *Case Digests* is to work through an example. Assume that you are continuing to work on the memo discussed in chapter 8. It reads as follows:

> Our client in Toronto, Ontario has a cocker spaniel that barks constantly. One day last month, her neighbour went to her apartment to complain. When our client opened the door, the dog rushed out to attack the neighbour, who fell backwards and broke his leg. The neighbour is now suing your client for the injuries caused by the dog. Can our client be held legally responsible?

In chapter 8, we used the *Canadian Encyclopedic Digest* to find a general statement of the law relating to injuries caused by dogs, and we found both case law and statute law there. Now we want to find case law using the *Case Digests* instead.

Using the General Index To Find the Relevant Case Digests

Start by looking up the word "dog" in the index. You will be referred to "animals," which is the relevant subject title. This part of the index is set out in figure 11.1. Next, look up the word "animals" in the general index. You will be referred to all the topics and subtopics under this subject title. This part of the index is set out in figure 11.2. Note the following:

• "Animals" is the main subject title. "Liability of owner or possessor" is a main subtopic under this subject title. "Injury by domestic animals" is a more specific subtopic and "injury by dog" is an even more specific subtopic.
• Bullets are used to identify the level of each topic under the main subject title "animals." Main topics have one bullet, subtopics under this main topic have two bullets, and sub-subtopics under this subtopic have three bullets.

The index gives you the relevant volume number and case digest numbers in those volumes that deal with your specific topic. For cases dealing with the liability of an owner for injuries caused by his or her dog, you are referred to digest numbers

FIGURE 11.1   **Case Digests General Index Showing "Dog"**

Divorce   General Index

- • cruelty
- • • evidence, **FAM 44**.520-531; **FAM 44Supp.**2
- • • mental cruelty, **FAM 44**.532-636
- • • physical cruelty, **FAM 44**.637-666
- • • tests and definitions, **FAM 44**.434-518
- • generally, **FAM 44**.258-264
- • living separate and apart
- • • calculation of time period, **FAM 44**.323-345
- • • interruption of separation, **FAM 44**.346-364
- • • what constitutes, **FAM 44**.265-322; **FAM 44Supp.**1
- jurisdiction of court
- • determining ordinary residence, **FAM 44**.218-257
- • duties and powers of court
- • • generally, **FAM 44**.170-212
- • • on appeal, **FAM 44**.213-217
- miscellaneous issues, **FAM 44**.1164; **FAM 44Supp.**11
- practice and procedure
- • abridging waiting period, **FAM 44**.949-967
- • appeals
- • • extending time for appeal, **FAM 44**.1044-1067
- • • generally, **FAM 44**.1001-1043
- • discovery, **FAM 44**.895-914
- • miscellaneous issues, **FAM 44**.1068-1158; **FAM 44Supp.**7-10
- • parties
- • • generally, **FAM 44**.813-818; **FAM 44Supp.**3
- • • parties under legal disability, **FAM 44**.819-829
- • pleadings
- • • amendment, **FAM 44**.861-894
- • • generally, **FAM 44**.831-860
- • setting aside decree or judgment, **FAM 44**.968-1000; **FAM 44Supp.**6
- • summary judgment, **FAM 44**.915-948; **FAM 44Supp.**4-5
- reconciliation
- • communications to assistreconciliation, **FAM 44**.685-687
- • generally, **FAM 44**.667-684

Dock, *see* Harbours and docks

Doctors
- • generally, *see* Physicians
- • hospital privileges, *see* Hospitals

Documentary evidence. *see* Children in need of protection; Evidence; Intellectual property, copyright, evidence; Motor vehicles, evidence

Dog, *see* Animals   ◄

Doing act intended to cause bodily harm to Her Majesty, *see* Treason and related offences

Doing act with intent to alarm Her Majesty, *see* Treason and related offences

Domestic animal, *see* Animals

Domestic contracts
- effect of contract
- • miscellaneous issues, **FAM 43**.3100-3144; **FAM 43Supp.**200-202
- • on child support, **FAM 43**.2700-3010; **FAM 43Supp.**183-192
- • on custody and access, **FAM 43**.3011-3099; **FAM 43Supp.**193-199
- • on division of family property
- • • generally, **FAM 43**.1756-1962; **FAM 43Supp.**155-159
- • • matrimonial home, **FAM 43**.1963-2055; **FAM 43Supp.**160-162
- • • pensions, **FAM 43**.2056-2087; **FAM 43Supp.**163-164
- • on spousal support
- • • cost of living adjustments, **FAM 43**.2696-2699
- • • effect on application under dependants' relief legislation, *see* Dependant's relief legislation
- • • under Divorce Act, **FAM 43**.2088-2601; **FAM 43Supp.**165-181
- • • under provincial legislation, **FAM 43**.2602-2695; **FAM 43Supp.**182
- enforcement
- • effect of death, **FAM 43**.3689-3706; **FAM 43Supp.**231
- • effect of divorce, **FAM 43**.3669-3688
- • effect of electing alternate remedy, **FAM 43**.3750-3766
- • effect of reconciliation, **FAM 43**.3707-3744
- • effect of release against estates, **FAM 43**.3745-3749

144

FIGURE 11.2   Case Digests General Index Showing "Animals"

Alternative dispute resolution   General Index

- • variation or exclusion of statutory provisions, **ADR 2.**164
- • what is arbitrable, **ADR 2.**13-36

Altering highways, *see* Roads

Amalgamations, *see* Corporations, amalgamation

Ambiguity

- • in boundaries, *see* Boundaries, description in deed or grant, resolving ambiguities
- • in charities, *see* Charities, uncertainty
- • in contract, *see* Contracts, construction and interpretation
- • in municipal by-law, *see* Municipal by-laws, attacks on
- • in statutes, *see* Statutes, interpretation
- • in will, *see* Wills

Amicus curiae, *see* Lawyers, relationship with client

Amortization, *see* Debtors and creditors, payment by debtor; Mortgages

Ancillary letters probate, *see* Estates

▶ **Animals**

- • bailment and hire
- • • agistment, **CML 21.**2889-2917
- • • carriage of animals, **CML 21.**2918-2952
- • • generally, **CML 21.**2854-2888; **CML 21Supp.**72-73
- • • horses, **CML 21.**2953-2974; **CML 21Supp.**74
- • cruelty to animals
- • • fighting or baiting of animals, **R9E Reis.**19878-19880
- • • injuring or endangering cattle, **R9E Reis.**19881-19900
- • • keeping cock-pit, **R9E Reis.**19901
- • • killing, injuring or endangering animals other than cattle
- • • • charging, **R9E Reis.**19919
- • • • elements, **R9E Reis.**19902-19918; **R9E Supp.**46
- • • • sentencing, **R9E Reis.**19928-19933; **R9E Supp.**48-50
- • • • specific defence: legal justification, **R9E Reis.**19920-19927; **R9E Supp.**47
- • • mistreatment of animals, **R9E Reis.**19934-19950; **R9E Supp.**51-57
- • • shooting captive birds, **R9E Reis.**19951

- • diseases of animals
- • • compensation, **R1 Reis.**3694-3705; **R1 Supp.**405-410
- • • destruction of animals, **R1 Reis.**3687-3693; **R1 Supp.**395-404
- • • generally, **R1 Reis.**3681-3686; **R1 Supp.**394
- • injury to animals
- • • by railway, **R1 Reis.**2871-3036
- • • generally, **R1 Reis.**2759-2783; **R1 Supp.**314-321
- • • malicious injury, **R1 Reis.**3037-3088; **R1 Supp.**326
- • • on highway
- • • • duty of motorist, **R1 Reis.**2819-2870; **R1 Supp.**324-325
- • • • generally, **R1 Reis.**2808-2818; **R1 Supp.**323
- • • stray animals, **R1 Reis.**2784-2807; **R1 Supp.**322
- • liability of owner or possessor
- • • criminal liability, **R1 Reis.**3408-3420; **R1 Supp.**372-375
- • • distress damage feasant, **R1 Reis.**3359-3407; **R1 Supp.**371
- • • injury by domestic animals
- • • • at common law, **R1 Reis.**3089-3119; **R1 Supp.**327-329
- • • • injury by dog, **R1 Reis.**3124-3215; **R1 Supp.**332-355
- • • • on highway, **R1 Reis.**3216-3296; **R1 Supp.**356-367
- • • • under by-law or statute, **R1 Reis.**3120-3123; **R1 Supp.**330-331
- • • injury by wild animals, **R1 Reis.**3297-3304
- • • liability for nuisance, **R1 Reis.**3421-3433; **R1 Supp.**376-377
- • • miscellaneous issues, **R1 Supp.**386-393
- • • regulation of dangerous animals, **R1 Reis.**3434-3450; **R1 Supp.**378-385
- • • trespass by animals, **R1 Reis.**3305-3358; **R1 Supp.**368-370
- • miscellaneous issues, **R1 Supp.**412
- • property in animals
- • • domestic animals, **CML 21.**2603-2614
- • • liens and security on animals
- • • • chattel mortgages, **CML 21.**2667-2691
- • • • conditional sales, **CML 21.**2627-2655

16

3124-3215 in volume R1 Reis. (the hardcover volume) and digest numbers 332-355 in R1 Supp. (the corresponding supplement volume).

Using the Key and Research Guide To Find the Relevant Case Digests

The *Case Digests* divides the law into main subject titles, and every topic falls under one of these subject titles. If you look up a word or topic that is not an actual subject title, you will be referred to the subject title under which your word or topic falls.

A subject titles table, found at the beginning of the key and research guide, lists all the subject titles in the *Case Digests* and refers you directly to the pages in the key that contain information about each title. If you already know that "animals" is the subject title relevant to your issue, you can look at the subject titles table; it refers you to page 2-27 of the key (see figure 11.3). If you don't know the subject title, use the index portion of the key to look up "dogs." It refers you to the relevant subject title, "animals" (see figure 11.4). Look at page 2-27 of the key, set out in figure 11.5. It tells you that the subject is dealt with in volume R1 Reissue and breaks down, or "classifies," the subject title into increasingly more specific subtopics.

Once you find the most specific subtopic relevant to your issue, you can determine the classification number for that topic. In our example, the subject title "animals" is broken down into the following main topics:

> II. Injury to Animals
> III. Liability of Owner or Possessor of Animals
> VI. Diseases of Animals
> VII. Stray Animals
> VIII. Miscellaneous Issues

If you then look under topic III, you will find this topic broken down into subtopics and sub-subtopics, as follows:

> III. LIABILITY OF OWNER OR POSSESSOR OF ANIMALS
>   1. Injury by domestic animals
>   a. At common law
>   b. Under by-law or statute
>   c. Injury by dog
>   i. At common law
>   ii. Under by-law or statute

Using this information, you can "classify" your topic. In our example, you are looking for cases dealing with a dog owner's liability under the relevant Ontario statute. The classification number for this specific topic is III.1.c.ii. All the case digests dealing with this specific topic will have the same classification number.

You now know to look in volume R1 Reis. for the digests found under key classification number III.1.c.ii.

Finding and Reading the Text

Once you have identified your specific topic using one of the finding tools discussed above, locate the appropriate volume—that is, R1 Reis.—and refer to the digest numbers (3124-3215) obtained from the general index, or the key classification number (III.1.c.ii.) obtained from the key and research guide.

FIGURE 11.3   **Case Digests Subject Titles Table Showing "Animals"**

SUBJECT TITLES TABLE

EDITOR'S NOTE: The list of subject titles below is supplemented in the Key by an extensive system of cross-references. The cross-references appear in bold-face and may be of assistance in locating specific topics or related issues. In addition, each subject title includes a Scope Note describing its contents and the location of related issues in other subject titles.

Subject Title	Page
Aboriginal Law	2-3
Actions	2-9
Administrative Law	2-11
Agency	2-19
Alternative Dispute Resolution	2-23
▶ Animals	2-27
Armed Forces	2-31
Auctions and Auctioneers	2-37
Aviation and Aeronautics	2-39
Bailment and Warehousing	2-43
Bankruptcy and Insolvency	2-47
Barristers and Solicitors	2-61
Bills of Exchange and Negotiable Instruments	2-67
Boundaries and Surveys	2-77
Burial and Cemeteries	2-81
Business Associations	2-83
Carriers	2-99
Chattel Mortgages and Bills of Sale	2-107
Choses in Action	2-113
Churches and Religious Institutions	2-117
Civil Practice and Procedure	2-121
Commercial Law	2-161
Communications Law	2-177
Conflict of Laws	2-181
Conspiracy	2-189
Constitutional Law	2-191
Construction Law	2-203
Construction Law Professionals	2-209
Contracts	2-213

i   Key & Research Guide 2004-2

FIGURE 11.4   **Case Digests Key and Research Guide Index Showing "Dogs"**

DOWER

DOCKS — *see Maritime law VII; Waters and watercourses*

DOCTORS — *see Health law III*

DOCUMENTARY EVIDENCE — *see Criminal law VI.21.c.iv.D; Evidence IX; Motor vehicles XI.1.a.ii*

DOCUMENTS — *see Civil practice and procedure X.2; Contracts; Criminal law VI.49, VI.55.d.i.B, VI.55.g.i.A; Evidence IX*

▶ **DOGS** — *see Animals*

DOMAIN NAME — *see Information technology II*

DOMESTIC CONTRACTS — *see Family law III*

DOMESTIC TRIBUNALS — *see Administrative law*

DOMICILE — *see Business associations III.5.a; Conflict of laws*

DOMINANT TENEMENT — *see Easements*

DONATIO MORTIS CAUSA — *see Estates and trusts I.15.d.iii, IV.1.b*

DOUBLE ASPECT — *see Constitutional law VII.5.d; Crown*

DOUBLE JEOPARDY RULE — *see Criminal law IV.28*

DOUBLE POSSIBILITIES — *see Estates and trusts IX.2*

DOWER — *see Civil practice and procedure XXII.3.b.ii; Family law II.8; Mortgages*

FIGURE 11.5   **Case Digests Key and Research Guide, Pages 2-27 and 2-28**

ANIMALS
1996 REISSUE

CONTENTS   VOLUME

II. Injury to animals   *R1 Reissue*

III. Liability of owner or possessor of animals   *R1 Reissue*

VI. Diseases of animals   *R1 Reissue*

VII. Stray animals   *R1 Reissue*

VIII. Miscellaneous issues   *R1 Reissue*

RELATED TITLES

• Insurance of livestock — see INSURANCE VII.2.h, VII.11, VIII.3.n

LOCATION

A complete search of case digests requires a search of the following:

• Volume R1 Reissue (to April 1996)

• Most recent R1 Annual Supplement volume (current to December of previous year)

• Issues of Canadian Current Law — Case Digests published after most recent hardcover volume or Annual Supplement volume

TABLE OF CLASSIFICATION

II.   INJURY TO ANIMALS

— *criminal offence, see CRIMINAL LAW* VI.34
1. **General**
2. **Stray animals**
3. **On highway**
   — *liability of public authority for failure to maintain or repair highway, see HIGHWAYS AND STREETS* VI
   a. General
   b. Duty of motorist
4. **By railway**
5. **Malicious injury**

III.   LIABILITY OF OWNER OR POSSESSOR OF ANIMALS

1. **Injury by domestic animals**
   a. At common law
   b. Under by-law or statute

c. Injury by dog
   i. At common law
   ii. Under by-law or statute
   iii. Injury to other animals
d. On highway
e. Injury to other animals
2. **Injury by wild animals**
3. **Trespass by animals**
4. **Distress damage feasant**
5. **Criminal liability**
   — *criminal offences generally, see CRIMINAL LAW*
6. **Liability for nuisance**
7. **Regulation of dangerous animals**
8. **Miscellaneous issues**

VI.   DISEASES OF ANIMALS

— *sale of diseased animals, see* IV.2

FIGURE 11.5   **Concluded**

ANIMALS VI.1

1. General
2. Destruction of animals
3. Compensation

VII. STRAY ANIMALS

— *see also* III.1.d; *injury to stray animals, see* II.2

VIII. MISCELLANEOUS ISSUES

Scan the appropriate digests, and write down the names and citations of important cases.

If you used the general index, look for appropriate case digest numbers in the upper left corner of each digest. From your research of this issue in the *Canadian Encyclopedic Digest* (see chapter 8), you know that there is statute law, the *Dog Owners' Liability Act*, governing this issue. As a result, you can go directly to the digest entries dealing with liability under statute law. The first digest under this heading is number 3160. If you used the key and research guide, look for the key classification number that appears at the upper right hand corner of each digest. All the case digests dealing with your research topic will be under classification number III.1.c.ii. The relevant digests are reproduced in figure 11.6.

Updating Your Research

Look in the R1 supplement volume of the *Case Digests* for digests of any cases that may have been reported after the cut-off date of the R1 reissue permanent volume. If you used the general index as your finding tool, it gave you the digest numbers in the supplement volume—in this case digest numbers 332-355. If you used the key and research guide, find your subject title—in this case animals—and then look under the relevant classification number—in this case III.1.c.ii.

To update beyond the supplement's cut-off date (the end of the previous calendar year), check each monthly softcover issue of *Canadian Current Law: Case Digests*, starting with January of the current calendar year. To find the digests in these issues, look up "animals" in the index found at the back of each monthly issue. The subject titles are set out in alphabetical order. The March, June, September, and December issues contain a cumulative index of all digests that have appeared to that date during the year, so begin your search with the most current volume that contains a cumulative index. Then check each subsequent monthly issue. You can then refer to the relevant case digests contained in these issues.

You can also use the case law update section provided in the general index to direct you. The "scope note" at the start of the case law update section sets out the *Canadian Current Law: Case Digests* issues covered in the update section. (See figure 11.7.) Look for your subject title and classification number.

LOOKING FOR CASES INTERPRETING A STATUTE

You can consult a number of different sources to find cases that have interpreted or applied a statute, including

- the *Canadian Abridgment Canadian Statute Citations*,
- statute citators, and
- annotated statutes.

Canadian Statute Citations

Canadian Statute Citations is part of the *Canadian Abridgment* and contains citations of cases that interpret both federal and provincial statutes. Federal and provincial statutes are located in separate volumes. First, locate the hardcover volumes for Canada or the province in which you are interested; then find the name of the statute. Look up the statutory provision by statute name and then by section

FIGURE 11.6   Case Digests Classification Number III.1.c.ii

[3159 - 3162]   LIABILITY OF OWNER   III.1.c.ii

disposition was shown in evidence to have been exhibited, once in the presence of defendant and once in the presence of defendant's son. Held, there was ample evidence for the jury that defendant harboured the dog with knowledge of its vicious propensities.

Vaughan v. Wood (1890), 18 S.C.R. 703, affirming (1889), 28 N.B.R. 472 (C.A.).

3159.   (III.1.c.i)
Liability of owner or possessor of animals – Injury by domestic animals – Injury by dog – At common law – Dog biting person – Evidence of previous and subsequent attacks by dog – Admissibility thereof – Owner's knowledge of dog's vicious propensity – Negligence. In an action brought for an injury inflicted by a dog, it is necessary to allege and prove that defendant had knowledge of the animal's vicious propensity. As soon as that knowledge is shown, the same responsibility attaches to the owner to keep him from doing mischief, as the keeper of an animal, naturally ferocious, would be subject to, and there is no necessity for proving negligence. Plaintiff was bitten by defendant's dog. In an action for damages, 1 witness testified that he had been bitten by the dog one year previously and that he informed defendant of it and another witness testified that he had been bitten by the same dog subsequently to the action having been brought. Held, the evidence with reference to the dog's biting on the occasion subsequent to the action having been started, was improperly received, but since the trial Judge expressly withdrew it from the consideration of the jury, the verdict should not be interfered with.

Wilmot v. Vanwart (1877), 17 N.B.R. 456 (C.A.).

ii.   Under by-law or statute

3160.   (III.1.c.ii)
Liability of owner or possessor of animals – Injury by domestic animals – Injury by dog – Under by-law or statute – Rural Municipality Act, S.S. 1989-90, c. R-26.1, s. 222. Infant plaintiff was bitten in the face by defendants' dog while playing in their yard. Before the enactment of the new Act, a plaintiff in an action involving injury by a domestic animal was required to prove that the defendant knew of the animal's dangerous propensities, unless the defendant was otherwise negligent. S. 222 of the new Act removed the defence of lack of knowledge. Plaintiff sued defendants after the new Act came into force, and parties applied for a determination of whether s. 222 applied. Held, the section did not apply. A defence to an action was a matter of substance, and removal of the defence was an interference with a vested right. There was a presumption that a prospective enactment was bad only if it affected vested rights in ambiguous terms;

the intention to affect vested rights had to be stated clearly. In enacting s. 222 the Legislature would have known that, except for an infant, the limitation period for commencing a personal injury action in the province was two years. There was nothing in s. 222 indicating that the Legislature intended to eliminate vested legal rights which existed in isolated circumstances only. The word "action" in s. 222 meant one arising after the section's enactment and the presumption operated so as not to interfere with defendants' vested legal rights.

Karras v. Richter, [1995] 7 W.W.R. 406, 133 Sask. R. 40 (Q.B.).

3161.   (III.1.c.ii)
Liability of owner or possessor of animals – Injury by domestic animals – Injury by dog – Under by-law or statute – Strict liability – No contributory negligence – Dog Owners' Liability Act, R.S.O. 1990, c. D-16, s. 2(1), (3). Animal control officer while responding to a call about a stray dog was bitten by the dog. The bite was incurred when officer bent down to determine the sex of the dog. The dog was later claimed by owner. Officer's action against owner for damages for personal injury was dismissed by the trial judge. Officer appealed the decision. Held, the appeal was allowed. Under the ss. 2(1) and 2(3) of the Act, owner of the dog was strictly liable for damages caused by that dog as long as it was proven that that person was the owner of the dog and that that dog had bitten plaintiff. The scents on the officer and his actions did not in any way amount to contributory negligence.

Michalik v. Khan (1995), 80 O.A.C. 353 (Div. Ct.).

3162.   (III.1.c.ii)
Liability of owner or possessor of animals – Injury by domestic animals – Injury by dog – Under by-law or statute – Application for summary judgment – Plaintiff's affidavits proving case – Defendant merely denying allegations – Dog Act, R.S.N. 1990, c. D-26, s. 8. Plaintiff was walking past defendant's house when she was bitten by a small white dog. Plaintiff's son saw the same dog inside defendant's house and defendant admitted that he had a white dog which was a nuisance at times. Plaintiff brought an action against defendant under s. 8 of the Act, for damages for personal injuries. Defendant denied that his dog had bitten plaintiff. Plaintiff applied for summary judgment. Held, the application was allowed. The issues were the identification of the dog that attacked plaintiff and the ownership of that dog. The affidavits of plaintiff and her son clearly proved that a dog owned by defendant attacked plaintiff. Defendant did not provide a bona fide defence, or raise an issue to be tried, merely by denying the allegations and putting plaintiff to her proof.

627

FIGURE 11.6   Concluded

III.1.c.ii   ANIMALS   [3163 - 3166]

Abbott v. Sharpe   (1994), 121 Nfld. &
P.E.I.R. 57, 377 A.P.R. 57 (Nfld. T.D.).

3163.   (III.1.c.ii)
**Liability of owner or possessor of animals
– Injury by domestic animals – Injury by
dog – Under by-law or statute –
"Harbouring" requiring some degree of
care or control – Dog Owners' Liability
Act, R.S.O. 1990, c. D.16, ss. 1, 2(1), (3).** T.
was the owner of two dogs. B. and S. owned
a home in which they lived. They allowed
T. to stay in the home and to bring his dogs
when he was working in the area. B. and
S. never fed, walked, or supervised the dogs
and they had no special facilities for the dogs.
P. was a neighbour of B. and S. T. was walking his dogs when they ran across the street
and attacked P. P. was very frightened and,
while she was fleeing from the scene, her coat
was sprayed by a skunk. At the time, B. and
S. were away for the weekend and T. was
staying at their home with his dogs. Ss. 2(1)
and 2(3) of the Act conferred absolute
liability on the owner of a dog who attacked a
person. S. 1 defined the owner of a dog to
include a person who harboured the dog. A
default judgment was obtained against
T. P. brought an action against B. and S.,
arguing that they were liable for having harboured the dogs. Held, the action was dismissed. To harbour a dog within the meaning
of s. 1 required more than the simple act of
allowing it to be in the home together with its
owner. Harbouring required the exercise of
some degree of care or control over the dog.

Purcell v. Taylor   (1994), 120 D.L.R. (4th)
161 (Ont. Gen. Div.).

3164.   (III.1.c.ii)
**Liability of owner or possessor of animals
– Injury by domestic animals – Injury by
dog – Under by-law or statute – Damages –
Dog Owners' Liability Act, R.S.O. 1990, c.
D.16, s. 2.** Child was bitten by a dog when he
went to give it a hug. The dog was on a leash
that was long enough to allow it to come onto
the church property where child was playing.
Child's mother took him to an emergency
department of the hospital where a doctor su-
tured three lacerations around and about the
right corner of child's mouth. Although the
lacerations healed well, scars developed. A
specialist in plastic surgery stated 1 year later
that the scarring would be permanent and always obvious. Subsequent to the incident,
child had nightmares, bed-wetting problems
and was fearful of dogs. Child brought an
action for damages under the Act. Held, the
action was allowed. No degree of fault or
negligence was ascribed to child which would
have caused or contributed to the damages.
The hug given to the dog by child did not
constitute a contributing cause that would
warrant a reduction of the damages. Child
was left with a permanent cosmetic deformity
and suffered mental distress as a result of the

physical injuries. He was entitled to non-
pecuniary damages of $22,000 and his
parents were entitled to $4,968 in special
damages.

Strom (Litigation Guardian of) v. White
(*sub nom.* **Strom v. White**) (1994), 21 O.R.
(3d) 205 (Gen. Div.).

3165.   (III.1.c.ii)
**Liability of owner or possessor of animals
– Injury by domestic animals – Injury by
dog – Under by-law or statute – Summary
judgment granted to dismiss part of claim
where statutory provisions not applying to
defendants.** Where the Court determined
that defendants were not owners within the
meaning of the Dog Owners' Liability Act,
that part of the claim alleging liability under
the Act was dismissed. It was alleged by
plaintiff that two dogs belonging to
R. attacked her on a public sidewalk. R. was
the brother of one of the defendants. R. had
an arrangement with defendants to the effect
that R. could stay at defendants' house with
his two dogs when he was working in the
area. R. had taken advantage of the arrangement about a dozen times in the previous 3
years. When the alleged incident occurred,
defendants were not at home and were un-
aware that R. and the dogs were in the house.
Plaintiff's claim was based on liability under
the Act and negligence and breach of duty.
Defendants moved for summary judgment to
have the claim against them dismissed. An
order was granted dismissing the claim based
on the Act. With respect to the claim in
negligence and breach of duty, the motion by
defendants for summary judgment was dismissed. On the question of liability of defendants under the Act, the Court was satisfied
that there was no genuine issue for trial. The
Court found that defendants were not the
owners of the two dogs and thus could not be
found liable under the Act. There must be
some degree of care or control of the dogs on
the part of the person who it is said is harbouring the animals before that person can be
said to have harboured them in a way that
makes him or her an owner for the purposes
of liability under the Act.

Purcell v. Taylor   (December 1, 1992), Doc.
92-CQ-16622 (Ont. Gen. Div.).

3166.   (III.1.c.ii)
**Liability of owner or possessor of animals
– Injury by domestic animals – Injury by
dog – Under by-law or statute – Minor dog
bite – Systemic infection not foreseeable.**
Owner of a dog tied it to a wharf so that the
dog would not interfere with water-skiers, as
it was wont to do. The dog broke loose and
gave a skier a very minor bite which punc-
tured the skin. Several days later, the skier
died from a bacteria commonly found in
dogs' mouths. However, medical knowledge
of this bacteria at the time of the bite was
scant and it was not generally understood by

628

FIGURE 11.7   **Case Digests Scope Note and Case Law Update**

CASE LAW UPDATE

SCOPE NOTE

This update provides names and citations of cases digested in Canadian Current Law – Case Digests after the last Canadian Abridgment Case Digests Supplement, organized by Canadian Abridgment classification.

The current tables refer to:

- [2005] Canadian Current Law – Case Digests, Issues 1 – 3 (January – March 2005):

  Issue 1 . . . . digests 1-3717
  Issue 2 3718-7036
  Issue 3 7037-10144

- [2004] Canadian Current Law – Case Digests, Issues 1 – 12 (January – December 2004):

  Issue 1 . . . . digests 1-3544
  Issue 2 3545-7345
  Issue 3 7346-11049
  Issue 4 11050-13834
  Issue 5 13835-18560
  Issue 6 18561-21043
  Issue 7 21044-24307
  Issue 8 24308-26960
  Issue 9 26961-29660
  Issue 10 29661-32333
  Issue 11 32334-35299
  Issue 12 35300-37644

To locate cases digested prior to January 2004 consult:

- 2003 Case Digests Annual Supplement (Second Edition - Volumes R1 Supp. to R35 Supp. and Third Edition - Volumes 1 to 28)

- Main Work (Third Edition) - Volumes 1 to 59

- Main Work (Second Edition) - Volumes R1 to R35

i   General Index Binder 2005-2

FIGURE 11.7 **Concluded**

ANIMALS III.1.c.i | Case Law Update

	Weeks v. Baloniak (2003), 2003 CarswellBC 2796, 2003 BCSC 1684 (B.C. S.C.)	11254
(III.1.c.ii)	Pagourov v. Mowbray (2003), 2003 CarswellOnt 4297 (Ont. C.J.)	32377
	R. v. Beaulieu (2004), 2004 CarswellNWT 13, 2004 NWTSC 19 (N.W.T. S.C.)	21415
	R. v. Brenhouse (2003), 2003 CarswellOnt 4938 (Ont. C.J.)	7573
(III.1.d)	Borstmayer v. Mackrell (2004), 2004 SKPC 84, 2004 CarswellSask 508 (Sask. Prov. Ct.)	32378
	Porter v. Pond (2004), 2004 CarswellNB 297, 2004 NBCA 47, 2004 CarswellNB 401 (N.B. C.A.)	32379
(III.4)	McDougall v. British Columbia Society for the Prevention of Cruelty to Animals (2003), 2003 CarswellBC 2600, 2003 BCSC 1604 (B.C. S.C.)	3718
(III.7)	Hall, Re (2004), 2004 CarswellBC 297, 2004 BCPC 27 (B.C. Prov. Ct.)	14153
	Prince George (City) v. MacLeod (2004), 2004 CarswellBC 143, 2004 BCPC 8 (B.C. Prov. Ct.)	14154
(III.8)	Beynon v. Ontario Society for the Prevention of Cruelty to Animals (2004), 2004 CarswellOnt 472 (Ont. S.C.J.)	14155
	Manitoba Public Insurance Corp. v. Lamb (2004), 2004 CarswellMan 234, 2004 MBQB 128, 185 Man. R. (2d) 128 (Man. Q.B.)	24475
(VI.2)	Cervinus Inc. v. Canada (Minister of Agriculture) (2002), 296 N.R. 234, 2002 CarswellNat 3865, 2002 CAF 398, 2002 CarswellNat 2874, 2002 FCA 398, 233 F.T.R. 270 (note) (Fed. C.A.)	178
	Siclo c. Canada (Ministère de l'Agriculture & de l'Agroalimentaire) (2004), 2004 CarswellNat 1876, 2004 CF 871, 2004 FC 871, 2004 CarswellNat 4172 (F.C.)	26999
(VI.3)	Begg v. Canada (Minister of Agriculture) (2004), 2004 CarswellNat 1311, 2004 FC 659, 2004 CarswellNat 3298, 2004 CF 659 (F.C.)	24476
	Siclo c. Canada (Ministère de l'Agriculture & de l'Agroalimentaire) (2004), 2004 CarswellNat 1876, 2004 CF 871, 2004 FC 871, 2004 CarswellNat 4172 (F.C.)	27000
(VIII)	R. c. Charest (2004), 2004 CarswellOnt 1486, 2004 ONCJ 4 (Ont. C.J.)	18735

ARMED FORCES

(II.2.a)	Donoghue v. Canada (Minister of National Defence) (2004), 2004 CarswellNat 1504, 2004 FC 733, 2004 CarswellNat 2791, 2004 CF 733 (F.C.)	24477
(II.2.c)	Spiegelberg v. Hubley (2004), 2004 CarswellBC 401, 2004 BCCA 92 (B.C. C.A. [In Chambers])	14156
	Stieber v. Canada (Department of National Defence) (2004), (sub nom. Stieber v. Canada (Attorney General)) 317 W.A.C. 26, 194 B.C.A.C. 26, [2004] 5 W.W.R. 83, 24 B.C.L.R. (4th) 49, 21 C.C.L.T. (3d) 245, 2004 CarswellBC 118, 2004 BCCA 44 (B.C. C.A.)	14157
(II.2.d)	White v. Canada (Attorney General) (2002), [2002] B.C.J. No. 1821, 4 B.C.L.R. (4th) 161, 2002 CarswellBC 1890, 2002 BCSC 1164 (B.C. S.C. [In Chambers])	21416
(IV.3)	Duplessis v. R. (2004), 2004 CarswellNat 328, 2004 CF 154, 2004 FC 154, 2004 CarswellNat 2191 (F.C.)	18736
(VI.2)	Tremblay c. R. (2004), 2004 CarswellNat 1277, 2004 CAF 172, 2004 FCA 172, [2004] F.C.J. No. 787, 2004 CarswellNat 3374 (F.C.A.)	27001
(VI.3.a)	Aylsworth v. Ewan (2004), 2004 CarswellBC 1357, 2004 BCSC 739, 29 B.C.L.R. (4th) 345 (B.C. S.C.)	27002
	De Quoy c. Canada (Procureur Général) (2004), 2004 CF 654, 2004 CarswellNat 1320, [2004] F.C.J. No. 793 (F.C.)	24478

number. Cases considering statutes as a whole appear at the beginning of the entry for that statute under the heading "generally." The statutes are listed alphabetically and then, within that order, chronologically by statute revision. Make sure that you look under the correct revision of the statute (1990, 1980, 1970, etc.). You will have to concord the statutory revision (see chapter 9) to find cases that were decided under earlier revisions of the statute. After looking in the hardcover volume of *Canadian Statute Citations*, check the corresponding supplement volume to find cases decided after the cut-off date of the permanent volume. You should check the corresponding supplement volume even if you don't see the name of the statute or the section of the statute you are looking for in the hardcover volume, since cases may have been decided after the cut-off date of the hardcover volume. Complete your search by consulting the monthly issues of *Canadian Statute Citations*.

Each case citation is preceded by a code inside a small circle that indicates the court's treatment of the statute. See figure 11.8.

FIGURE 11.8   Treatment Symbols for Statutes

Symbol	Meaning
(U)	Unconstitutional—The case decided that a section of the statute was unconstitutional or invalid.
(C)	Considered—The case analyzed or interpreted a section of the statute.
(P)	Pursuant to—The case was brought pursuant to a section of the statute.
(R)	Referred to—The case mentions a section of the statute in passing, but does not consider it directly.

Statute Citators

Statute citators provide another way of looking for cases interpreting a statute or a specific provision of a statute. The citator will refer you to important cases dealing with a statute. For cases involving federal statutes, consult the *Canada Statute Citator*. For cases involving Ontario statutes, consult the *Ontario Statute Citator*. Cases are listed under the statutory provision to which they are related. The citator is not comprehensive and should be used only with another source.

Annotated Statutes

There is also a third way of looking for cases interpreting a statute. A commercially published annotated version of the statute will list relevant cases under the section of the statute that the cases considered.

LOOKING FOR CASES CONSIDERING A WORD OR PHRASE

The *Canadian Abridgment* has a set of volumes called *Words and Phrases Judicially Defined in Canadian Courts and Tribunals*. Use this source to find cases that have considered particular legal terms or phrases. Words and phrases are arranged alphabetically in the volumes. Each entry includes an extract from the judgment in which the word or phrase was considered. It also gives you the name, citation, and jurisdiction for each case. First check the hardcover volumes of *Words and Phrases Judicially Defined in Canadian Courts and Tribunals*; next look in the supplement volumes to update your search for cases reported after the cut-off date of the hardcover volume.

TREASURE HUNTING

Sometimes you can't find a case that you're looking for because you have been given a wrong or partial citation.

Finding a Case When You've Been Given the Wrong Citation

One of the most tedious aspects of legal research is that, when looking for a case, chances are about 50–50 that you have an incorrect citation. Either you have copied it down wrong, the person who gave you the citation copied it down wrong, or the text from which you got the citation contains a misprint that was not caught by a proofreader. What do you do when you track down the case report volume in the citation you've been given and the case you're looking for is nowhere to be found?

To find the correct case name, try looking in either the *Consolidated Table of Cases* or the *Canadian Case Citations* volumes of the *Canadian Abridgment*. Cases are arranged alphabetically by name and are cross-referenced by alternate case names and by the defendant's name.

If you cannot find the name of a case in the hardcover volumes, check the supplement volumes. It may be that the case you are looking for was decided or reported after the cut-off date of the main volume.

NOTE: Before you do the above, you may wish to check (1) the table of cases in the case report volume you pulled that was *supposed* to contain the case but didn't, and/or (2) the index volume of that case report series. Incorrect citations are often a matter of a wrong page number or volume number.

If the above steps do not work, recheck the source of the citation, because you may have the wrong name.

"Find me this case—I think it's called Smith, or maybe it's Jorgensen"

Another tedious aspect of legal research is dealing with lawyers who expect a case to be found given little information. Here's a suggestion. Look up the supposed name of the case in the *Consolidated Table of Cases* or *Canadian Case Citations* permanent volumes and all supplements.

If you still cannot find the correct name, you probably have been given a completely wrong name reference. Find out exactly the subject of the case, and proceed to research the matter as you would research a subject. You eventually may come across the case under a variation of the originally suggested name.

"Find me a case that says ..."

Research the matter as you would research a subject.

LOOKING FOR UNREPORTED CASES

Many more cases are decided than are reported. Lawyers used to think that an unreported case was not worth showing to the court, but that has now changed, partly because so many decisions are handed down that not all the important ones can be reported, and partly because computer databases have made it possible to find more and more unreported decisions.

Unreported cases may be found in digest services or legal newspapers.

Digest Services

Digest services are published on a weekly or monthly basis and contain summaries of recent cases of interest. An unreported decision is usually available on request from the publisher of the service. There are various digests available:

- General digests—*Canadian Current Law: Case Digests*, *Dominion Report Service*, and *Canadian Weekly Law Sheet*.
- Civil cases digests, from all jurisdictions—*All Canada Weekly Summaries* (A.C.W.S.).
- Topical digests, with cases from all jurisdictions—for example, the *Family Law Digest*, the *Weekly Criminal Bulletin* (W.C.B.), and the *Weekly Digest of Civil Procedure* (W.D.C.P.).
- Supreme Court digests—*Supreme Court of Canada Bulletin*, *Supreme Court of Canada Summaries*, *Supreme Court of Canada Reports Service*, and *Supreme Court of Canada Decisions*.

Legal Newspapers

Unreported decisions are available from legal newspapers on request; the digest section of each paper provides phone and fax numbers of the newspaper. *The Lawyers Weekly* covers all of Canada and contains news articles about recent decisions and case digests in every issue; it produces *The Lawyers Weekly Reports* as a supplement, which gives the full text of selected recent decisions that have not yet been reported. The *Law Times*, published weekly, covers Ontario cases only and, as with *The Lawyers Weekly*, prints both articles about decisions and case digests.

LOOKING FOR THE TEXT OF A CASE: UNDERSTANDING A CASE CITATION

Once you have found the name and citation of relevant cases, you still need to find the text. To do this, you must understand case citations.

Case Citations

A correct legal citation of a case consists of several parts as illustrated in the following examples, explained below:

1	2	3	4	5	6	7
Malette v. Shulman	(1990),	67	D.L.R.	(4th)	321	(Ont. C.A.)
Pettkus v. Becker,	[1980]	2	S.C.R.		834	

1. Style of Cause or General Heading

The **style of cause** of the citation sets out the names of the parties (last names only). The names of *all* the parties to the action are not always included in the citation. In a reported case, the editors of the report series will have given the case a short style of cause as well as the complete one if it is long. The names of the parties are separated by "v." (which is Latin for "versus," meaning against) and are italicized.

style of cause
names of the parties in an action

2. Year

The year in which the case is decided or reported—that is, published in a report series—follows the style of cause and will be in either round or square brackets.

Some report series number their volumes sequentially no matter what the year, and it is not essential to know the year in which the case was reported in order to find it in the report series. In that case the year is placed in round brackets—( )—and is followed by a comma.

Other report series start a new set of volume numbers each calendar year, and it is essential to know the year in order to find the case in the report series. In this case, the year appears in square brackets—[ ]—and is preceded by a comma. For example, in each calendar year, the first volume of the Supreme Court Reports is volume 1. To find a case that is located in volume 1, you must know the year in which the case was reported to find the appropriate volume 1.

3. Law Report Volume Number

This number tells you the volume number of the report series in which your case can be found. Some law report volumes are identified simply by volume number (as in the first example above), while others are identified also by the year in which the volume was published. More than one volume may be published in one year as illustrated in the second example above. If the report series starts a new sequence of volume numbers each year, then you must make sure you look for the volume number for the correct year. In the example of *Pettkus v. Becker* above, you are looking for volume 2 for the year 1980.

4. Name of the Law Report Series

This part of the citation tells you the name of the law report series in which the case is reported. Abbreviations are generally used. In the example of *Malette v. Shulman* above, D.L.R. stands for the *Dominion Law Reports*. In the example of *Pettkus v. Becker*, S.C.R. stands for the *Supreme Court Reports*.

See the appendix for a list of standard abbreviations covering most Canadian report series.

5. Law Report Series Number

Many reports will not continue past a certain number of volumes. When the report reaches, for example, volume 75 or volume 100, that series ends and a new one begins. Subsequent editions are identified by 2d, 3d, 4th, and so on (*not* 2nd, 3rd). If a series or edition number is provided in a citation, be sure that you have the right series as well as the right volume number of the report. In the *Malette v. Shulman* citation above, the case can be found in the 67th volume of the 4th series of the D.L.R.s.

6. Page Number

This number tells you the page number on which the case begins in the report volume. In a correct citation no abbreviation such as p., pp., or pg. is used before the page number.

7. Jurisdiction and Court

The abbreviation for jurisdiction and the level of court is found in round brackets following the page number of the case. This information is omitted if the jurisdiction and/or court level is obvious from the name of the reporter series.

If the citation refers to a report series that includes cases for one province only, such as the *Ontario Reports* or the *British Columbia Reports*, only the level of court is set out. For example, the citation of a Court of Appeal case published in the *Ontario Reports* will end with (C.A.). The citation for the same case in the *Dominion Law Reports* (which publishes cases from across Canada) will end in (Ont. C.A.).

If the citation refers to a report series for one court only, the level of court will not be included in the citation. For example, the *Supreme Court Reports* cover only Supreme Court of Canada decisions. Therefore a citation for that report series will omit both the jurisdiction and level of court, as illustrated in the example of *Pettkus v. Becker* above.

Sometimes the name of the judge or judges who decided the case is included in the citation. For example (Ont. C.A.—Robins J.). The J stands for judge or justice; it is not the initial of the judge's first name. JJ. stands for justices and JJ.A. stands for justices of appeal. C.J. stands for Chief Justice. A judge's own initial is used only if it is necessary to distinguish between two judges with the same last name, for example R.E. Holland J. and J. Holland J.

Parallel Citations

Cases may be reported in more than one report series, in which case "parallel" citations are given. A parallel citation tells you about other reports where the same case report can be found. The citation for any official report series is given first. For example:

R. v. Carosella, [1997] 1 S.C.R. 80, 142 D.L.R. (4th) 595, 112 C.C.C. (3d) 289.

This citation means that the case can be found in the *Supreme Court Reports*, the *Dominion Law Reports*, and *Canadian Criminal Cases*. Parallel citations are separated by commas.

When parallel citations are given, you need to choose only one of the report series to find the text of the case. However, if the case has been reported in an official report series, you should read and copy the case from that report series, if it is available to you.

Using the Case Citation To Find the Text of the Case

The citation of a case contains all the information you need to find the actual case report, by providing the name and volume numbers of the report series in which the case has been published.

Start your search for a cited case by finding the law report series, including the correct series number. Then look for the appropriate volume number. Finally, turn to the page number set out in the citation. The case starts on that page.

UPDATING CASES

Once you find relevant case law, you must make sure that it is current, by updating each case to find out

- the case's **appeal history** or case history—has it been confirmed or overturned on appeal; what was the highest court that reviewed the decision; and
- how has the case been treated by other judges—has it been followed or not; has it been distinguished?

A case in your favour is useless if it has been reversed on appeal; a case that has not been followed by other judges has less persuasive value than one that has been followed consistently.

If a case has been appealed to higher courts, the citation you have in hand may include a complete appeal history or case history of the journey of the case through the court system. For example:

> *Queen v. Cognos Inc.*, [1993] 1 S.C.R. 87, rev'g. (1990), 74 O.R. (2d) 176 (C.A.), aff'g. (1987), 63 O.R. (2d) 389 (H.C.J.).

This citation tells you that the 1993 Supreme Court of Canada decision reversed the 1990 decision from the Ontario Court of Appeal, but affirmed the 1987 decision of the Ontario High Court of Justice.

If you don't have a full citation showing the case history, or if you think the case may still be in play so the citation is not complete, use either the *Consolidated Table of Cases* or the *Canadian Case Citations* (both series are part of the *Canadian Abridgment*) to find the history of the case. *Canadian Case Citations* may be slightly more thorough in listing cases. For either series, look in both the hardcover main volumes and the paperback supplementary volumes. To find out whether a case has been followed by other judges, use *Canadian Case Citations*.

Figure 11.10 reproduces a page from *Canadian Case Citations*. Note how the cases are listed alphabetically with parallel citations. If a case has been mentioned in other cases, those cases are listed at the end of the entry. Each case is preceded by an explanatory letter in a circle, as shown in figure 11.9.

appeal history
history of a case—for example, whether the case has been confirmed or overturned on appeal and the name of the highest court that reviewed the decision

FIGURE 11.9   Treatment Symbols for Cases

Symbol	Meaning
(F)	Followed—This case followed the principal of law in the cited case.
(D)	Distinguished—This case distinguished the cited case—that is, the principle of law was not applied because of a difference in facts or law).
(N)	Not Followed/Overruled—This case ruled that the cited case was wrongly decided.
(C)	Considered—This case considered or mentioned the cited case.

FIGURE 11.10 Canadian Case Citations Sample Page

CCC/RJC   *Stewart v. Rundle*

(1961), 38 C.R. 19 (B.C. Co. Ct.)

Stewart v. R.
(March 11, 1902)
(1902), 32 S.C.R. 483 (S.C.C.)

Cases citing S.C.C.
- Ⓕ Lawson v. W.R. Carpenter Oversea Shipping Ltd., [1945] 1 W.W.R. 5 (B.C. C.A.)
- Ⓖ Klimack Construction Ltd. v. Belleville (City), [1951] O.W.N. 705 (Ont. H.C.)

Stewart v. R.
(1901), 7 Ex. C.R. 55 (Can. Ex. Ct.)

Cases citing Can. Ex. Ct.
- Ⓖ Klimack Construction Ltd. v. Belleville (City), [1951] O.W.N. 705 (Ont. H.C.)

Stewart; R. c., *see R. c. Stewart*

Stewart; R. v., *see R. v. Stewart*

Stewart v. R. (No. 2)
(1977), 35 C.C.C. (2d) 281 (Ont. C.A.)

Cases citing Ont. C.A.
- Ⓕ Myers v. R. (1991), 65 C.C.C. (3d) 135 (Nfld. C.A.)
- Ⓖ R. v. Pearson (1978), 7 C.R. (3d) 175 (Que. S.C.)
- Ⓒ Desbiens v. Québec (Procureur général), [1986] R.J.Q. 2488 (Que. S.C.)
- Ⓖ R. v. Skogman, [1984] 2 S.C.R. 93 (S.C.C.)
- Ⓖ Stolar v. R. (1983), 32 C.R. (3d) 342 (Man. C.A.)
- Ⓖ Bourget v. Northwest Territories (1982), 47 A.R. 220 (N.W.T. S.C.)

Stewart v. Ray
(October 27, 1941)
[1941] 3 W.W.R. 881, [1941] 4 D.L.R. 718 (Sask. C.A.)

Stewart v. Reavell's Garage
[1952] 2 Q.B. 545, [1952] 1 All E.R. 1191 (Eng. Q.B.)

Cases citing Eng. Q.B.
- Ⓕ Walsh Insurance & Real Estate Ltd. v. Trans North Holdings Ltd. (1978), 20 A.R. 108 (Alta. T.D.)
- Ⓕ Raiche's Steel Works Ltd. v. J. Clark & Son Ltd. (1977), 16 N.B.R. (2d) 535 (N.B. Q.B.)
- Ⓕ Scott Maritimes Pulp Ltd. v. B. F. Goodrich Canada Ltd. (1977), 19 N.S.R. (2d) 181 (N.S. C.A.)

Stewart v. Rempel
(November 5, 1991), Doc. Vancouver B880462
[1991] B.C.W.L.D. 2603 (B.C. S.C.)

Stewart v. Rennie
(1836), 5 U.C.Q.B. (O.S.) 151

Stewart v. Rhodes
[1900] 1 Ch. 386 (Eng. Ch. Div.)

Cases citing Eng. Ch. Div.
- Ⓒ Jacobson Brothers v. Anderson (1962), 48 M.P.R. 29 (N.S. C.A.)

Stewart v. Richard
(1885), 3 Man. R. 610 (Man. Q.B.)

Cases citing Man. Q.B.
- Ⓕ Canada Settlers Loan Co. v. Fullerton (1893), 9 Man. R. 327 (Man. C.A.)
- Ⓑ Morris (Rural Municipality) v. London & Canadian Loan & Agency Co. (1890), 7 Man. R. 128 (Man. C.A.)

Stewart v. Richardson
(February 18, 1870)
(1870), 17 Gr. 150

Stewart v. Richardson Securities of Canada
(February 12, 1982), Doc. GDC-3210
(1982), 35 Nfld. & P.E.I.R. 325, 99 A.P.R. 325 (P.E.I. S.C.)

Stewart v. Richardson Sons & Co.
(June 10, 1920)
[1920] 3 W.W.R. 134, 30 Man. R. 481, 53 D.L.R. 625 (Man. C.A.)

Stewart; Robertson v., *see Robertson v. Stewart*

Stewart; Robichaud v., *see Robichaud v. Stewart*

Stewart v. Rogers
(June 30, 1905)
(1905), 6 O.W.R. 195 (Ont. H.C.)

Stewart v. Roop
(1983), 58 N.S.R. (2d) 407, 123 A.P.R. 407 (N.S. T.D.)

Stewart v. Ross
Doc. Q.B. J.C.R. 4226/86
(1988), 64 Sask. R. 271 (Sask. Q.B.)

Stewart v. Rounds
(1882), 7 O.A.R. 515

Cases citing 1st level
- Ⓕ Weaver v. Sawyer & Co. (1889), 16 O.A.R. 422 (Ont. C.A.)
- Ⓖ Bate v. Canadian Pacific Railway (1888), 15 O.A.R. 388

Stewart v. Routhier
(December 21, 1971)
(1971), 4 N.B.R. (2d) 340 (N.B. Q.B.)
affirmed / confirmé (March 9, 1972) (1972), 4 N.B.R. (2d) 332, 26 D.L.R. (3d) 752 (N.B. C.A.)
which was reversed / qui a été infirmé (1973), [1975] 1 S.C.R. 566, 7 N.B.R. (2d) 251, 45 D.L.R. (3d) 383, 1 N.R. 183 (S.C.C.)
which was varied / qui a été modifiée (April 2, 1974) (1974), [1975] 1 S.C.R. 588, 7 N.B.R. (2d) 558, 53 D.L.R. (3d) 77, 1 N.R. 630 (S.C.C.)

and which was reversed / et qui a été infirmé (1973), [1975] 1 S.C.R. 566, 7 N.B.R. (2d) 251, 45 D.L.R. (3d) 383, 1 N.R. 183 (S.C.C.)
which was varied / qui a été modifiée (April 2, 1974) (1974), [1975] 1 S.C.R. 588, 7 N.B.R. (2d) 558, 53 D.L.R. (3d) 77, 1 N.R. 630 (S.C.C.)

Cases citing S.C.C.
- Ⓕ Bate v. Kileel Enterprises Ltd. (1976), 14 N.B.R. (2d) 204 (N.B. C.A.)
- Ⓕ Brekka v. Reid (1975), 14 N.S.R. (2d) 677 (N.S. C.A.)
- Ⓕ Lessard v. Paquin, [1975] 1 S.C.R. 665 (S.C.C.)
- Ⓑ Lewis Realty Ltd. v. Skalbania (1980), 25 B.C.L.R. 17 (B.C. C.A.)

Cases citing S.C.C.
- Ⓑ Canadian Aero Service Ltd. v. O'Malley (1975), 10 O.R. (2d) 239 (Ont. H.C.)

Stewart v. Rowlands
(1864), 14 U.C.C.P. 485

Stewart v. Rowsom
(1892), 22 O.R. 533

Stewart v. Royal Bank
(1930), 1 M.P.R. 302, [1930] 2 D.L.R. 617 (N.S. C.A.)
reversed / infirmé (June 11, 1930), [1930] S.C.R. 544, [1930] 4 D.L.R. 694 (S.C.C.)

Cases citing N.S. C.A.
- Ⓒ Laidlaw Waste Systems Ltd. v. C.U.P.E., Local 1045 (1993), 37 L.A.C. (4th) 146 (Ont. Arb. Bd.)
- Ⓒ Landymore v. Hardy (1991), 21 R.P.R. (2d) 174 (N.S. T.D.)
- Ⓒ Landymore v. Hardy (December 23, 1991), Doc. S.H. 77533/91 (N.S. T.D.)

Cases citing S.C.C.
- Ⓕ El-Zayed v. Bank of N.S. (1988), 87 N.S.R. (2d) 171 (N.S. T.D.)
- Ⓖ Booth Fisheries Canadian Co. v. Banque provinciale du Canada (1972), 7 N.B.R. (2d) 138 (N.B. Q.B.)
- Ⓖ Levasseur v. Banque de Montréal, [1978] C.S. 1157

Stewart; Royal Bank v., *see Royal Bank v. Stewart*

Stewart; Royal Trust Co. v., *see Royal Trust Co. v. Stewart*

Stewart v. Royds
(1904), 118 L.T. 176

Cases citing 1st level
- Ⓕ Richardson v. McCaffrey (1919), 45 O.L.R. 153 (Ont. C.A.)

Stewart v. Rundle
(April 13, 1940)

KEY TERMS

appeal history
case digest
general index
key and research guide
key classification system
reported case
style of cause
unreported case

CHAPTER 12

Library Exercises

Now that you know more than you want to about paper-based legal research, it's time to apply your knowledge to research in a law library.

Below are sample questions, but an exercise is not useful unless it involves looking for recent changes to the law *and* takes into account the available materials. Therefore, ask your professor for an exercise that requires you to update statutes, regulations, and cases and includes questions that require you to find the following:

- a provincial or federal statute on a given subject;
- whether a specific provincial or federal statute has yet come into force;
- whether a regulation has been made under a specific provincial or federal statute;
- whether a specific statutory provision has been repealed or amended;
- whether a specific statutory provision has been interpreted by case law;
- whether a specific case has been cited in other cases; and
- a specific case that has been given to you as an incorrect citation.

SAMPLE QUESTIONS
Read the questions below, and for each one

- identify the kind of information you're being asked for (a statute, a regulation, a case, an update, or other?);
- decide which research tool(s) you will need;
- in the library, find out which tools are available; and
- answer the question. Cite correctly any statute, regulation, or case that you are asked to find.

1. Is there an Ontario statute that governs transplanting of human organs after death?

   a. What kind of information are you being asked for?

   b. Which research tools will you need?

   c. Which tools are available in your library?

   d. Your answer to the question.

2. Find the federal statute that deals with the sentencing of young offenders.

    a. What kind of information are you being asked for?

    b. Which research tools will you need?

    c. Which tools are available in your library?

    d. Your answer to the question.

3. The federal *Tobacco Products Control Act* is no longer in force. On what
   date was it repealed and by what statute?

   a. What kind of information are you being asked for?

   b. Which research tools will you need?

   c. Which tools are available in your library?

   d. Your answer to the question.

4. Find the *Criminal Code* section that deals with possession of prohibited weapons and update it to the present.

    a. What kind of information are you being asked for?

    b. Which research tools will you need?

    c. Which tools are available in your library?

    d. Your answer to the question.

5. Are there any cases in your province that followed the Supreme Court of Canada decision in *Crocker v. Sundance Northwest Resorts Ltd.*, [1988] 1 S.C.R. 1186?

   a. What kind of information are you being asked for?

   b. Which research tools will you need?

   c. Which tools are available in your library?

   d. Your answer to the question.

6. Was the 1992 Ontario case *Dunn v. Dunn Estate* appealed? If so, what happened on appeal?

    a. What kind of information are you being asked for?

    b. Which research tools will you need?

    c. Which tools are available in your library?

    d. Your answer to the question.

7. Find two recent texts on torts that are available in the library in which you are working. Give the author's name, book title, publisher, and date of publication.

a. What kind of information are you being asked for?

b. Which research tools will you need?

c. Which tools are available in your library?

d. Your answer to the question.

8. Are there any Manitoba Court of Appeal cases dealing with renewal of franchising contracts?

    a. What kind of information are you being asked for?

    b. Which research tools will you need?

    c. Which tools are available in your library?

    d. Your answer to the question.

9. Choose a specific provision of the Ontario *Limitations Act* and then find out if that provision has been cited in case law. Remember that you may have to concord the provision to trace the same section back through previous statute revisions.

   a. What kind of information are you being asked for?

   b. Which research tools will you need?

   c. Which tools are available in your library?

   d. Your answer to the question.

10. Are there any cases that have cited s. 181(2) of the 1985 federal *Bankruptcy and Insolvency Act*?

   a. What kind of information are you being asked for?

   b. Which research tools will you need?

   c. Which tools are available in your library?

   d. Your answer to the question.

11. Find the Ontario statute that provides information about who may adopt infants and children. Are there any regulations made under it?

    a. What kind of information are you being asked for?

    b. Which research tools will you need?

    c. Which tools are available in your library?

    d. Your answer to the question.

12. Your firm's client resides in British Columbia. She recently defaulted in her mortgage payments and the mortgagee is suing for a final order for foreclosure. Which B.C. statute provides information about the effect of a final order for foreclosure? Find the text of this statute.

   a. What kind of information are you being asked for?

   b. Which research tools will you need?

   c. Which tools are available in your library?

   d. Your answer to the question.

13. There is a 1982 Alberta Court of Appeal case involving Holt Renfrew and another corporation. Find the name and citation of this case. Locate the case report and provide the names of all the judges.

   a. What kind of information are you being asked for?

   b. Which research tools will you need?

   c. Which tools are available in your library?

   d. Your answer to the question.

Computer-Assisted Legal Research

In part IV of this book you learned about using paper sources for legal research. By the time you got from the beginning of chapter 7 to the end of chapter 12, you felt as though a library shelf full of books had fallen on top of you—and you were thinking (if not shouting) that there must be an easier way to do legal research.

Well, there *is* another way, and it is often an easier way, although it's not always the best way. In this part of the book, we explain how to use a computer to do legal research.

As with paper sources, there are usually several different ways to find answers to your questions when you do your research using a computer. You may be used to thinking of access to information via computer as free—but many of the computerized legal research sources are "subscription" sources, for which a library or a law firm has to pay. So, once again, you may find you won't have a lot of choice about which tool to use—there may be one computerized tool in the office or library for finding statutes, one for regulations, and one for cases, and you won't know which one until you get to the library or office. Just as with paper sources, you need to know something about all the available computerized sources. Then, when you sit down to work, you'll know how to deal with whatever tools are available.

CHAPTER 13

An Overview of Computerized Sources

When you conduct legal research using computerized sources, your purpose is the same as when you conduct legal research using paper sources—to find binding law that is relevant to a legal problem you need to solve. The law that you are looking for will be in the form of statutes, regulations, and/or cases. These primary sources, whether in paper or computerized form, are not especially user-friendly, and it is usually wise to start your research with secondary sources, using them to gain an understanding of the law and as finding tools to direct you to the primary sources that actually create the law.

This chapter begins to examine the process of finding law that is binding, using computerized primary and secondary sources. We will look at the various computerized legal research sources according to the purpose they serve or the job that they do and discuss the following topics:

- finding tools,
- primary sources,
- updating tools, and
- working with computerized sources.

The various sources are discussed more fully in chapters 14, 15, 16, and 17.

FINDING TOOLS

Generally speaking, you will start your computerized legal research using secondary sources we call "finding tools." Finding tools are used to help you find

- a general statement of the law,
- specific statutes,
- specific regulations, and
- specific cases.

General Statement of the Law

When you use computerized sources, just as when you use paper sources, it is best to start your research by looking for a general statement of the law as it applies to the problem to be solved. As we said in chapter 7, legal encyclopedias such as the *Canadian Encyclopedic Digest*, or CED, not only provide you with a summary of the law, but refer you to the relevant statutes, regulations, and cases from which the principles of law are derived, so they are a good place to begin.

Looking for a general statement of the law with the computerized version of the CED is discussed in more detail in chapter 14.

Specific Statutes and Regulations

Some computerized finding tools are designed specifically to help you find statutes and/or regulations on a particular subject or area of law. These finding tools include

- the Index to Federal and Ontario Statutes Online,
- government website search templates,
- Westlaw*e*CARSWELL's LawSource,
- Quicklaw, and
- the Canadian Legal Information Institute (CanLII) website.

Looking for statutes using computerized sources is discussed in more detail in chapter 15.

Looking for regulations using computerized sources is discussed in more detail in chapter 16.

Specific Cases

Legal encyclopedias, textbooks, and articles refer you only to the leading cases on a particular subject. When you want to find additional cases, there are computerized finding tools designed specifically to help you. The two main finding tools are the *Canadian Abridgment*'s *Canadian Case Digests* (CCD) and Quicklaw, both of which can be used to find

- cases dealing with a specific subject or legal issue,
- cases that have interpreted a statute or a section of a statute,
- cases considering a word or a phrase,
- cases when you have only a partial or incorrect citation (treasure hunting), and
- unreported cases.

Looking for cases using computerized sources is discussed in more detail in chapter 17.

PRIMARY SOURCES

You cannot rely on secondary sources alone. Use them to gain an understanding of the law and as finding tools to direct you to the primary sources that actually create the law. Finding tools will give you the names of relevant statutes, regulations, and cases and sometimes a summary of their provisions. You must then go to the primary sources they refer you to, read them, and understand what they say.

Looking for the text of statutes using computerized sources is discussed in chapter 15. Looking for the text of regulations using computerized sources is discussed in chapter 16. Looking for the text of cases using computerized sources is discussed in chapter 17.

UPDATING TOOLS

Once you have found the relevant statutes, regulations, and/or cases, you must make sure that the statutes and regulations have not been amended or repealed and that the cases have not been overturned on appeal and their legal principles changed by subsequent cases. You do this using secondary sources that we call "updating tools."

The following computerized sources will help you update statutes:

- Canada or Ontario Citator Service,
- *Canada Gazette* website (for federal statutes only),
- Library of Parliament website (for federal statutes only), and
- Legislative Assembly of Ontario website (for Ontario statutes only).

These updating tools are discussed more fully in chapter 15.

The following computerized sources will help you update regulations:

- *Canada Gazette* website (for federal regulations only), and
- *Ontario Gazette* website (for Ontario regulations only).

These updating tools are discussed more fully in chapter 16.

The following computerized sources will help you update cases:

- Quicklaw's QuickCite, and
- LawSource's KeyCite.

These updating tools are discussed more fully in chapter 17.

CATEGORIES OF COMPUTERIZED SOURCES

As you can see, you can use computerized sources to do anything that you can do using paper sources. Before starting to work with computerized sources, however, you must know a little bit about their categories.

Computerized sources can be categorized by

- format,
- organization, and
- function.

Format

Computerized sources come in a variety of different formats.

Sources available in CD-ROM format include:

- *Canadian Encyclopedic Digest*, and
- *Canadian Case Digests*—the CD-ROM equivalent of the *Canadian Abridgment Case Digests.*

Sources available through free-access websites include:

- Canada and Ontario government websites for statutes and regulations—the online equivalents of the Revised Statutes of Canada, Statutes of Canada, *Canada Gazette*, Revised Statutes of Ontario, Statutes of Ontario and *Ontario Gazette*;
- various court websites providing access to the text of case reports; and
- the Canadian Legal Information Institute (CanLII) website.

Sources available through pay-for-use subscription services include:

- Westlaw*e*CARSWELL's LawSource, which includes access to the *Canadian Encyclopedic Digest* and the *Canadian Case Digests*
- Quicklaw
- Ontario Citator Service and Canada Citator Service—the online version of the statute citators
- Index to Federal and Ontario Statutes Online—the online version of *McLean's Index.*

Organization

Human editors have organized the information in the paper sources that we have looked at in various ways, be it by topic or chronologically. When you work with paper sources, you retrieve information by browsing through the source or by using an index or table of contents.

Computerized sources, on the other hand, may or may not be edited. Information in all computerized sources is stored in databases. If the source is not edited, its information is stored randomly and you can retrieve it only by searching through the database for specific words. If the source is edited, you can also browse through it and use a table of contents.

Function

Computerized research sources serve the same functions as paper research sources. They may act as finding tools, primary sources, or updating tools, and you have seen examples of each listed above. In addition, online services such as Westlaw*e*CARSWELL's LawSource and Quicklaw combine secondary-source finding tools with access to the primary-source texts of statutes and case reports as well as updating tools.

KEYWORD SEARCHING

Computerized research sources will provide you with the same information as paper sources. However, although the information is the same in both print and computerized sources, the methods of getting access to the information differ for the two types of sources.

Information in paper sources is edited and organized, usually by topic. A researcher uses an index or table of contents to locate information. So, when you work with paper sources, you must analyze the facts of your legal research problem in an attempt to identify categories of law and/or legal concepts that may be relevant to your problem. You then use those categories and concepts to locate the information you are looking for in an index or table of contents.

Computerized sources store information randomly in databases. A researcher "asks" the computer to locate information in the database by searching for words that we call **keywords**. A computerized search is a request for all documents that contain requested keywords. When the researcher enters the keywords, the computer searches the entire database for appropriate matches.

Computerized sources usually use **Boolean** searching (named for a British mathematician, George Boole) to locate documents. In a Boolean search, the computer hunts through thousands of documents to locate requested combinations of words or phrases. Since information is not arranged in a database by subject, the only way the computer can locate a document is to locate words within the document.

When you work with computerized sources, you must analyze the facts of your legal research problem in an attempt to identify keywords that are likely to appear in the statutes, regulations, or court decisions that deal with your problem. It is important to understand that when you conduct a keyword search, you will get only what you ask for. The quality of your research will depend on how well you choose your keywords. You will not be able to see the surrounding material about your subject that would jump out at you from a print source.

keywords
words by which researchers search computerized sources for information stored randomly in databases

Boolean search
method by which the computer hunts through thousands of documents to locate requested combinations of words or phrases

The Role of Legal Knowledge and Analysis

When you do computerized legal research you are asking the computer to find cases that are relevant to your particular legal issue by searching the database for statutes, regulations, or court decisions that contain the keywords you have identified. In order to choose your keywords you must have some idea of the words that are likely to be found in a judge's decision in a case or a statute or regulation that deals with your issue. This means that you must know enough about the law to identify the legal issue(s) involved, and you must be familiar enough with the wording of statutes and the language of cases to be able to choose useful keywords.

The first step in this process is to place your legal problem within the relevant area of the law. Each area of law has terms and expressions that are commonly used, and you must know enough about the area of law you are researching to know what keyword to use. If you use inappropriate keywords you risk retrieving far too many documents and/or missing what you are looking for entirely. Once you retrieve some statutes, regulations, and/or cases, you must review them to decide whether they are relevant to the issue you are researching.

Here's an example. Your client wants to sue her doctor. She went to the doctor because she had a broken arm, and the doctor made the break worse. You have to conduct a keyword search for relevant cases. If you don't know the relevant area of the law, your choice of keyword is limited to "arm," "broken," and "doctor." A search using these terms will retrieve every case that contains those words in it, regardless of the area of law the case deals with. You'll get criminal cases about assault victims with broken arms who were examined by the doctor, and you'll get product liability cases about broken armrests in doctored automobiles. If you know that the area of law is tort law, you can be more specific and add terms such as "medical malpractice" or "negligence" to your keyword search that will reduce the number of unwanted cases that you retrieve.

Coming Up with Keywords

In a Boolean search, you are asking the computer to search for statutes, regulations, or case decisions containing keywords you have chosen. You have to guess what words the documents you're looking for might contain. In order to choose useful keywords, try thinking about common words or phrases used within this area of law, either from your general knowledge of law or from research you have done using secondary sources.

Usually there are several possible keywords you can try. For example "drunk driving" is also known as "impaired driving," "operating a motor vehicle while impaired," or "driving over 80." If you choose just one keyword, you will not retrieve any of the cases that have referred to the matter in a different way. You increase your chances of getting the most accurate results when you search using a range of keywords.

For example, in a Boolean search involving medical malpractice in the setting of a broken arm, you might start off with the keywords "doctor," "medical malpractice," and "broken arm." However, the computer will search only for these specific words or phrases. If a case on the same subject uses different words or phrases instead, such as "physician" or "surgeon" instead of "doctor," or "negligence" instead of "malpractice," the computer will *not* find the case. So you want to search for cases that contain the word "doctor," "physician," *or* "surgeon" PLUS the word "arm," "radius," *or* "ulna" PLUS the words "medical malpractice," "negligence," or "negligent." You have to look for all these synonyms because it is impossible to know in advance whether a particular written decision spoke of a *doctor* who was *negligent* in splinting a *radius* or of *medical malpractice* involving a *surgeon* who did not set an *arm* properly.

Keyword Example

Marsha Steward had a party at her cottage, Loon Hill, in Muskoka. During the party one of her guests slipped on the staircase leading from the dock to the cottage. In keeping with the theme of her party—decorating with butter—Marsha had placed butter carvings of Ontario birds all along the stairs. Unfortunately, the carvings melted in the heat, making the staircase slippery. The guest has sued Marsha, and Marsha wonders if she will be held liable. She would like you to give her some advice. You decide you will research relevant case law.

1. What area of law does this case involve?
   Tort law.

2. What kind of torts decisions are you looking for?
   Cases dealing with negligence generally, but in particular with occupier's liability.
3. What words might you expect to find in a decision about occupier's liability? Think of all the synonyms and variations of each term.
   a. occupier's liability;
   b. negligent, negligence, negligently;
   c. owner, homeowner, occupier;
   d. guest, invitee; and
   e. slip, fall, trip.

Boolean Connectors

When you conduct a Boolean search using keywords, it is not enough simply to come up with the correct keywords. You must also think about the combinations of the words that interest you. Do you want to see case decisions that contain *any* of your keywords, or only those decisions that contain *all* of your keywords?

Boolean searching is based on principles of Boolean logic—the logical relationship among search terms. Boolean searching uses three basic connectors:

- OR,
- AND, and
- NOT.

These connectors allow you to direct the computer to search for any of your keywords or for all of your keywords.

The OR Connector

The OR connector directs the computer to search for documents that contain either term or both (or all) terms. For example, if you're looking for information about incarceration, you can search for two terms, *jail* OR *prison*. This search will retrieve documents in which at least one of the search terms is present—documents with either *jail* or *prison* or both in them. In figure 13.1, the shaded circle with the word *jail* represents all the documents that contain the word *jail*; the shaded circle with the word *prison* represents all the documents that contain the word *prison*; and the shaded overlap area represents all the documents that contain both *jail* and *prison*. An OR search will retrieve all these documents.

FIGURE 13.1   **OR Search with Two Terms**

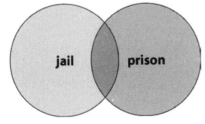

The OR connector is most commonly used to search for different ways of saying the same thing. The more terms or concepts combined in a search with the OR connector, the more documents the search will retrieve. For example, you can search for *jail* OR *prison* OR *penitentiary*, as illustrated in figure 13.2. This search will retrieve documents that contain any one, any two, or all three words.

FIGURE 13.2   **OR Search with Three Terms**

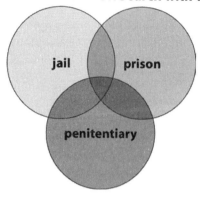

The AND Connector

The AND connector directs the computer to search only for documents that contain both or all search terms. For example, if you're interested in researching the relationship between alcohol and abuse, you would search *alcohol* AND *abuse*.

This search will retrieve only documents in which BOTH of the search terms are present. In figure 13.3 this is represented by the shaded area in which the two circles overlap. The search will not retrieve documents containing only *alcohol* or only *abuse*.

FIGURE 13.3   **AND Search**

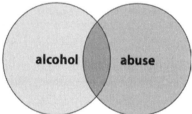

The more terms or concepts you combine in a search with the AND connector, the fewer documents you will retrieve.

The NOT Connector

The NOT connector is used when you want to retrieve documents that include one term, but not if the documents also include a second term. For example, if you want to see information about support, but want to avoid seeing anything about interim support, you would search *support* NOT *interim*. The search will retrieve documents in which *only* the word support is present. In figure 13.4, the circle on the left represents all the documents that include the word *support*. The area of overlap represents documents that include the words *support* and *interim*. The shaded area represents the documents that contain the word *support* but not the word *interim*.

FIGURE 13.4   **NOT Search**

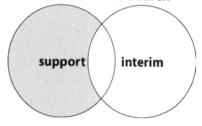

The NOT connector excludes documents from your search results. You must be careful when using the NOT connector because the term you are searching for may be present in relevant documents that also contain the word you wish to avoid.

More Advanced Boolean Searching

Once you have the hang of the simple connectors, you can move on to somewhat more complicated search methods.

Searching for a Phrase

None of the Boolean connectors discussed above will retrieve documents containing a phrase—a series of words in a set order. To search for a phrase, enclose the phrase in quotation marks. For example, if you search for "*child support*" you will retrieve only documents that contain that specific phrase.

Here's a Boolean search using the medical malpractice situation set out earlier in this chapter. To find cases that contain the word *doctor*, *physician*, or *surgeon* PLUS the words *medical malpractice*, *negligent*, or *negligence* PLUS the word *arm*, *radius*, or *ulna*, use the following Boolean language:

> doctor OR physician OR surgeon AND "medical malpractice" OR negligent OR negligence AND arm OR radius OR ulna

Proximity Connectors

When you're doing a Boolean search, to make sure you retrieve cases that are really about your topic, you may need to specify that certain words be close together.

If you are looking for cases on sexual harassment, for example, you can ask for cases where *sexual* and *harassment* both appear by joining the two words with the AND connector. A search query for *sexual* AND *harassment* will bring up cases where both words appear in the case, but those words may appear anywhere in the document. For example, you may retrieve a case in which there was a criminal sexual assault on a victim who also claimed there was harassment by the investigating police officers. You can retrieve cases where *sexual* and *harassment* are joined as a phrase by putting the phrase in quotation marks: "*sexual harassment.*"

You can also ask for cases where words are not beside each other in a phrase, but appear reasonably close to each other in the document. If you are searching for cases on the right to counsel under the Charter of Rights, for example, you would want cases that contain the phrase "*right to counsel*" but you would probably also want cases that contain the words *right to retain counsel* and *right to contact and obtain advice from counsel*. Proximity connectors allow you to limit your search to documents in which the terms you are searching for appear close to each other—for example within 10 words of each other (in some sources by entering *right/10 counsel*) or in the same paragraph (in some sources by entering *right/p counsel*).

Substitution and Truncation

Most computerized sources use substitution and truncation symbols to make the job of searching all possible search terms a little easier.

SUBSTITUTION

Because your keywords may be spelled in more than one way (*offence* and *offense*), you can ask the computer to search for the word spelled either way by using a

substitution symbol
symbol used in a
computerized search
that replaces a single
letter to find keywords
spelled in more than
one way

truncation symbol
symbol used in a
computerized search to
find all possible endings
of a root word

substitution symbol—for example, "*" (an asterisk) for the letters that may change: *offen*e.*

TRUNCATION

Because your keywords may have different endings (*dismiss, dismissing, dismissed,* and *dismissal*), you can ask the computer for all these words by using a **truncation symbol**—for example, "!" (an exclamation mark): "*dismiss!.*"

Search Syntax

All the sources you will use for computerized legal research rely on the same Boolean logic, and all require you to have the same skills in determining and combining the appropriate keywords. But different sources may have different "search syntax"—that is, different rules for setting up the search. You will find that Boolean logic is used in one of three ways, depending on the source:

- Full Boolean logic with the use of connectors. You must use the connectors OR, AND, or NOT between your search terms.
- Implied Boolean logic. You enter search terms, but you don't use Boolean connectors. The space between the keywords defaults to either OR or AND, depending on the source. This is what is most commonly found in internet searching. Many well-known search engines traditionally defaulted to OR but as a rule are moving away from that practice and defaulting to AND.
- Predetermined language. Some sources offer a search template that sets out connectors for you to choose from a drop-down menu.

Each computerized source has its own search syntax and rules that you must learn before you use the source. You must find out whether the words you enter

- are searched as a phrase,
- are searched as though there were an OR between them,
- are searched as though there were an AND between them, or
- require the Boolean connectors to be written out.

You must also learn what, if any, proximity connectors and truncation symbols are used. Most computerized sources contain a help feature that explains the search syntax for that source.

KEY TERMS

Boolean search
keywords
substitution symbol
truncation symbol

CHAPTER 14

Finding a General Statement of the Law: The Canadian Encyclopedic Digest

The general approach to legal research using computerized sources is the same as that for paper sources. It is best to start your research by using a secondary source, such as a legal encyclopedia, to find a general statement of the law as it applies to the legal problem you need to solve.

As we said in chapter 8, the *Canadian Encyclopedic Digest*, or CED, is an excellent place to begin your research. In chapter 8 we talked about the print version of the *Canadian Encyclopedic Digest*. In this chapter we discuss the computerized version of the CED.

WHAT IS THE CED?

The CED is a legal encyclopedia that provides a general overview of most areas of law. It's an excellent starting point for your research when you know very little about the area of law that you are researching. The CED is available in two computerized formats: CD-ROM and online. Both are organized in the same way as the print version.

The computerized versions of the CED are made up of over 220 subject titles, arranged alphabetically, and they combine the contents of the Ontario and Western editions of the CED in print. The subject titles are broad topics or general areas of law—for example, animals, contracts, evidence, and income tax. Each subject title contains parts, sections, subsections, and sub-subsections, breaking the title down into increasingly more topic-specific areas of information.

THE CED ON CD-ROM

The CD-ROM version of the CED consists of a single disc that contains the Ontario and Western editions of the CED—material equivalent to more than 60 volumes of information. The CED is available on an annual subscription basis, with an updated CD-ROM disc being provided quarterly to subscribers.

When you launch the program, you have access to the full text of the CED, which you can then scroll through and read from beginning to end, if you're so inclined. There are, however, more efficient ways to locate the information you are looking for.

The two main tools for finding information are

1. the table of contents, and
2. keyword searching.

Table of Contents

The table of contents allows you to browse through all the subject titles in the CED. You can expand the topics contained within a subject title (as explained below) to get more and more specific information. This allows you to get a broad under-standing of the relevant area of law and narrow down the specific topic you want to research. You can view the table of contents either alone, as shown in figure 14.1, or in a split-screen side by side with the text, as shown in figure 14.2.

The table of contents lists all the subject titles in the CED in alphabetical order, the same order in which the text of the CED appears. The table of contents has several levels. Whenever you click the + sign next to a heading, you open up the table of contents to the next level, and the information gets more specific. The table of content levels are organized in the same way as in the print version of the CED. Each subject title is given a name and a title number. Each subject title is then divided into parts that are given both a number (in uppercase roman numerals) and a name. Each part is divided into sections that are given both a number and a name. Each section may be further divided into headings (subtopics) that are given a letter and a name. Each heading may be further divided into subheadings that are given a number (lowercase roman numerals) and a name. Each section is divided into numbered paragraphs (not named).

In figure 14.1, the table of contents has not been expanded at all. In figure 14.2, the subject title Animals has been opened up to the paragraph level under Part IX—Dogs.

Once you find the paragraph dealing with your research topic, double-click on the text to display the entire paragraph. If you are working in the full-screen view of the table of contents, the screen will now show a full-screen view of the para-graph in question. If you are working in a split-screen view of the table of contents, the paragraph in question will be shown in the right-hand part of the screen, as illustrated in figure 14.2.

FIGURE 14.1 CED on CD-ROM Unexpanded Table of Contents: Full-Screen View

FIGURE 14.2 CED on CD-ROM Expanded Table of Contents: Split-Screen View

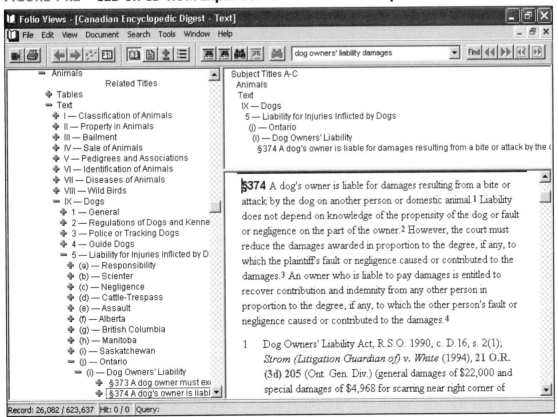

Once you get into the text of the CED, you can scroll up and down and read any of the surrounding paragraphs to see if they contain information that is useful for your research, just as you could skim through the pages of the print version of the CED.

Keyword Searching

The CED on CD-ROM is a searchable database, which you can search using keywords. For this type of search you must be familiar with Boolean search concepts (see chapter 13).

You can conduct keyword searches of the CED in several different ways, including:

- **advanced query**—accessible through the search menu on the toolbar, this function allows you to search the full database by crafting a Boolean search using keywords, which you can select from a "word wheel," and Boolean connectors and expanders (called **search operators**);
- **query box**—this small box located on the toolbar works like the advanced query; however, you have much less space in which to craft your query and you do not have access to the word wheel; and
- **query templates**—the title-search query template and the classification query template are accessible through the search menu on the toolbar; these templates allow you to narrow your search to specific parts of the database.

As we said in chapter 13, every computerized source has its own search syntax. Figure 14.3 sets out the main search operators used in the CED on CD-ROM.

advanced query
function accessible through the search menu on the toolbar that allows you to search the full database using a Boolean search

search operators
keywords and Boolean connectors and expanders

query box
small box located on the toolbar that works like the advanced query, but with less space in which to craft your query and without access to the word wheel

query templates
accessible through the search menu on the toolbar; allow you to narrow your search to specific parts of the database

FIGURE 14.3   CED on CD-ROM Search Operators

To Find	Enter	Example
one keyword **OR** another	**or** or **|**	**business** or **profits**
one keyword **AND** another	**space**, **&**, or **and**	**business profits**, **business & profits**, or **business and profits**
one keyword but **NOT** another	**not** or **^**	**business not profits** or **business ^ profits**
a phrase	the phrase in quotation marks (" ")	**"best interests of the child"**
variant letters (substitution in chapter 13)	**?** in place of the variant letter	**m?n** finds man and men
various suffixes (truncation in chapter 13)	***** at the end of a root word in place of the possible endings	**craft*** finds crafted, crafting, crafty

THE CED ONLINE

The CED is also available on the Internet as part of LawSource, a subscription service offered by Westlaw*e*CARSWELL.

The content of the CED through LawSource is the same as that of the CED on CD-ROM. However, unlike the CD-ROM, you cannot get access to the full text of the CED to scroll through from beginning to end. Instead, your access is limited to retrieving material by using the various search tools of the program, discussed below.

There are two main tools for finding information in the online version of the CED:

1. the table of contents, and
2. custom search templates.

Table of Contents

The table of contents is similar to that of the CD-ROM. It lists all the subject titles in the CED in alphabetical order. It has several levels and each new level can be reached by clicking on the + sign next to a heading. It is not possible to view the table of contents in a split-screen side by side with the text.

You can get access to the table of contents by clicking on the CED link under the heading "Browse Tables of Contents" on the left side of the home page. Figure 14.4 illustrates how the subject title Animals is broken down in the table of contents.

Once you find the paragraph dealing with your research topic, click on the text to display the entire paragraph. The text will be displayed in a separate window. You will have access only to the text of the paragraph you clicked on. You will not be able to scroll through the text and read any of the surrounding paragraphs to see

FIGURE 14.4   Online CED Table of Contents in LawSource

if they contain useful information for your research. To look at adjoining paragraphs, you will have to return to the table of contents and click on each paragraph one at a time.

Custom Search Templates

There are three custom search templates available:

1. a standard search,
2. a terms and connectors search, and
3. a natural language search.

standard search
allows you to search for information using keywords and a connector that is selected from the drop-down menu

The **standard search** template allows you to search for information using keywords. You get access to this template by clicking on the Canadian Encyclopedic Digest (CED) link on the right side of the home page, under the heading "Custom Search Templates." Enter the keywords and then select the desired connector from the drop-down menu within the template. You can search for

- any of the keywords you entered,
- all the keywords you entered,
- the exact phrase you entered,
- all the keywords you entered within five words of each other,
- all the keywords you entered in the same sentence, or
- all the keywords you entered in the same paragraph.

The template also allows you to search the entire CED or to limit your search to a specified subject title, classification, or citation. Figure 14.5 illustrates the Standard Search Template.

FIGURE 14.5   Online CED Standard Search Template

The **terms and connectors search** allows you to construct a Boolean search using keywords and your own Boolean connectors and expanders. It is therefore not as limiting as the standard search template. You get access to this search tool by clicking on the terms and connectors search link at the top right side of the standard search template screen. You can use it to search the entire CED or you can limit your search to parts of the CED by adding field and date restrictions to your search. Figure 14.6 illustrates the terms and connectors search screen.

sidebar

terms and connectors search not as limiting as the standard search template; allows you to construct a Boolean search using keywords and your own Boolean connectors and expanders

FIGURE 14.6   Online CED Terms and Connectors Search Screen

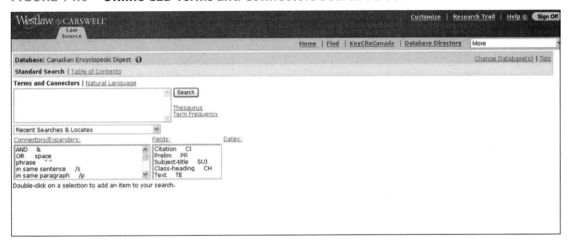

The search syntax for the online version of the CED is not exactly the same as the syntax for the CD-ROM. Figure 14.7 sets out the main search operators used in the online version of the CED.

FIGURE 14.7   Online CED Search Operators

To Find	Enter
one keyword **AND** another	**&**
one keyword **OR** another	**Space**
a phrase	**" "**
keywords in same sentence	**/s**
keywords in same paragraph	**/p**
keywords within a specified number of words	**/n (n = 1-255)**
various suffixes (truncation in chapter 13)	**!**
variant letters (substitution in chapter 13)	*****
one term but **NOT** another	**%**

The terms and connectors search template contains a built-in thesaurus that provides related terms for all the keywords you enter. It also contains a term frequency option that lets you specify how many times your keyword must appear. There is a link to both these features beside the terms and connectors search window.

natural language search
allows you to search for information by asking your question using plain language

The **natural language search** allows you to search for information by asking your question using plain language. You get access to this search tool by clicking on the natural language search link at the top right side of the standard search template screen. You can also get a link to this search at the top of the search window while you are in the terms and connectors search template. You simply enter your question in the description box. You do not need to use any operators or connectors. "Are dog owners in Ontario liable for injuries caused by their dog?" is an example of a natural language search. Figure 14.8 shows the natural language search screen.

FIGURE 14.8   Online CED Natural Language Search Screen

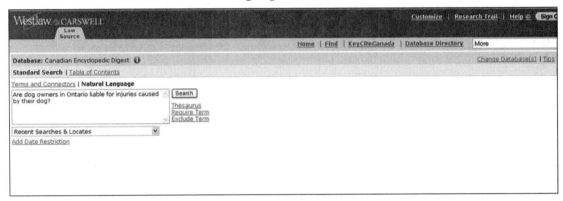

The natural language search template, like the terms and connectors search template, contains a built-in thesaurus and a term frequency option.

Linking to the Text

Using any of the above search methods will lead you to the paragraph(s) in the CED that provide an overview or summary of the relevant law. Results are displayed on the left side of the screen. Each result provides an excerpt from the paragraph with the search keywords highlighted. Results are numbered and provide the subject title, part, section(s), and paragraph number. Figure 14.9 illustrates the results of a natural language template search.

Each result number is a hyperlink to the text of the entire paragraph. To view the text of the paragraph, click on the number in the result list that contains the paragraph you want to read. Each paragraph includes a reference to the relevant legislation and leading cases. The paragraphs also provide a hyperlink to the text of the cases. By clicking on the hyperlink, you can retrieve the full text of the case.

Figure 14.10 shows a paragraph from the CED.

FIGURE 14.9   Results of a Natural Language Template Search

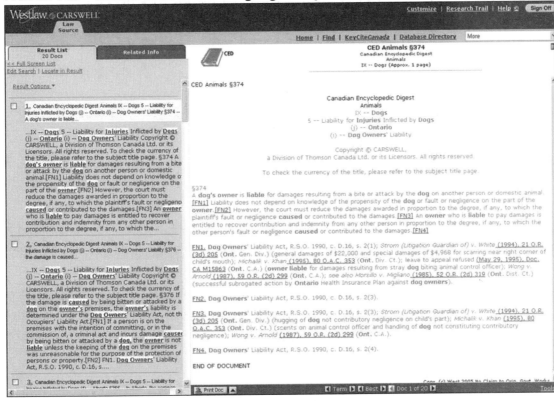

FIGURE 14.10   Paragraph from the Online CED

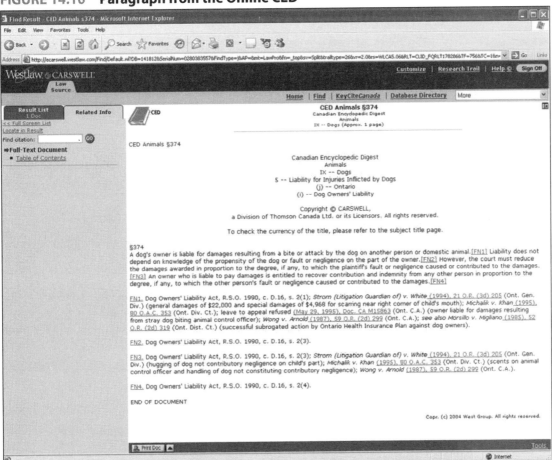

KEY TERMS

advanced query

natural language search

query box

query templates

search operators

standard search

terms and connectors search

CHAPTER 15

Finding and Updating Statutes

When you are doing legal research using computerized sources, your first priority is to find out whether there is a statute that is relevant to the issue. In chapter 14 we saw that you may be able to do this by looking in the *Canadian Encyclopedic Digest*. There are also computerized finding tools, which we'll talk about in this chapter. Once you determine that there is a statute relevant to your issue, you have to be able to locate the text of that statute, which we'll also discuss.

This chapter addresses the following topics:

- how statutes are published in computerized format,
- computerized finding tools for statutes,
- finding the text of the statute using the computer,
- updating statutes using the computer, and
- legislative history.

HOW STATUTES ARE PUBLISHED IN COMPUTERIZED FORMAT

In chapter 9, we discussed how statutes are published in paper format by both the federal and provincial governments and noted that the official text of the statutes is contained only in the government revised statutes or annual statute volumes. However, the federal and Ontario (as well as other provincial) governments also publish their statutes on their websites, but they do this as a matter of convenience only. For the moment, the official text is still the paper text, even if the computerized text is a lot easier for everyone to find. (However, under legislation introduced on October 27, 2005, Ontario's computerized statutes will also be considered official text.)

Federal Statutes

You can find federal statutes at the federal Department of Justice website: http://laws.justice.gc.ca/en/. This site contains consolidated versions of the federal statutes, organized alphabetically by title. "Consolidated" means that the version incorporates all amendments that have been made to the text of the statute, to the most recent update. It is important to note that the consolidated statutes are updated approximately every four months, usually in April, August, and December. Each update is about four months old when posted, so, for example, the update current to April 30th is not usually posted until August. (If you are looking for more recent legislation, you should check the website for the *Canada Gazette* at http://canadagazette.gc.ca/index-e.html.)

The Department of Justice website also

- provides direct links to several important or frequently accessed statutes;
- contains a list of repealed acts (acts that are no longer active, but may be useful for historical legal research purposes);
- contains a table of private acts (a historical index showing all private acts of Canada, other than those dealing with divorces, that have been enacted since 1867 and that appear in the Statutes of Canada from 1867 to December 31, 1997); and
- a table of public statutes (a historical index with information on specific statutes, such as the dates of enactment and the responsible ministers as well as a detailed listing of amendments, including repealed sections).

The site contains several search tools, which are discussed further below under the heading Computerized Finding Tools for Statutes.

Figure 15.1 shows the home page for the website as of August 15, 2005.

Ontario Statutes

You can find Ontario statutes at the Ontario government's e-Laws website: http://www.e-laws.gov.on.ca. This website contains the current consolidated version of most of Ontario's public statutes (the statutes that don't appear are listed in the site's table of unconsolidated and unrepealed public statutes).

The statutes are organized alphabetically by name. The government's goal is to provide consolidated statutes that are up to date within 10 business days of enactment of a new law or amendment of an existing law. But if 10 business days isn't good enough for you, the site provides information that allows you to arrive at a consolidation that is up to date to within 2 business days. At the beginning of each consolidated statute, there is a notice of currency stating whether there are outstanding amendments to be consolidated into the statute or whether the consolidation is current. The notice also gives information about proclamations that have been issued, naming a day on which provisions of the statute come into force (in cases where that information is not already reflected in the consolidated statute). Notices of currency are usually up to date to within 2 business days. For even more

FIGURE 15.1   Department of Justice Laws Home Page

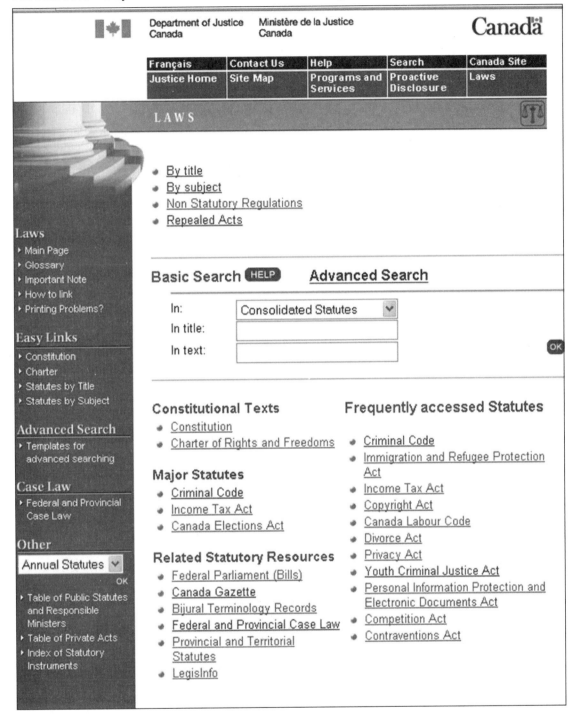

current amendment information, the notices of currency direct you to the site's table of public statutes—legislative history overview.

In addition to consolidated statutes, the website also contains:

- Public and private statutes as enacted, dating back to January 1, 2000 (referred to as "source law")—these include new statutes and amending, repealing, or revoking statutes. They are organized first by the year in which the statute was enacted, and then alphabetically by name.

- Annual consolidations beginning in 2003. This provides an annual snapshot of all of Ontario's consolidated public statutes as of January 1st of each year.
- Historical versions (a consolidated version of a statute as it read immediately before a change) of statutes amended since January 1, 2004.
- The text of repealed statutes, if the statute was in the *Revised Statutes of Ontario, 1990* or enacted after 1990 and repealed on or after January 1, 2004.

Figure 15.2 shows the home page for the website as of September 10, 2005.

FIGURE 15.2   e-Laws Home Page

COMPUTERIZED FINDING TOOLS FOR STATUTES

As we noted in chapter 9, the challenge with respect to statute law is not so much finding the text of the statute as it is finding whether, in fact, a relevant statute exists. The easiest way to find whether a relevant statute exists is by researching your subject using the CED. When you find the general statement of the law dealing with your specific topic, it will refer you to the relevant legislation, if any.

There are other computerized ways to find whether a relevant statute exists, including

- the Index to Federal and Ontario Statutes Online, and
- government website search templates.

Index to Federal and Ontario Statutes Online

Mary McLean's *Index to Federal and Ontario Statutes*, published in print format until 2001, is now published in an online version by Captus Press. The Index to Federal and Ontario Statutes Online is a computerized subscription service that allows you to search for statutes by subject matter. Like the print version, it gives lists of statutes under general topic headings, but does not break down topics thoroughly or give specific information about what a statute might contain. As a result, you may find yourself confronted with several statutes under one heading with no way of telling which one is relevant to your research.

Government Website Search Templates

Both the federal Department of Justice and the Ontario e-Laws websites include search templates that allow you to search for current statutes using keywords—that is, by entering words that may appear in either the title or text of a statute. This method is not always easy or reliable because you may find more than one statute containing the keywords you entered. You will then have to scan each statute carefully to determine if it is in fact relevant to your research topic.

The Department of Justice site contains two search templates:

- The basic search template allows you to search for keywords in either the text or the title of a statute.
- The advanced search template allows you to limit your search to a specific subject area by choosing from a drop down menu of subject titles.

The Ontario e-Laws site contains a standard search template that allows you to search for keywords within the titles alone of all the consolidated statutes or within the contents, including titles, of all the consolidated statutes.

FINDING THE TEXT OF A FEDERAL STATUTE

Once you know the name of the federal statute that is relevant to the issue you are researching, it is easy to find the text of the statute. Use any of the following sources:

- the Department of Justice website,
- Westlaw*e*CARSWELL's LawSource,
- Quicklaw, or
- the Canadian Legal Information Institute (CanLII) website.

Department of Justice Website: http://laws.justice.gc.ca

When you know the name of the statute you are looking for you can go to the "Laws" site, and click on the link "By title." Select the letter of the alphabet that corresponds to the first letter of the name of the statute you are looking for. All statutes that begin with that letter are displayed. Scroll down the list until you find your statute and then click on its name. Figure 15.3 is a copy of the Search by Title page for the letter "A."

Assume, for example, that you want to find the text of the *Canada Health Act*. Click on the letter "C" and then click on the name of the statute. You can then link either to the text of the entire Act (by clicking the name of the statute) or to a

FIGURE 15.3   Search by Title Page

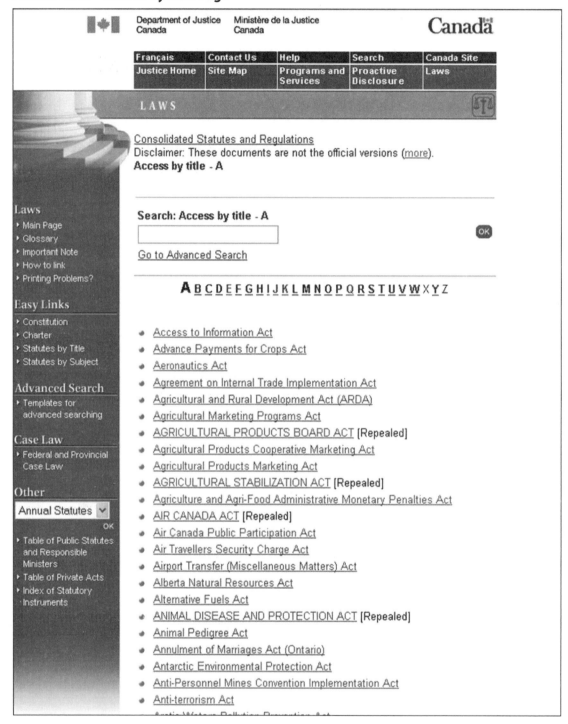

specific section only (by clicking on the desired heading). The search also generates a link to related regulations and related information. Figure 15.4 illustrates the search results for this statute.

WestlaweCARSWELL's LawSource

The text of federal statutes is available on the Internet as part of LawSource, a subscription service offered by WestlaweCARSWELL. If you know the name of the

FIGURE 15.4   Search Results for the Canada Health Act

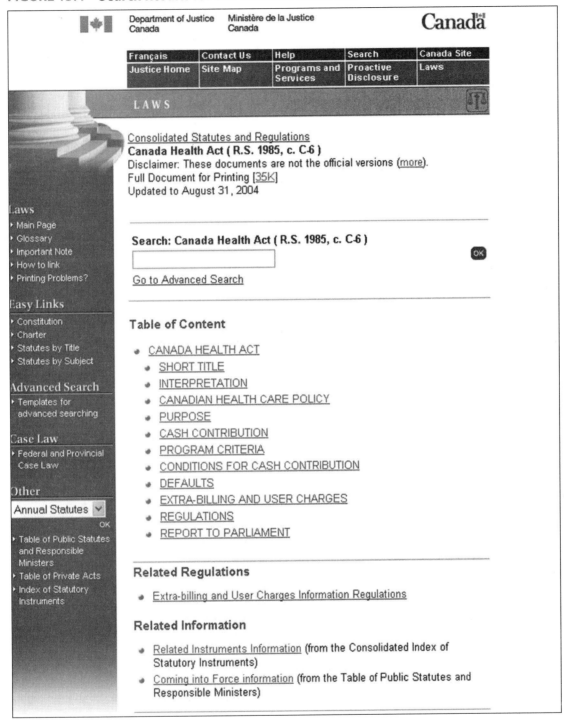

statute you are looking for you can use the "Find/KeyCite a Document" template on the bottom of the LawSource homepage.

For example, to find the *Canada Health Act*, enter "Canada Health Act" under "Title" and choose "Federal" for Jurisdiction. You can also include a section number to find a specific section of the statute. Figure 15.5 shows the completed Find/KeyCite a Document template for finding the text of the *Canada Health Act*. Figure 15.6 shows the results of the search for the *Canada Health Act*.

FIGURE 15.5   Completed Find/KeyCite a Document Template

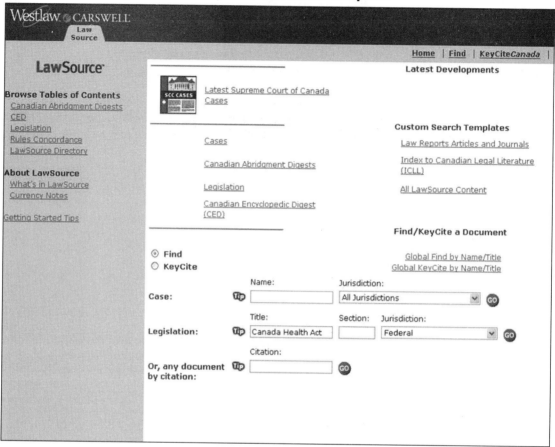

FIGURE 15.6   Results of Search for the Canada Health Act

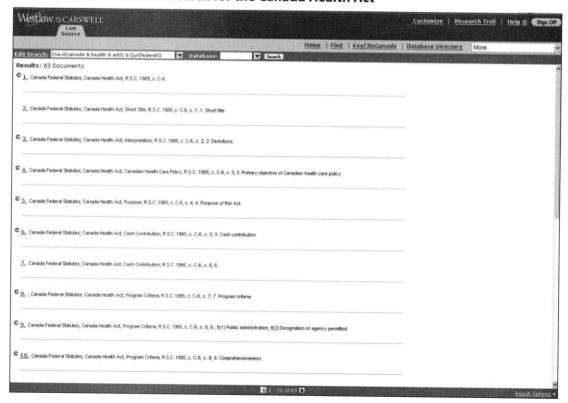

Click on the section of the Act that you want to look at. LawSource displays the text of statutes by sections only; you cannot view the text of the entire statute at once. The letter "c" next to a section indicates that citing references for that section are available, in which case you can link directly to case law citing that section. Figure 15.7 illustrates the text of s. 2 of the *Canada Health Act*.

FIGURE 15.7 Text of Section 2 of the Canada Health Act

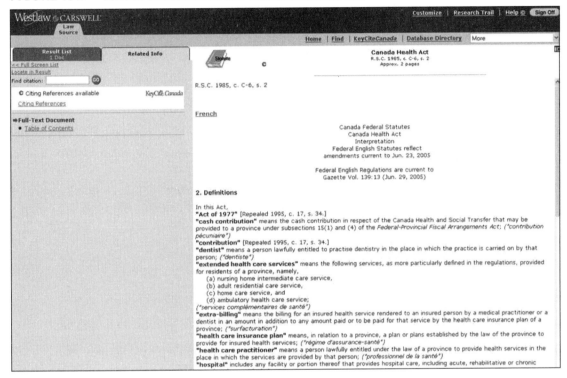

Quicklaw

The text of federal statutes is also available on the Internet as part of the Quicklaw subscription service. Quicklaw's RSC (Revised Statutes of Canada) database provides access to all federal consolidated and annual statutes. Quicklaw is discussed more fully in chapter 17.

Canadian Legal Information Institute (CanLII)

The Canadian Legal Information Institute (CanLII) maintains a website at www.canlii.org. This website provides access to the text of federal statutes under the heading "Canada." Click on the Statutes and Regulations link, then scroll down to Consolidated Statutes of Canada—Alphabetical List.

FINDING THE TEXT OF AN ONTARIO STATUTE

Once you know the name of an Ontario statute, it is easy to find the text of the statute. Use any of the following sources:

- the Ontario e-Laws website,
- Westlaw*e*CARSWELL's LawSource,
- Quicklaw, or
- the Canadian Legal Information Institute (CanLII) website.

Ontario e-Laws Website: www.e-laws.gov.on.ca

To find the text of a statute, use the Browse by Title link at the top of the home page. Choose the Statutes and associated Regulations link under the heading "Consolidated Law." Click on the + sign beside the letter that is the same as the first letter of the name of the statute you want to find.

For example, to find the text of the *Dog Owners' Liability Act*, click on the + sign beside the letter "D" and scroll down to the name of the statute. Click on the name of the statute to view the text of the entire statute. Figure 15.8 illustrates the Browse by Title link. Figure 15.9 illustrates how the text of the statute is displayed. A notice of currency appears at the top of the page indicating whether there are any amendments yet to be consolidated into the statute and the date those amendments will come into force. Amendments that have been passed but have not yet come into force are displayed in greyed-out text in the statute, as illustrated in figure 15.10.

FIGURE 15.8   e-Laws Browse by Title Link

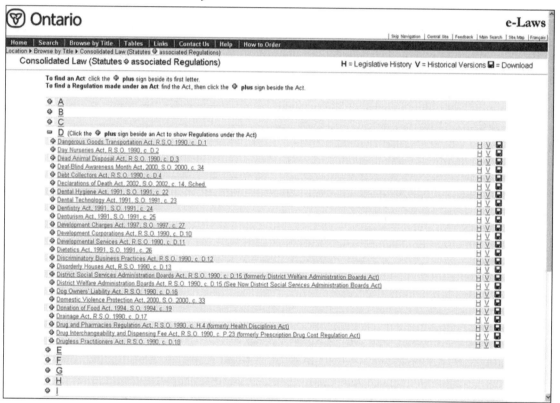

WestlaweCARSWELL's LawSource

The text of Ontario statutes is available on the Internet as part of LawSource, a subscription service offered by WestlaweCARSWELL. If you know the name of the statute you are looking for you can use the "Find/KeyCite a Document" template on the bottom of the LawSource homepage.

Enter the name of the statute you are looking for under "Title" and choose "Ontario" for Jurisdiction. You can also include a section number to find a specific section of the statute. Click on the section of the Act that you want to look at. LawSource displays the text of statutes by sections only; you cannot view the text of the entire statute at once.

FIGURE 15.9   Text of the Dog Owners' Liability Act

Français

Dog Owners' Liability Act

R.S.O. 1990, CHAPTER D.16

Notice of Currency: *   All amendments have been incorporated into this document.

A proclamation has been issued naming August 29, 2005 as the day on which the amendments made by 2005, c. 2, s. 1 come into force. This is not yet reflected in this document.

*This notice is usually current to within two business days of accessing this document. For more current amendment information, see the Table of Public Statutes – Legislative History Overview.

Amended by: 2000, c. 26, Sched. A, s. 6; 2005, c. 2, s. 1.

SKIP TABLE OF CONTENTS

CONTENTS

FIGURE 15.10   Amendments Passed But Not Yet in Force

20.   Regulations

Note: On a day to be named by proclamation of the Lieutenant Governor, the Act is amended by the Statutes of Ontario, 2005, chapter 2, subsection 1 (1) by adding the following heading:

INTERPRETATION

See: 2005, c. 2, ss. 1 (1), 3.

Definition

   1. In this Act,

   "owner", when used in relation to a dog, includes a person who possesses or harbours the dog and, where the owner is a minor, the person responsible for the custody of the minor. R.S.O. 1990, c. D.16, s. 1.

Note: On a day to be named by proclamation of the Lieutenant Governor, section 1 is amended by the Statutes of Ontario, 2005, chapter 2, subsection 1 (2) by adding the following definitions:

   "pit bull" includes,

       (a)   a pit bull terrier,

       (b)   a Staffordshire bull terrier,

       (c)   an American Staffordshire terrier,

       (d)   an American pit bull terrier,

       (e)   a dog that has an appearance and physical characteristics that are substantially similar to those of dogs referred to in any of clauses (a) to (d); ("pit-bull")

   "pound" has the same meaning as in the *Animals for Research Act*; ("fourrière")

   "regulation" means a regulation made under this Act. ("règlement")

See: 2005, c. 2, ss. 1 (2), 3.

Note: On a day to be named by proclamation of the Lieutenant Governor, section 1 is amended by the Statutes of Ontario, 2005, chapter 2, subsection 1 (3) by adding the following subsection:

Same

   (2) In determining whether a dog is a pit bull within the meaning of this Act, a court may have regard to the breed standards established for Staffordshire Bull Terriers, American Staffordshire Terriers or American Pit Bull Terriers by the Canadian Kennel Club, the United Kennel Club, the American Kennel Club or the American Dog Breeders Association. 2005, c. 2, s. 1 (3).

See: 2005, c. 2, ss. 1 (3), 3.

Note: On a day to be named by proclamation of the Lieutenant Governor, the Act is amended by the Statutes of Ontario, 2005, chapter 2, subsection 1 (4) by adding the following heading:

CIVIL LIABILITY

See: 2005, c. 2, ss. 1 (4), 3.

Quicklaw

The text of Ontario statutes is also available on the Internet as part of the Quicklaw subscription service. Quicklaw's RSO (Revised Statutes of Ontario) database provides access to all Ontario consolidated and annual statutes. Quicklaw is discussed more fully in chapter 17.

CanLII

The Canadian Legal Information Institute (CanLII) website at www.canlii.org. provides access to the text of Ontario statutes under the heading "Ontario." Click on the Statutes and Regulations Link, and then scroll down to Consolidated Statutes of Ontario—Alphabetical List.

FINDING THE TEXT OF STATUTES OF PROVINCES OR TERRITORIES OTHER THAN ONTARIO

You can find the statutes of other provinces as well:

- Most provinces and territories have a government website that provides access to provincial statutes. An easy place to start when you're looking for the website for any of the provinces or territories is the Government of Canada link to all of them at http://canada.gc.ca/othergov/prov_e.html.
- Quicklaw provides a link to legislation databases for all provinces.
- The CanLII website provides a link to the statutes of all the provinces.

UPDATING STATUTES

Most computerized sources are quite current. However, to fully update a statute, you must make sure that there have been no legislative changes since your source was last updated, and you must check for the status of any bills that refer to that statute.

Federal Statutes

If you find the text of the statute on the Department of Justice website, it is important to note (as we did above, but there's no harm in mentioning it twice) that the consolidated statutes are updated approximately every four months (usually in April, August, and December). Each update is already about four months old when posted. Check the website for the *Canada Gazette* at http://canadagazette.gc.ca/index-e.html for more recent legislation or amendments.

To find out whether there are any bills pending (a bill is a statute that has not yet been passed by Parliament) that might affect a statute you're interested in, check the LEGISINFO of the Library of Parliament at http://www.parl.gc.ca/LEGISINFO/. The status of bills section is updated daily. You can also check Quicklaw's federal Status of Bills database. This database is usually kept current to within one or two days.

In addition, you can update statutes using the Canada Citator Service, the computerized equivalent of the *Canada Statute Citator*, available online by subscription from Canada Law Book.

Ontario Statutes

If you find the text of the statute on e-Laws, be sure to check the notice of currency (at the beginning of the statute) that states whether there are outstanding amendments to be consolidated into the statute or whether the consolidation is current. The notice also gives information about proclamations naming a day on which provisions of the statute come into force, if that information is not already reflected in the consolidated statute. Notices of currency are usually up to date to within two business days. For more current amendment information, the notices of currency direct you to the site's table of public statutes—legislative history overview.

To find out whether there are any bills pending that might affect a particular statute, check the website for the Legislative Assembly of Ontario at http://www.ontla.on.ca.The status of bills section (bills before the House) is updated daily. You can also check Quicklaw's status of bills database for Ontario. This database is usually kept current to within one or two days.

In addition, you can update statutes using the Ontario Citator Service, the computerized equivalent of the *Ontario Statute Citator*, available online by subscription from Canada Law Book. However, this service is not as up to date as the Ontario e-Laws site.

CHAPTER 16

Finding and Updating Regulations

As we stated in chapter 10, regulations are as important as statutes and sometimes may be more important. Once you learn that a statute is relevant to the area of law you are researching, you must find out if any regulations have been made under that statute. If you determine that a regulation is relevant to your research, you must be able to locate the text of that regulation. Fortunately, once you know how to find the text of a statute using computerized sources, it is easy to find and update any regulations made under that statute.

In chapter 10 we talked about how to find and update regulations using paper sources. In this chapter we tell you how to find and update regulations using computerized sources.

HOW REGULATIONS ARE PUBLISHED IN COMPUTERIZED FORMAT

As we mentioned in chapter 10, regulations are published in paper format by both the federal and Ontario governments; the official text of the regulations is contained only in the government revised regulations volumes and gazettes. However, as a matter of convenience, the federal and Ontario (as well as other provincial) governments publish their regulations on the same statute websites discussed in chapter 15. As with statutes, the website version of the regulations is not the official version. (However, the Ontario government introduced legislation on October 27, 2005 that will make computerized regulations official.)

Federal Regulations

Federal regulations are available at the federal Department of Justice website: http://
laws.justice.gc.ca/en/. The site contains consolidated versions of the federal regulations ("consolidated" means that the version incorporates all amendments made to
the text of the regulation up to the most recent update). Regulations are organized
alphabetically under the title of the statute pursuant to which they were made.

Like the consolidated federal statutes (see chapter 15), consolidated regulations
are updated approximately every four months, usually in April, August, and December. Each update is about four months old when posted—for example, the
update current to April 30th is typically not posted until August. If you are looking
for more recent regulations, check the website for the *Canada Gazette Part II* at
http://canadagazette.gc.ca/partII/index-e.html.

See figure 15.1, chapter 15, for the website's home page as of August 15, 2005.

Ontario Regulations

Ontario regulations are available at the Ontario government's e-Laws website:
www.e-laws.gov.on.ca. This website contains current consolidated versions of most
Ontario regulations. (Exceptions are listed in the site's table of unconsolidated and
unrevoked regulations.)

Consolidated regulations are organized alphabetically by the name of the statute under which they were made. The government intends to provide consolidated
regulations that are up to date within 10 business days of enactment of a new
regulation or amendment of an existing regulation; the site provides information
with each consolidated regulation that allows you to arrive at a consolidation that
is up to date to within 2 business days. At the beginning of each consolidated
regulation, a notice of currency states whether there are outstanding amendments
to be consolidated into the regulation or whether the consolidation is current. If a
provision of the regulation is to come into force when a statute or a provision of
a statute is proclaimed in force, the notice also gives information about the day on
which the statute or statutory provision will be proclaimed in force. Notices of
currency are usually up to date to within 2 business days. For more current
amendment information, the notices of currency direct you to the site's table of
regulations—legislative history overview.

In addition to consolidated versions of the regulations, the website also contains:

- All regulations as they read when filed under the *Regulations Act*, dating
  back to January 1, 2000 (referred to as "source law"). These are organized
  first by the year in which the regulation was filed and then alphabetically
  by the name of the statute under which the regulation was made.
- Annual consolidations of regulations beginning in 2003. This provides an
  annual snapshot of all Ontario consolidated regulations as of January 1st
  of each year.
- Historical versions (a consolidated version of a regulation as it read
  immediately before a change to the regulation) of regulations that have
  been amended since January 1, 2004.
- The text of some repealed, expired, or spent regulations.

FINDING FEDERAL REGULATIONS

Use any of the following sources to find out, first, if regulations have been made under a federal statute, and, next, the text of the regulations:

- the Department of Justice website,
- WestlaweCARSWELL's LawSource,
- Quicklaw, or
- the Canadian Legal Information Institute (CanLII) website.

Generally, you will use the same source that you used to find the statute itself.

Department of Justice Website: http://laws.justice.gc.ca

When you use the Department of Justice website to find statute law (see chapter 15), you do not have to conduct a separate search for regulations. When you find the statute you are looking for, you will also find a link to any regulations made pursuant to the statute.

When you retrieve the statute you are looking for, the search results page lists all related regulations below the table of contents. Figure 16.1 illustrates the results of a search for the *Canada Health Act*. It shows that there is one related regulation, dealing with extra-billing and user charges information.

Click on the text to link to the regulation. You will be sent to a page that provides the table of contents of the regulation (see figure 16.2). If you click on the title of the regulation, you will be taken to a page that sets out the full name, citation, and text of the regulation.

There is also an advanced search template that lets you search directly for consolidated regulations. Figure 16.3 is a copy of the Search Consolidated Regulations template.

WestlaweCARSWELL's LawSource

The text of some federal regulations is available on WestlaweCARSWELL's LawSource. To research federal regulations, click on the legislation link under "Browse Tables of Contents," on the left side of the home page. Click on "Canada" and then expand the heading "Legislation." Choose "Federal" and then click on "Regulations." Figure 16.4 illustrates the table of contents.

An alphabetical list of statute names will appear. Click on the name of a statute to see a list of regulations made pursuant to that statute. Click on the name of the regulation to link directly to the text of the regulations. Figure 16.5 illustrates a list of regulations made under the *Divorce Act*.

If you know the name of the regulation you are looking for, you can use the "Find/KeyCite a Document" template on the bottom of the LawSource homepage. Type in the name of the regulation, choose "Federal" under the jurisdiction drop-down menu and click "Go." Your regulation will then appear in a result list.

Quicklaw

The text of federal regulations is available on the Internet as part of the Quicklaw subscription service. Quicklaw's SOR (Statutory Orders and Regulations) database

FIGURE 16.1   **Search Results for the Canada Health Act**

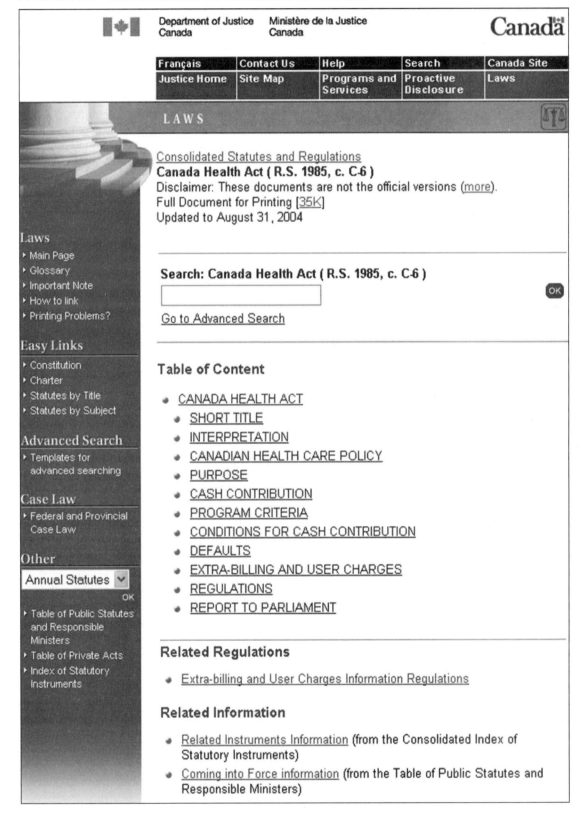

FIGURE 16.2   Table of Content of Regulation Under the Canada Health Act

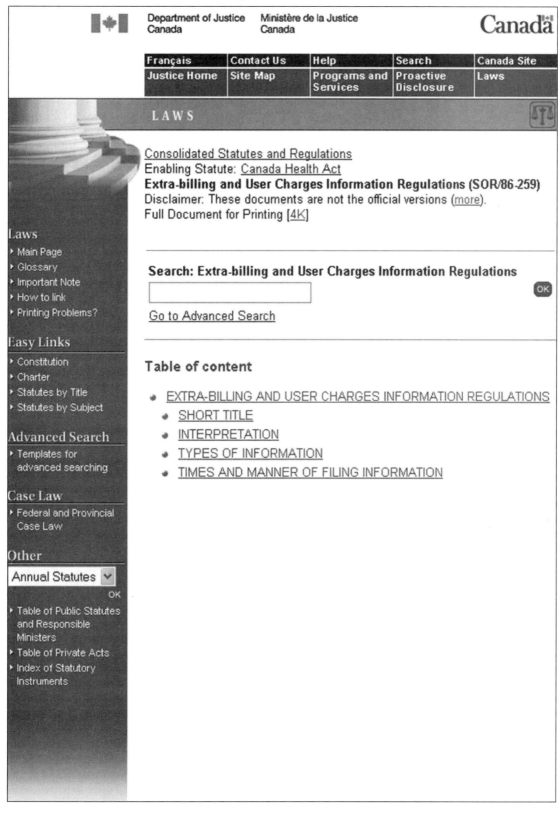

FIGURE 16.3   **Search Consolidated Regulations Template**

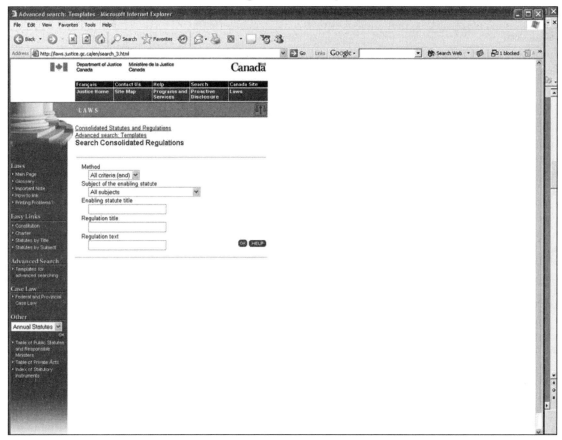

FIGURE 16.4   **LawSource Table of Contents**

FIGURE 16.5   Regulations Under the Divorce Act

provides access to all federal regulations. Quicklaw is discussed more fully in chapter 17.

Canadian Legal Information Institute (CanLII)

The Canadian Legal Information Institute (CanLII) maintains a website at http://www.canlii.org. This website provides access to the text of federal statutes under the heading "Canada." Click on the "Statutes and Regulations" link, and then scroll down to Consolidated Regulations of Canada—Alphabetical List.

FINDING ONTARIO REGULATIONS

Use any of the following sources to find out if regulations have been made under an Ontario statute and then to find the text of the regulations:

- the Ontario e-Laws website,
- WestlaweCARSWELL's LawSource,
- Quicklaw, or
- the Canadian Legal Information Institute (CanLII) website.

Generally, you will use the same source that you used to find the statute itself.

Ontario e-Laws Website: www.e-laws.gov.on.ca

When you use the Ontario e-Laws website to find statute law (discussed in chapter 15), you do not have to conduct a separate search for regulations. When you find the statute you are looking for, you will also find a link to any regulations made pursuant to that statute. When you find the name of the statute you are looking for, you will see that there is a + sign next to it. (See figure 15.8, chapter 15, for an illustration.) By clicking on the + sign, you will generate a list of all regulations made pursuant to the statute. Figure 16.6 shows that there is one regulation under the *Dog Owners' Liability Act*, dealing with pit bulls. Click on the name of the regulation to retrieve the text of the regulation.

FIGURE 16.6   Regulations Under the Dog Owners' Liability Act

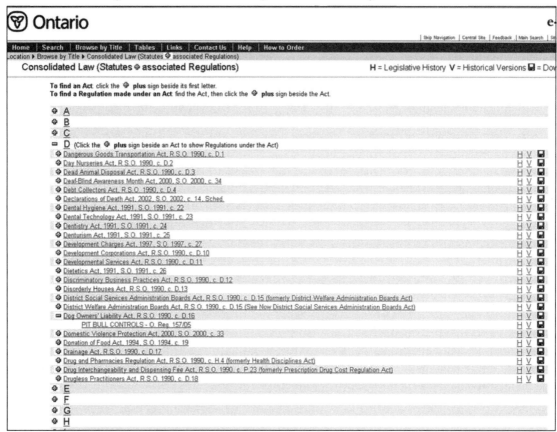

WestlaweCARSWELL's LawSource

The text of some Ontario regulations is available on LawSource. In the table of contents, choose "Ontario" and click on "Regulations." An alphabetical list of Ontario statutes will be displayed. Click on the name of the statute to see a list of regulations. Expand the name of the regulation to link directly to the text of the regulation.

If you know the name of the regulation you are looking for, you can use the "Find/KeyCite a Document" template on the bottom of the LawSource homepage. Type in the name of the regulation, choose "Ontario" under the jurisdiction drop-down menu, and click "Go." Your regulation will then appear in a result list.

Quicklaw

The text of Ontario regulations is also available on the Internet as part of the Quicklaw subscription service. Quicklaw's OREG (for Ontario Regulations) database provides access to all Ontario regulations. Quicklaw is discussed more fully in chapter 17.

CanLII

The Canadian Legal Information Institute (CanLII) website at www.canlii.org provides access to the text of Ontario regulations under the heading "Ontario." Click on the "Statutes and Regulations" link, and then scroll down to "Regulations of Ontario—Alphabetical List."

FINDING REGULATIONS OF PROVINCES AND TERRITORIES OTHER THAN ONTARIO

You can find the regulations of other provinces and the territories as well:

- Most provinces and territories have a government website that provides access to regulations as well as provincial statutes. An easy place to start when you're looking for the website for any of the provinces or territories is the Government of Canada link to all of them at http://canada.gc.ca/othergov/prov_e.html.
- Quicklaw provides a link to regulation databases for all provinces.
- The CanLII website provides a link to the statutes and regulations of all the provinces.

UPDATING REGULATIONS

Regulations are issued and amended on a regular basis. Even though computerized sources tend to be fairly current, it is important to find the most current version of a regulation. The best source for updating regulations is a gazette—the *Canada Gazette* for Canadian regulations and the *Ontario Gazette* for Ontario regulations (the other provinces and territories have gazettes as well).

Federal Regulations

Federal regulations are published in the *Canada Gazette Part II*, available online at http://canadagazette.gc.ca/partII/index-e.html.

Ontario Regulations

Ontario regulations are published in the *Ontario Gazette*, available online at http://www.ontariogazette.gov.on.ca/.

CHAPTER 17

Finding and Updating Cases

Once you've determined whether there are any statutes or regulations relevant to the issue you are researching, then (as we said in chapter 11) you must find out whether there is any relevant case law. You may be able to do this by looking in the *Canadian Encyclopedic Digest*, the computerized version of which we discussed in chapter 14, but there are other computerized finding tools as well. If the finding tools tell you that there is case law relevant to your problem, you must be able to locate the text of the cases, and you can also use computerized sources to do this.

FINDING TOOLS: ARE THERE ANY RELEVANT CASES?

In chapter 11 we discussed finding cases using paper legal research sources. We told you about a number of different secondary sources you can use to find case law on the issue you are researching; the source you use will depend on whether you are looking for

- cases dealing with a specific subject or legal issue,
- cases that have interpreted a statute or a section of a statute,
- cases considering a word or a phrase,
- cases when you've got only partial or incorrect citations (treasure hunting), or
- unreported cases.

When you're using computerized legal research sources, the two most comprehensive case finding tools are the *Canadian Abridgment*'s *Canadian Case Digests* (CCD) and Quicklaw, both of which can be used in all the above situations. Both sources allow you to find relevant case law using keyword searches. Unlike Quicklaw, the CCD is an edited source, so it also allows you to browse through a table of contents related to your topic. This feature makes it easier to focus your search by looking for a specific issue within the relevant subject title.

Canadian Case Digests

case digest
summary of how a legal issue was decided in a particular case

The *Canadian Case Digests* (CCD) contain **case digests**, or summaries of cases, from all Canadian courts and many tribunals, and organizes them by subject area. Each digest gives a brief summary of how a legal issue was decided in a particular case, together with a summary of all necessary background facts and the reasons for the decision. Each digest deals with only a single legal issue. If a case covers several legal issues, there is a separate digest for each issue.

key classification system
multi-level classification system

The CCD is available in two computerized formats: CD-ROM and online. Both are organized in the same way as the print version. Topics or main areas of law are arranged alphabetically, by subject title. Each subject title is then broken down into increasingly more detailed subtopics, according to a multi-level classification system, called the **key classification system**. Each individual digest has a key classification number and a specific case digest number. The classification and digest numbers are the same as in the print version. See chapter 11 for a complete discussion of the key classification system in the CCD.

CCD ON CD-ROM

The CD-ROM version of the CCD comes on one disc that contains the contents of all the volumes of the print version of the *Canadian Abridgment Case Digests* (see chapter 11). The CCD is available on an annual subscription basis, and an updated CD-ROM disc is provided quarterly. The CD-ROM version of the CCD uses the same software and works in the same way as the CD-ROM version of the CED (see chapter 14).

When you launch the program, you have access to the full text of the CCD, which you can then scroll through all the way from top to bottom. However, it's unlikely you'll have either the time or the inclination to do that, and you'll want to use one of the CCD's tools in order to do your research efficiently. The two main tools for finding information are the table of contents and keyword searching.

Table of Contents

The table of contents allows you to browse through all the subject titles in the CCD. You can expand the topics contained within a subject title (as explained below) to get information that's progressively more specific. This allows you to get a broad understanding of the relevant area of law and narrow down the specific topic you want to research.

The opened table of contents lists all the subject titles in the CCD in the same alphabetical order in which the content appears. In addition, the table of contents contains several levels; whenever you click the + sign next to a heading, you move to the next level and get more specific information. The table of contents levels are organized the same way electronically as they are in the print version of the CCD (see chapter 11). You can view the table of contents either alone or in a split-screen side by side with the text.

Figure 17.1 shows a full-screen view of the table of contents that has not been expanded at all. In figure 17.2, the subject title ANIMALS has been opened up to classification number III.1.c. Note that the number of case digests on each topic is shown in round brackets.

Once you find the topic you want to research, double-click on the words to display the text of the actual case digests. If you are working in the full-screen view of the table of contents, the screen will now show a full-screen view of the case digests in question. If you are working in a split-screen view of the table of contents, the case digests will be shown in the right-hand part of the screen, as illustrated in figure 17.3.

Keyword Searching

The CCD on CD-ROM is a searchable database. You can search it using keywords associated with your research topic. For this type of search you must be familiar with Boolean search concepts (see chapter 13).

You can conduct keyword searches of the CCD in several different ways, including:

- **advanced query**—accessible through the search menu on the toolbar, this function allows you to search the full database by setting up a Boolean search using keywords and Boolean connectors and expanders (called **search operators**);
- **query box**—small box located on the toolbar that works like the advanced query, but with less space in which to craft your query and without access to the word wheel; and

advanced query
function accessible through the search menu on the toolbar that allows you to search the full database using a Boolean search

search operators
keywords and Boolean connectors and expanders

query box
small box located on the toolbar that works like the advanced query, but with less space in which to craft your query and without access to the word wheel

FIGURE 17.1   CCD on CD-ROM Unexpanded Table of Contents: Full-Screen View

FIGURE 17.2   **CCD on CD-ROM Expanded Table of Contents: Full-Screen View**

FIGURE 17.3   **CCD on CD-ROM Expanded Table of Contents: Split-Screen View**

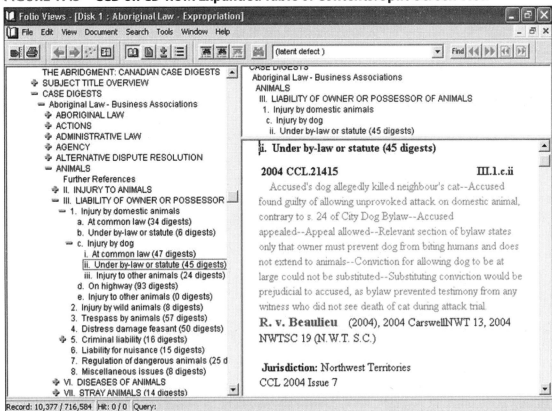

- **query templates**—the keyword and field query template and the case citation query template, accessible through the search menu on the toolbar, allow you to narrow your search to specific parts of the database; the **keyword and field query template** allows you to limit your keyword search to specific jurisdictions, specific years, and/or specific subject areas and/or classification phrases; the **case citation query template** allows you to search by case name or citation.

As we said, and then proceeded to show, in chapter 13, every computerized source has its own search syntax. The CCD uses the same search syntax as the CED. Figure 14.3 in chapter 14 sets out the main search operators used in the CED and CCD on CD-ROM.

CASE DIGESTS ONLINE

The *Canadian Abridgment Case Digests* is also available online via the Internet as part of LawSource, a subscription service offered by WestlaweCARSWELL. The CCD on CD-ROM acts as a finding tool only, allowing you to learn the names and citations of relevant cases. The *Case Digests* online goes further: it gives you access to the text of the cases by linking directly to LawSource's large database of case decisions.

The content of the *Case Digests* through LawSource is the same as that of the CCD on CD-ROM. However, unlike the CD-ROM, you cannot get access to the full text of the *Case Digests*, which you can then scroll through and read from beginning to end. Instead, your access is limited to the specific case digests you retrieve when you use the various search tools of the program, discussed below.

There are two main tools for finding relevant case law using the online version of the *Canadian Abridgment Case Digests*:

1. table of contents, and
2. custom search templates.

Table of Contents

The table of contents is similar to that of the CD-ROM. It lists all the subject titles in alphabetical order. It is made up of several levels that you can reach by clicking on the + sign next to a heading. You can view the table of contents alone only. It is not possible to view it in a split screen side by side with the text. You can get access to the table of contents by clicking on the "Canadian Abridgment Digests" link under the heading "Browse Tables of Contents" on the left side of the home page. Figure 17.4 illustrates how the subject title Animals is broken down in the table of contents.

Once you have identified your research topic in the table of contents, click on the words to display the relevant case digests. The text of all case digests dealing with the topic will be displayed in a separate window.

Custom Search Templates

Three custom search templates are available:

1. standard search,
2. terms and connectors search, and
3. natural language search.

---

query templates
accessible through the search menu on the toolbar; allow you to narrow your search to specific parts of the database

keyword and field query template
allows you to limit your keyword search to specific jurisdictions, specific years, and/or specific subject areas and/or classification phrases

case citation query template
allows you to search by case name or citation

FIGURE 17.4   Online Case Digests Table of Contents

standard search
allows you to search for information using keywords and a connector that is selected from the drop-down menu

The **standard search** template allows you to search for information using keywords associated with your research problem. You get access to this template by clicking on the "Canadian Abridgment Digests" link on the right side of the home page, under the heading "Custom Search Templates." Enter the relevant keywords and then select the desired connector from the drop-down menu within the template. You can choose to search for

- any keyword you entered,
- all the keywords you entered,
- the exact phrase you entered,
- all the keywords you entered within five words of each other,
- all the keywords you entered in the same sentence, or
- all the keywords you entered in the same paragraph.

The template allows you to limit your keyword search to

- the subject title,
- a classification number or phrase,
- the name of the case,
- the citation of the case, or
- the year of the decision.

You can also limit your search to a specified jurisdiction and date range. Figure 17.5 illustrates the standard search template.

FIGURE 17.5   Online Case Digests Standard Search Template

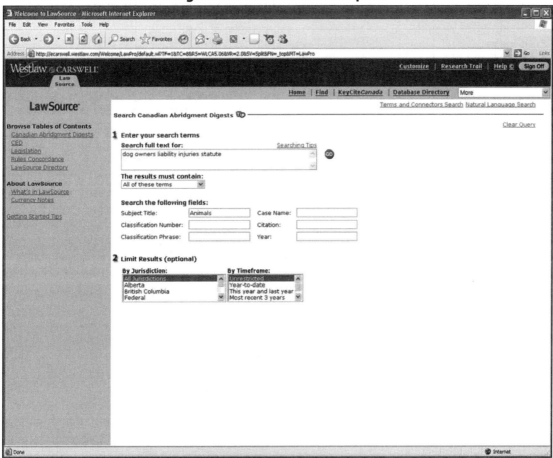

The **terms and connectors search** allows you to construct a Boolean search using keywords and your own Boolean connectors and expanders. It is therefore not as limiting as the standard search template. You get access to this search tool by clicking on the "Terms and Connectors Search" link at the top right side of the standard search template screen. You can use this tool to search all the *Case Digests* or you can limit your search to parts of the *Case Digests* by adding field and date restrictions to your search. Figure 17.6 illustrates the terms and connectors search screen.

The search syntax for the online version of the Abridgment is not exactly the same as the syntax for the CD-ROM. Figure 17.7 sets out the main search operators used in the online version of the *Case Digests*.

The terms and connectors search template contains a built-in thesaurus that provides related terms for all the keywords you enter. It also contains a term-frequency option that lets you specify how many times your keyword must appear. There is a link to both of these features beside the terms and connectors search window.

The **natural language search** allows you to search for information by asking your legal question using plain language. You get access to this search tool by clicking on the "Natural Language Search" link at the top right side of the standard search template screen. You can also get access to this link at the top of the search window while in the terms and connectors search template. You simply enter your question in the description box. You do not need to use any operators or connectors. "Are dog owners in Ontario liable for injuries caused by their dog?" is an example of a natural language search. Figure 17.8 shows the natural language search screen.

terms and connectors search
not as limiting as the standard search template; allows you to construct a Boolean search using keywords and your own Boolean connectors and expanders

natural language search
allows you to search for information by asking your question using plain language

FIGURE 17.6   Online Case Digests Terms and Connectors Search Screen

FIGURE 17.7   Online Case Digests Search Operators

Desired Operation	Enter
AND	&
OR	Space
a phrase	" "
in same sentence	/s
in same paragraph	/p
within a specified number of words	/n (n = 1-255)
various suffixes	!
variant letters	*
NOT	%

Linking to the Text

Any of the above methods will find the case digests that are relevant to your research topic. Results are displayed on the left side of the screen. Each result provides an excerpt from the case digest with the search keywords highlighted. Results are numbered and provide the name and citation of the case being digested. Figure 17.9 illustrates the results of a natural language search.

FIGURE 17.8 Online Case Digests Natural Language Search Template

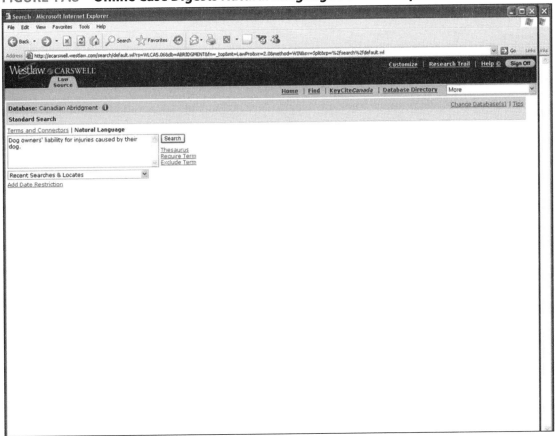

FIGURE 17.9 Results from Natural Language Search Template

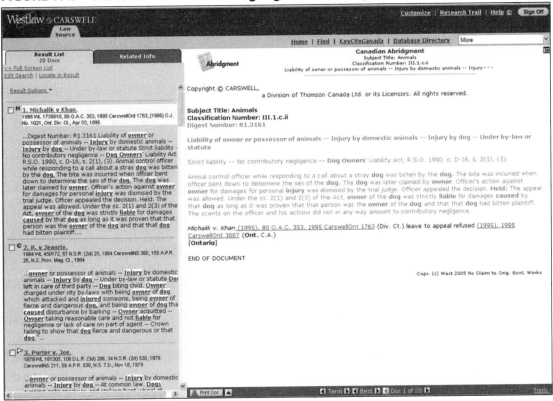

Each result number is a hyperlink to the text of the entire case digest. To view the text of a particular digest, simply click on the number in the result list that contains the digest you want to read. Figure 17.9 displays the first case digest in the results list. Each digest provides a summary of the point of law discussed in the case and includes the name, citation, and jurisdiction of the case being summarized. The citation provides a hyperlink to the text of the case. By clicking on the hyperlink, you can retrieve the full text of the case.

You will likely find many case digests that are relevant to your research topic. You will have to scan them all to determine which cases you should read in full.

LAWSOURCE'S CASE DATABASE FINDING TOOLS

LawSource, as we mentioned above, is a subscription service offered by Westlaw*e*CARSWELL that maintains a large database of case decisions. The CCD finding tools provide a direct link to the text of the cases in the LawSource database. The CCD is only one of the many finding tools available to search that database. Others are set out below.

Search Cases Custom Search Template

This tool allows you to conduct a keyword search of the LawSource database directly. It is particularly useful if you have a specific case in mind, have some information about it, but don't know the complete citation. Click on the "Cases" link under "Custom Search Templates" on the home page. Enter your keywords and choose the desired relationship between those keywords from the drop-down menu of choices. Enter any information you have about the name, court, jurisdiction, judge, counsel, or year of the case and LawSource will search for your keywords only in cases with the name, court, judge, or counsel you have specified.

For example, assume you are looking for an Ontario case about dog owners' liability and you know that one party's name is Strom. Enter the keywords "dog," "owner," and "liability" in the text box and choose "all of these terms" from the drop-down menu. Enter "Strom" in the case name field. Choose "Ontario" to limit your search to this jurisdiction only. Figure 17.10 illustrates this search template. Figure 17.11 illustrates the results of this search. Note how the full case report is displayed with the search keywords highlighted.

Find/KeyCite a Document

This tool allows you to search for case law that cites a statute generally or a specific section of a statute. Use the "Find/KeyCite a Document" link on the home page. Enter the name, section number(s), and jurisdiction of the statute you are researching. Figure 17.12 illustrates the KeyCite search template completed to request cases citing section 2(1) of the *Dog Owners' Liability Act*. Figure 17.13 illustrates the results of the search displaying the name and citation of cases citing this statute.

This tool also allows you to find a case when you know either part or all of the case name. Again, use the "Find/KeyCite a Document" link on the home page. Enter the information you have about the case name, including the jurisdiction, if you know it. The results list displays all the cases that contain the name(s) you have entered in that jurisdiction, and provides a breakdown of the subject matter using

FIGURE 17.10   LawSource Search Cases Template

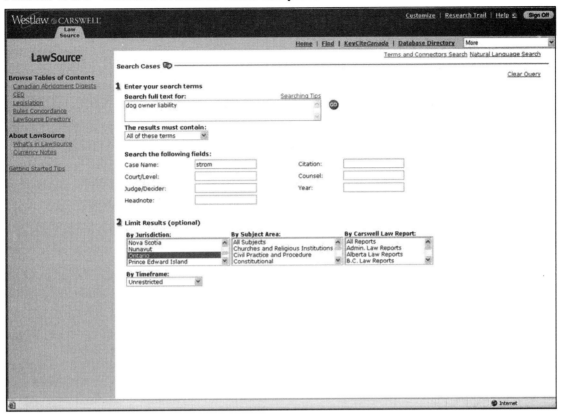

FIGURE 17.11   Law Source Search Cases Results

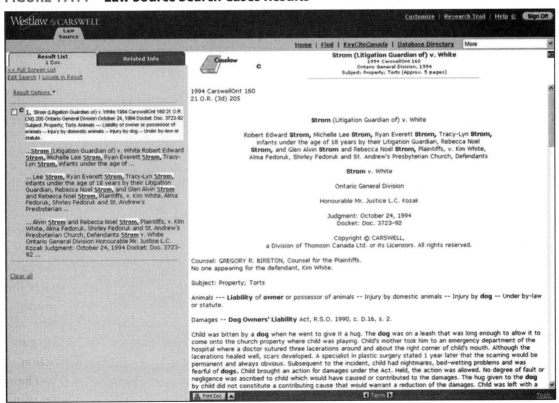

FIGURE 17.12   **LawSource KeyCite Search Template**

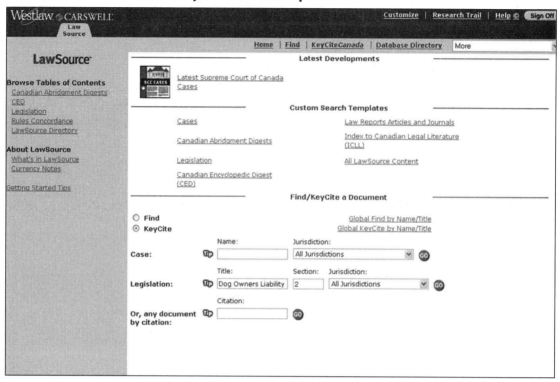

FIGURE 17.13   **LawSource KeyCite Search Results**

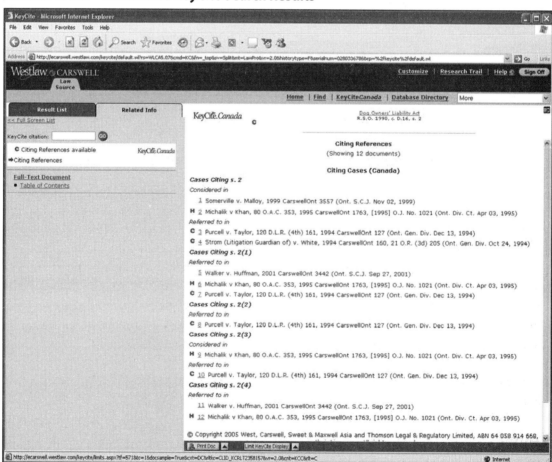

the CCD's key classification system. (If you don't know the jurisdiction, you can search "All jurisdictions.") The results are numbered starting at one, and each number is a hyperlink to the text of the case. Skim the list for a case that looks relevant to your research. Using the earlier example again, assume you are looking for an Ontario case dealing with dog owners' liability and you know that one of the parties is named Strom. Enter "Strom" for the case name, choose "Ontario" under the jurisdiction drop-down menu, and click "Go." Figure 17.14 illustrates the results of that search. Note that case number 7 deals with the relevant subject—animals, in particular, dog owners' liability.

FIGURE 17.14 LawSource Find/KeyCite Search Results

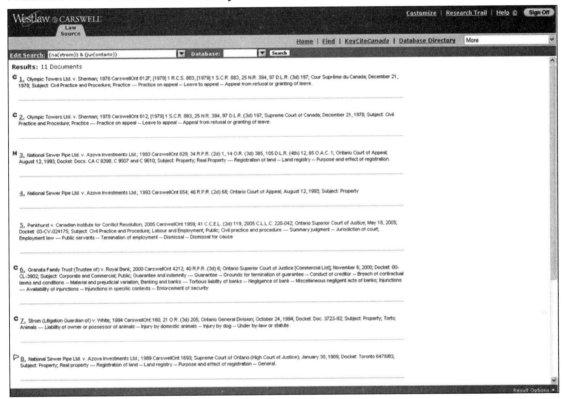

QUICKLAW

Quicklaw, a subscription service, is also a popular case finding tool. It provides access to a large number of cases collected in a number of databases. Each database contains cases from a particular report series, level of court, or jurisdiction. Quicklaw's databases are not edited, and so there is no table of contents to browse through. The only way to gain access to the contents of the database is by keyword searching. Quicklaw searches through the text of all cases in the database to find the keywords you enter. You must therefore search for keywords that are likely to appear in cases relevant to your research. Quicklaw matches the keywords you choose with the words contained in the database of cases. It will search for exact matches only. It will not automatically search for synonyms or alternate spellings of a word.

Keyword Searching

Two main ways to conduct a keyword search are by

- the template search, and
- a full Boolean search.

The first step with either search is to select the database of cases you want to search. Quicklaw provides a database directory, listing all the databases and their coverage by jurisdiction, court level, and date. Look through the database directory to find the appropriate database for your search. Once you select a database, Quicklaw will search for documents only within that database.

Use the **template search** only when you already have some information about a case you are looking for—for example, the case name, court, judge, or counsel. Enter your keywords and choose the desired relationship between those keywords from the drop-down menu of choices. Quicklaw will search for your keywords only in cases with the name, court, judge, or counsel you have specified.

Use a full **Boolean search** if you don't want to restrict your search by case name, court, judge, or counsel. A Boolean search allows you to define your search more specifically because it gives you greater choice in choosing the connectors between your keywords.

Quicklaw Search Syntax

Quicklaw search syntax provides a number of **root expanders** that instruct Quicklaw to search for different endings or spellings of words (see figure 17.15). Root expanders may be used for both template and Boolean searching.

FIGURE 17.15   Quicklaw Root Expanders

Command	Searches for	Example
! after the stem of a word (truncation)	All endings of a root word	**litig!** Searches for litigate, litigant, litigation, litigator, litigious
Suffix feature (ed, ing, tion)	Only specific endings of a root word	**Invest (ed, ment)** Searches for only invested or investment and NOT for investing, investor, investigate, etc.
* in place of a letter or number in a word	A variable letter or number	**Devi*e** Searches for devise or device **198*** Searches for any of 1980–1989

Figure 17.16 sets out the Boolean connectors used by Quicklaw for conducting a full Boolean search.

FINDING THE TEXT OF A CASE

Once you know the name and citation of a case, it is easy to find the text of the case using any of several computerized sources:

- Quicklaw and LawSource both offer a "find by citation" feature that allows you to retrieve the text of a case simply by providing its citation.
- The free CanLII website also provides access to the text of many Canadian cases. Once you select the jurisdiction and level of court, you can find the text of a case by its name or citation.

**Sidebar definitions:**

template search in a keyword search, used when you have some information about a case you are looking for—for example, case name, court, judge, or counsel

Boolean search in a keyword search, used when you don't want to restrict your search by case name, court, judge, or counsel

root expanders in a keyword search, used for both template and Boolean searching, to instruct Quicklaw to search for different endings or spellings of words

FIGURE 17.16   Quicklaw Boolean Connectors

Command	Searches for	Example
or (or **space**) between words	Documents that contain either word. If more than two words, searches for any of the words	**parent guardian relative** Searches for either *parent* or *guardian* or *relative*
and (or **&**) between words	Documents that contain all words entered	**child and support** Searches for both *child* and *support* (in no specific relationship to each other)
"..." Phrase connector	A specific phrase	**"blood relative"** Searches for the exact phrase *blood relative*
/n Word proximity connector	Words near each other, in any order	**child /2 support** Searches for *child* up to two words away from *support* **fraudulent negligent /5 misrepresentation** Searches for either *fraudulent* or *negligent* to be no more than five words away from *misrepresentation*
/p paragraph proximity connector	Words in the same paragraph, in any order	**Child /p support** Searches for documents in which the words *child* and *support* appear in the same paragraph

UPDATING CASES

In chapter 11 we told you that you have to update any relevant case you find to make sure that it is still useful to your research. By updating you will find out:

- Case history or appeal history—has the case been confirmed or overturned on appeal? What was the highest court that reviewed the decision?
- How has the case been treated by other judges—has it been followed, or not? Has it been distinguished?

See chapter 11 for a complete discussion of the importance of updating cases.

Both Quicklaw and LawSource have comprehensive case citators that allow you to update cases easily. Each source has its own codes to indicate the judicial treatment of a case, so you will need to know the citator treatment codes used by the source you are using.

Quicklaw

Quicklaw's citator is called QuickCite. You can get access to this tool any of the following ways:

- by using Quicklaw's "find by citation" link,
- by clicking the "note up with QuickCite" link while viewing the text of a case, or
- by searching the QuickCite database.

LawSource

Update cases in LawSource by using the KeyCite feature. The easiest way to get access to KeyCite is to use the "KeyCite a document" link at the bottom of the home page.

KEY TERMS

advanced query
Boolean search
case citation query template
case digest
key classification system
key word and field query template
natural language search
query box
query templates
root expanders
search operator
standard search
template search
terms and connectors search

CHAPTER 18

Legal Research on the Internet

Our discussion of computerized legal research wouldn't be complete if we didn't add a few more words about Internet research. In the preceding chapters, we talked about sources available on the Internet through both subscription services and free-access websites. Our discussion has been structured according to the legal research functions that the sources serve—that is, as finding tools, primary sources, or updating tools. This chapter focuses on free-access websites, and the issues that arise when you use them, whatever function they serve.

TYPES OF FREE-ACCESS SITES

There are many types of free-access websites that you can use when conducting legal research. In addition to websites that provide access to primary sources—statutes (discussed in chapter 15), regulations (discussed in chapter 16), and cases (discussed in chapter 17)—there are subject indexes and search engines, websites that contain law-related information, and bookmark lists.

Subject Indexes and Search Engines

Both subject indexes and search engines help a researcher locate Web documents or websites relevant to the topic being researched.

A **subject index**, also called a subject tree, is a website that categorizes or indexes Web documents or websites using subject classifications. Yahoo (at http://www.yahoo.com) is an example of a subject index. HierosGamos (at http://www.hg.org/index.html) is a legal subject index.

A **search engine** is an Internet site with a computer program that searches a database of Web documents or websites to match keywords that you supply. There are general search engines as well as specialized legal search engines.

The major general search engines are:

- AltaVista at http://www.altavista.com,
- Google at http://www.google.com,
- Lycos at http://www.lycos.com, and
- Yahoo at http://www.yahoo.com.

subject index
also called a subject tree, a website that categorizes or indexes Web documents or websites using subject clssifications

search engine
website with a computer program that searches a database of Web documents or websites to match supplied keywords

Catherine P. Best, who developed and maintains the Best Guide to Canadian Legal Research website, recommends Google because it has the largest database of indexed pages; it also ranks its results so that higher quality sites appear first.

The main legal search engines are:

- FindLaw LawCrawler at http://lawcrawler.findlaw.com. This American site focuses primarily on U.S. law, but has a link that allows you to search legal websites from Canada.
- LawRunner at http://www.ilrg.com. This American site is run by the Internet Legal Research Group. It acts as an interface for Google to find law-related sites in 238 countries, including Canada, but with emphasis on the United States.

Websites Containing Law-Related Information

Many websites contain law-related information.

Government Sites

In addition to their statute sites, the federal and provincial governments maintain websites that contain useful information for lawyers and law clerks.

The main Government of Canada site, at http://canada.gc.ca, provides information about government services for Canadians, non-Canadians, and Canadian businesses; it also provides information about the structure of the federal government and contains links to federal departments and agencies, provincial and territorial governments, and municipalities.

Other government of Canada websites that provide law-related information are:

- Statistics Canada at http://www.statcan.ca—for statistics, including the consumer price index, population rates, and unemployment rates;
- Canada Revenue Agency at http://www.cra-arc.gc.ca—for income tax and GST information and forms;
- Industry Canada's business information site, Strategis at http://www.strategis.ic.gc.ca—for information related to business.

Government of Ontario

The main government of Ontario site, at http://www.gov.on.ca, provides a complete services and offices directory, including all tribunals, boards, and agencies; a government of Ontario telephone directory; and links to specific ministries.

Other government of Ontario websites that provide law-related information are:

- Ministry of the Attorney General at http://www.attorneygeneral.jus.gov.on.ca—for information about, for example, going to court, getting a lawyer, family law matters, and Small Claims Court;
- Guide to Ontario Courts at http://www.ontariocourts.on.ca—for links to the Court of Appeal, Superior Court of Justice, and Ontario Court of Justice.

Other Provincial Governments

Each province and territory has a website similar to the government of Ontario website. You can find them individually—for example, by doing a Google search for "[name of province] government"—or you can link to each one of them through the federal government's website at http://canada.gc.ca/othergov/prov_e.html.

Municipal Governments

All major Canadian cities have their own websites with information about matters like bylaws and contact information for city administrators. You can find a city's website by doing a Google search for "city of [name of city]."

Legal Research Sites

A number of sites contain information about legal research, including:

- Best Guide to Canadian Legal Research at http://www.legalresearch.org. Run by Catherine Best, a research lawyer and adjunct professor with the University of British Columbia Faculty of Law, this site is an excellent source of information about legal research and contains links to legal sources.
- Bora Laskin Law Library at http://www.law-lib.utoronto.ca. Run by the University of Toronto Faculty of Law, this site contains guides to legal research, community legal information, and links to legal resources.
- William R. Lederman Law Library at http://library.queensu.ca/law/. Run by the Queen's University Faculty of Law, this site contains a comprehensive legal research manual. (However, you made the right decision by buying this book.)

General Legal Sites

Various law-related organizations maintain websites with access to information about the law, such as:

- Access to Justice Network at http://www.acjnet.org. A project of the legal studies program of the University of Alberta, this site provides access to public legal education articles.
- Canadian Legal FAQs at http://www.law-faqs.org. Also a project of the legal studies program of the University of Alberta, this site provides answers to commonly asked legal questions.

Most large law firms maintain websites that provide access to publications on legal topics written by members of their firms—for example:

- Davies, Ward, Phillips & Vineberg at http://www.dwpv.com;
- Gowling, Lafleur, Henderson at http://www.gowlings.com;
- McCarthy, Tetrault at http://www.mccarthy.ca; and
- Torys at http://www.torys.com.

You can get access to a comprehensive list of Canadian law firms, by practice area, by going to the Canadian Law List website at http://www.canadianlawlist.com.

Bookmark Lists

Bookmark lists are websites that provide a list of links to other sites. Canadian bookmark lists include:

- Best's Legal Bookmarks at http://legalresearch.org/docs/bookmark.html—part of the Best Guide to Canadian Legal Research site;
- CLE Legal Links at http://www.cle.bc.ca/links/pages/—maintained by the Continuing Legal Education Society of British Columbia;
- Jurist Canada at http://jurist.law.utoronto.ca—hosted by the University of Toronto Faculty of Law, but, in fact, a project of a law professor at the University of Pittsburgh; and

- LexUM at http://www.lexum.umontreal.ca/index.epl?lang=en—
maintained by the University of Montreal Law Faculty.

CONCERNS WHEN RESEARCHING ON THE INTERNET

Enormous amounts of information, legal and otherwise, are available on the Internet. This is the Internet's strength, but also its weakness as a research tool. The sheer volume of material can be overwhelming. The amount of information that comes back from a search request can be far too much to sift through and evaluate.

In addition, information on the Internet is not organized in any way. Add to that the fact that Internet sites change quickly, then, as the movie critic Roger Ebert said, "Doing research on the Web is like using a library assembled piecemeal by packrats and vandalized nightly." Or, as the Queen's University Law Library site says, "[Doing research on the Web is] like using a library in which all of the books have been dumped on the floor."

Internet research can be time-consuming. You must take the time to learn the search syntax used by search engines at different sites. If you use incorrect search syntax, you may miss relevant documents or retrieve many irrelevant documents. To add insult to injury, response times to searches can be slow if you are researching during times of heavy Internet traffic or if you are downloading large files.

Finally, as Catherine Best says, "There is no guarantee that information posted on the Internet for free access is comprehensive, current, or reliable." When you use free-access websites you must ask yourself:

- Who has written or edited the content for the website? Look for the author's or editor's name, credentials, and contact address.
- Is the site affiliated with a known, law-based organization?
- Is the site associated with an impartial organization, or with a political or advocacy group? Does the site show a bias?
- How current is the information on the site? How often is the site updated?

But, take heart. You can generally rely on information found on sites maintained by

- governments,
- universities,
- law schools, and
- courts.

KEY TERMS

search engine
subject engine

CHAPTER 19

Computer Exercises

It's once more time to apply your knowledge and do some legal research using computerized sources.

You often have a choice of computerized sources to find the information you are looking for. Once you have chosen your source, there may be more than one way to look for information with it. While it is best to become familiar with all finding tools a source has to offer, the choice of finding tool is up to you. However, whichever finding tool you use, you should find the same information.

The questions below require you to look for the same information you were looking for when using paper sources in chapter 12.

SAMPLE QUESTIONS

Read the questions below. For each one,

- identify the kind of information you're being asked for—for example, is it a statute, a regulation, a case, an update, or something other?
- decide what computerized source(s) you will need (given what you have access to, naturally);
- decide how you will look for the required information using your chosen computerized source; and
- answer the question, citing correctly any statute, regulation, or case you are asked to find.

1. Is there an Ontario statute that governs transplanting of human organs after death?

    a. What kind of information are you being asked for?

    b. Which research tools will you need?

    c. Which tools are available in your library?

    d. Your answer to the question.

2. Find the federal statute that deals with the sentencing of young offenders.

    a. What kind of information are you being asked for?

    b. Which research tools will you need?

    c. Which tools are available in your library?

    d. Your answer to the question.

3. The federal *Tobacco Products Control Act* is no longer in force. On what date was it repealed and by what statute?

   a. What kind of information are you being asked for?

   b. Which research tools will you need?

   c. Which tools are available in your library?

   d. Your answer to the question.

4. Find the *Criminal Code* section that deals with possession of prohibited weapons and update it to the present.

    a. What kind of information are you being asked for?

    b. Which research tools will you need?

    c. Which tools are available in your library?

    d. Your answer to the question.

5. Are there any cases in your province that followed the Supreme Court of Canada decision in *Crocker v. Sundance Northwest Resorts Ltd.*, [1988] 1 S.C.R. 1186?

a. What kind of information are you being asked for?

b. Which research tools will you need?

c. Which tools are available in your library?

d. Your answer to the question.

6. Was the 1992 Ontario case *Dunn v. Dunn Estate* appealed? If so, what happened on appeal?

   a. What kind of information are you being asked for?

   b. Which research tools will you need?

   c. Which tools are available in your library?

   d. Your answer to the question.

7. Find two recent texts on torts that are available in the library in which you are working. Give the author's name, book title, publisher, and date of publication.

   a. What kind of information are you being asked for?

   b. Which research tools will you need?

   c. Which tools are available in your library?

   d. Your answer to the question.

8. Are there any Manitoba Court of Appeal cases dealing with renewal of franchising contracts?

    a. What kind of information are you being asked for?

    b. Which research tools will you need?

    c. Which tools are available in your library?

    d. Your answer to the question.

9. Choose a specific provision of the Ontario *Limitations Act* and then find out if that provision has been cited in case law. Remember that you may have to concord the provision to trace the same section back through previous statute revisions.

   a. What kind of information are you being asked for?

   b. Which research tools will you need?

   c. Which tools are available in your library?

   d. Your answer to the question.

10. Are there any cases that have cited s. 181(2) of the 1985 federal
    Bankruptcy and Insolvency Act?

    a. What kind of information are you being asked for?

    b. Which research tools will you need?

    c. Which tools are available in your library?

    d. Your answer to the question.

11. Find the Ontario statute that provides information about who may adopt infants and children. Are there any regulations made under it?

   a. What kind of information are you being asked for?

   b. Which research tools will you need?

   c. Which tools are available in your library?

   d. Your answer to the question.

12. Your firm's client resides in British Columbia. She recently defaulted in her mortgage payments and the mortgagee is suing for a final order for foreclosure. Which B.C. statute provides information about the effect of a final order for foreclosure? Find the text of this statute.

   a. What kind of information are you being asked for?

   b. Which research tools will you need?

   c. Which tools are available in your library?

   d. Your answer to the question.

13. There is a 1982 Alberta Court of Appeal case involving Holt Renfrew and another corporation. Find the name and citation of this case. Locate the case report and provide the names of all the judges.

   a. What kind of information are you being asked for?

   b. Which research tools will you need?

   c. Which tools are available in your library?

   d. Your answer to the question.

PART VI

Putting It All Together

CHAPTER 20

The Best of Both Worlds

You now know about both paper and computerized legal research sources. You have learned (perhaps painfully) that there are usually several ways to find an answer when researching an issue using paper sources, and several more ways to find the same answer when using computerized sources.

In this chapter we look at how to choose between paper and computerized sources—how to have the best of both worlds.

ISN'T COMPUTER-ASSISTED RESEARCH ALWAYS BETTER?

In a word, no. There are advantages and disadvantages to working with computerized legal research sources, just as there are advantages and disadvantages to working with paper sources. When you use a computer in your research, or whether you use one at all, will depend on the particular research you are doing.

Advantages of Computerized Sources

Computerized sources have paper sources beaten hollow for some uses:

- Some computerized sources can give you immediate access to recently decided cases weeks or months before those cases are published in a report series. Several months pass from the time a case is decided until it is reported in a series.
- Some computerized sources can give you access to a digest or the full text of unreported decisions that will never be reported. Sometimes it is difficult or impossible to find unreported decisions any other way (this is particularly true of administrative tribunal decisions).

- Some computerized sources almost instantly provide information—for example, names of unreported cases, appeal history of a case, and judicial consideration of a case—that might take a researcher hours to find in paper sources.
- Computerized sources have the ability to search large amounts of data at one time—for example, to search a database for all cases containing certain words—or to search a statute database for specific words. Most paper statutes come with neither an index nor a table of contents.

Disadvantages of Computerized Sources

Computerized sources are not without their drawbacks:

- A particular computerized source may not always be available where you're doing your research—if you're working in a law library, do you go back to your office and use LawSource or Quicklaw, or do you use a paper resource that's available in the library and continue your work without interruption?
- Computerized sources can be frustrating to a researcher who is not experienced in online search techniques and, worse, an inexperienced researcher may miss important cases or statutes. For some research problems, if you do not know exactly what you're looking for, you will waste much time narrowing the vast amount of material that the database will provide.
- A computerized source may not cover all reported cases in a report series database; sometimes coverage extends back only into the 1980s, when publishing companies began computerizing. Check the starting date of the database. The incredibly important case relevant to your research may have been decided in 1953.
- Some computerized databases contain typographical errors. If you don't misspell your keyword in exactly the same way the database has misspelled the word you're looking for, you may miss an important case or statute. But if, for example, you're working with a paper source on a problem involving a surgeon's negligence and you see the word "malpratice," you carry on without missing a beat.
- Computerized subscription services can be expensive to use. Even though most law firms are on flat-rate accounts, usage will determine the renewal rate for the account, and each user is identifiable. If you're slow as molasses in January, there's no charge for reading paper sources.

Advantages of Paper Sources

Even though you may be itching to get your hands on a computer to do your research:

- Print sources are better at providing context and a sense of where a legal issue fits into an area of the law, because you can skim through surrounding material. If you're not really familiar with the area of law you're researching and you're doing more than updating a case, you're better off starting with the broad view that paper sources can give you.

- Print sources tend to be more comprehensive in coverage, especially for older cases and historical versions of statutes. In fact, as we pointed out above, for some cases and statutes paper sources are the only sources.
- Only the print volumes of annual and revised statutes have official status and can be used in court (although pending legislation in Ontario may change that). If the matter is going to end up in a courtroom, you're going to have to pull out the paper sources at some point.
- There is no charge to use print sources that are already in a library.

Disadvantages of Paper Sources

On the other hand, paper sources aren't perfect:

- Print sources tend not to be as current as computerized sources.
- It often takes longer to find information using print sources because more volumes must be consulted and there are often more steps involved.

A COMBINED APPROACH

The best approach to legal research combines paper and computerized sources in a way that is efficient and cost-effective. The following approach assumes that you have access to all possible sources. In reality, your approach will likely be determined by the sources that are available to you at the time of your search.

Use Paper Sources To Find a General Statement of the Law

As we've stated several times—in fact, it's starting to seem like nagging even to us—it is usually wise to start your research with secondary sources, using them to gain an understanding of the law and as finding tools to direct you to the primary sources that actually create the law. If you don't know much about the area of law you're researching, you should start by reading a legal encyclopedia or a text or article on the subject. This will give you an overview of the law in addition to the name of any relevant statute and the names of leading cases in the area. While encyclopedias, texts, and articles come in both paper and computerized formats, it is best to do your preliminary reading using paper sources. A computerized source gives you only what you ask for. Looking at a book allows you to skim through surrounding material, which may be where you find the key to your problem's solution.

Use Computerized Sources To Find and Update Statutes and Regulations

Once you have the name of a relevant statute, it is far easier to find the up-to-date text of that statute and any associated regulations with computerized sources than with paper sources.

Use Both Paper and Computerized Sources To Find Additional Cases

If you are looking for the names of cases dealing with a subject generally, your best source is the *Canadian Abridgment Case Digests*, which is available in both paper and computerized format. You may find it easier to work with the paper version so that you can browse through surrounding material. However, computerized sources are better if you are looking for

- cases that have interpreted a statute or a section of a statute;
- cases considering a word or a phrase;
- cases for which you've got only a partial or incorrect citation—that is, when you're treasure hunting; or
- unreported cases.

Use Paper or Computerized Sources To Locate the Text of Cases

Once you have the names of the cases you're interested in, you will have to locate the text of those cases in order to review them. Depending on the sources available to you, you can use either print law reports or computerized versions of the case. If you are using computerized sources, use a free-access website such as CANLII rather than a subscription service.

Use Computerized Sources To Update Cases

It is far faster to work with computerized sources—Quicklaw or LawSource—than with paper sources to update cases.

If you use our combined approach to research and make use of both paper and computerized sources at appropriate times, you will find that you get through your work efficiently. You won't miss important ideas about the law because you're starting off with too much focus (on the computer), and you won't miss important recent developments in case or statute law because you couldn't find one of the little update brochures (in the paper sources).

CHAPTER 21

Legal Writing

When you complete your legal research, you will most likely have to communicate your research findings in writing. It is important that you be able to do this in a clear and concise manner. This chapter talks about the requirements of good legal writing and discusses two types of legal writing: case briefs and memos of law.

WHAT IS LEGAL WRITING?

The term "legal writing" is used to describe the drafting of any type of law-related document; for example,

- court pleadings such as a statement of claim, a statement of defence, or a third-party claim;
- affidavits;
- contracts;
- wills;
- letters, including opinion letters to clients;
- case briefs; and
- memos of law.

Case briefs and memos of law are discussed in more detail below.

WHAT IS GOOD LEGAL WRITING?

Good legal writing does not require complex language and a lot of "legalese"—in fact it avoids both. It simply requires writing that is well-organized, easy to understand, and free of grammatical and spelling errors. In other words, good legal writing isn't very different from plain, ordinary, good writing.

To write well, you must pay attention to your

- audience,
- purpose,
- grammar, and
- spelling.

Audience

The audience for your writing is the intended reader. Ask yourself who will be reading your document, and then write for that reader. Your audience may be a legal professional such as a law clerk, articling student, lawyer, or judge or a layperson, such as a client. A legal professional will be more familiar and comfortable with legal terms and concepts than a layperson. Therefore, when you write for a legal professional, you can use legal terms and concepts without having to define, explain, or translate them as you would for a layperson. But, in either case, your writing should be as clear, simple, and straightforward as possible.

Whether your intended reader is a legal professional or a layperson, you should always keep in mind that you are writing for a business purpose. You should therefore maintain a level of formality in your writing, avoiding slang and colloquial language (such as "cops" for "police officers") and contractions (such as "isn't" for "is not").

Purpose

The purpose of the document you are writing could be, for example, to record the results of your research in the form of a memo to file or to another legal professional; to write a letter to a client requesting information; or to use your research to give the correct structure to an affidavit or a will that your client will sign. Whatever your purpose, you have to make sure that the content and organization of the document achieves that purpose.

Grammar

Good writing requires good grammar—properly constructed sentences using proper punctuation. Grammatically incorrect writing not only annoys people who know something about grammar (count among them judges, lawyers, and, often, clients), it is often unclear. Clarity is very important in legal documents, so that means that good grammar is also very important.

Spelling

Good writing also requires correct spelling. Improper spelling, just like incorrect grammar, not only makes the writer look unprofessional, but it can change the meaning of what you have written, even if the grammar, content, and organization of your document are otherwise flawless. You need to brush up on the spelling not only of your general vocabulary, but also of your legal vocabulary, which often includes words that nobody but legal professionals have ever heard of—for instance, "waive" and "enure," which are *never* to be confused with "wave" and "ensure." Check your documents for spelling errors by proofreading them thoroughly. Use the spell-check feature of your word processing software, but do not rely on it alone; it will not pick up words that are improperly spelled only in the context in which they are used and it will probably not tell you the correct spelling of unusual words like "enure."

WRITING A CASE BRIEF

A case brief is a document that provides a clear and concise summary of a court decision by setting out the facts of the case, the legal issues involved, the court's decision, and the reasons for that decision. See chapter 4 for a more complete discussion of the elements that make up a court decision or case.

There is no standard format for a case brief, but it should contain all of the following:

1. the citation of the case (see chapter 11 if you don't remember what a citation is);
2. a summary of the facts of the case;
3. a summary of the issues in the case (or, if there are many issues and some are clearly irrelevant to your research, the relevant issues);
4. the disposition or judgment of each (relevant) issue in the case; and
5. a summary of the judge's reasons for his or her decision with respect to each (relevant) issue.

WRITING A MEMO OF LAW

The results of legal research are often recorded in a memorandum of law. In a memo of law, the writer sets out a question or a fact situation that he or she has been presented with and the law that relates to that question or fact situation; the writer may suggest possible courses of action and the legal consequences of each course of action.

Before you prepare a final memo of law in the format below, work your way through the memo according to the flow chart that appears below, under the heading "Flow Chart for a Memo of Law."

FORMAT OF A MEMO OF LAW

Most memos of law appear in the following format:

Memo

To:

From:

Re:

File No.:

Date:

Question(s)

The question(s) will be those that the client or lawyer has asked or the fact situation that he or she has described. If the lawyer is familiar with the field, the question asked may turn out to be the issue as well. If the lawyer knows little about the field, the question may not be the same as the legal issue that actually had to be researched.

Facts

These are facts that are relevant to the issue(s), in chronological order.

Issue(s)

What is the issue of law that must be examined here—that is, what problem must be solved in order to reach a solution? Issues are usually introduced by the word "whether." There may be just one issue, or several.

Law

Set out the relevant statutory or regulatory provisions as they appear in the statute or regulation with a full citation of the statute or regulation and section; set out the relevant passages from cases, with a full citation of each case. If there is more than one issue, restate each issue exactly as it appeared in the issue section before setting out the law on that issue.

Do not set out diverging lines of authority that you find in a case. You are quoting the case for the law the judge followed and the decision that the judge reached, not for the law the judge decided not to follow. If you think the law the judge did *not* follow is useful to you, get the cases and quote from them directly.

Discussion

Discuss or analyze the statute, regulation, and/or case law in light of the given fact situation. This is the appropriate place to discuss

1. whether the facts in the cases you have found are sufficiently similar to your client's situation for the law in those cases to be applicable to your fact situation;
2. the state of the law if it is changing, or if there are conflicting cases or conflicting statutory or regulatory provisions;
3. whether existing statutes, regulations, and cases in fact address the problem in your fact situation. Is yours a new or unusual point of law? If so, can you use existing law to suggest a likely solution to the problem?
4. whether previously unforeseen problems for the client arise out of your study of the law.

Be objective. A client will not be helped by a memo that ignores problems that arise in the law, nor will a client be helped by a memo that ignores possible solutions when the law generally seems to go against the client.

Conclusion

Draw together the facts and the law. State what you have concluded from applying the law to the facts in your situation. There should be one paragraph or section in the conclusion for each issue. Also point out any further information that is required or problems that need further research.

Attachments

Attach the cases and statutory and regulatory provisions that you refer to in your memo.

FLOW CHART FOR A MEMO OF LAW

1. Analyze the fact situation.
2. Research the law.
3. Prepare a draft memo of law. At this point, try to see the problem as a whole, which is necessary to prepare your memo. A draft memo of law gives you a chance to try out different ideas about what you think is going on from a legal point of view and settle on the true issues, the important facts, and the relevant law. You may have to rework your draft once or twice before you're satisfied that you've approached the problem from the correct angle.

   In your draft memo, you should NOT start with the *facts* and work down. Start with the *question* asked by the client or lawyer.

   Then set out the legal *issues* that arise out of the question, out of the facts, and out of the law you have found in your research.

   Then set out the *law*.

   When you have done all this, you will be able to look at the facts and decide which ones are relevant to the principles of law involved. Delete irrelevant facts. Emphasize essential facts.

   Discuss the law as it relates to the facts in your particular case.

   Finally, reach a conclusion. Suggest possible action and potential consequences of such action.

4. Prepare a final memo of law in the format above. Remember that a memo of law is not a 5,000-word term paper; keep it short and to the point. The lawyer reading the memo is also going to read the attached statute, regulatory, and case law and draw his or her own conclusions.

EXERCISES

I. Prepare a memo of law from the information and materials provided below.

Memo

To: You

From: Lawyer

Re: *Giller and Keaton Estate*

Date: December 12, Year Zero

Elizabeth Giller is our 58-year-old client.

Elizabeth met Jack Keaton in Year Minus Six and they became involved with each other. Elizabeth had been separated from her husband for 12 years at that time (she is still not divorced from him). Jack was a widower and had two adult daughters from his marriage. For two years, she and Jack spent much time together, slept over at each other's residences, and went on vacations together, but did not live together. She decided to leave her apartment and move into his house in January, Year Minus Four, because his health was beginning to fail and they agreed that he shouldn't live alone. By early Year Minus Two, he was so ill that she quit her job to be with him full time. They were able to live fairly comfortably on his pension and investments, although Elizabeth ended up spending money looking after him and she now has debts. In August Year Zero, Jack died. In his will (which he never changed after meeting Elizabeth), he left everything to his two adult daughters.

Elizabeth was a senior secretary at an investment firm before she stopped working to look after Jack. She is starting to suffer from arthritis in her hands and finds it difficult to keyboard. She began looking for work after Jack's death but quickly realized that she would have a lot of trouble re-entering the work force at her age. She has saved a little money on which she is now living, and she will receive a pension, but not until she turns 65. Elizabeth believes that she would not be in financial trouble if she had not looked after Jack, of whom she was very fond. In addition, she was shocked and hurt that he left her nothing at all in his will.

Elizabeth wants to know if there is anything in law that can be done to help her. She would like an income, if possible—at least until she starts receiving pension benefits—and money to pay her debts that relate to looking after Jack.

Further information: The law of Ontario applies.

NOTE: Don't forget to consider in your memo

- whether the client has the legal status to make an application under the Act,
- what factors the court is likely to look at *in this case* to determine whether to order support, and
- whether the Act provides for what Elizabeth wants (an income and money to pay off debts).

Selected provisions of the *Succession Law Reform Act*, R.S.O. 1990, c. S.26:

PART V
SUPPORT OF DEPENDANTS

57. **Definitions**—In this Part,

"child" means a child as defined in subsection 1 (1) and includes a grandchild and a person whom the deceased has demonstrated a settled intention to treat as a child of his or her family, except under an arrangement where the child is placed for valuable consideration in a foster home by a person having lawful custody;

"cohabit" means to live together in a conjugal relationship, whether within or outside marriage;

"court" means the Ontario Court (General Division);

"dependant" means,
(a) the spouse of the deceased,
(b) a parent of the deceased,
(c) a child of the deceased, or
(d) a brother or sister of the deceased,
to whom the deceased was providing support or was under a legal obligation to provide support immediately before his or her death;

"letters probate" and "letters of administration" include letters probate, letters of administration or other legal documents purporting to be of the same legal nature granted by a court in another jurisdiction and resealed in this province;

"parent" includes a grandparent and a person who has demonstrated a settled intention to treat the deceased as a child of his or her family, except under an arrangement where the deceased was placed for valuable consideration in a foster home by a person having lawful custody;

"spouse" means a spouse as defined in subsection 1 (1) and in addition includes either of a man and woman who,
  (a) were married to each other by a marriage that was terminated or declared a nullity, or
  (b) are not married to each other and have cohabited,
    (i) continuously for a period of not less than three years, or
    (ii) in a relationship of some permanence, if they are the natural or adoptive parents of a child.

58.(1) **Order for support**—Where a deceased, whether testate or intestate, has not made adequate provision for the proper support of his dependants or any of them, the court, on application, may order that such provision as it considers adequate be made out of the estate of the deceased for the proper support of the dependants or any of them.

(2) **Applicants**—An application for an order for the support of a dependant may be made by the dependant or the dependant's parent.

(3) **Idem**—An application for an order for the support of a dependant may also be made by one of the following agencies:

(a) the Ministry of Community and Social Services in the name of the Minister;

(b) a municipal corporation, including a metropolitan, district or regional municipality, but not including an area municipality;

(c) a district welfare administration board under the *District Welfare Administration Boards Act*; or

(d) a band approved under section 15 of the *General Welfare Assistance Act*,

if the agency is providing or has provided a benefit under the *Family Benefits Act* or assistance under the *General Welfare Assistance Act* in respect of the dependant's support, or if an application for such a benefit or assistance has been made to the agency by or on behalf of the dependant.

(4) **Idem**—The adequacy of provision for support under subsection (1) shall be determined as of the date of the hearing of the application.

59. **Suspensory order**—On an application by or on behalf of the dependants or any of them, the court may make an order suspending in whole or in part the administration of the deceased's estate, for such time and to such extent as the court may decide.

60.(1) **Application**—An application under this Part may be made to the court by notice of application in accordance with the practice of the court.

(2) **Idem**—Where an application for an order under section 58 is made by or on behalf of any dependant,

(a) it may be dealt with by the court as; and

(b) in so far as the question of limitation is concerned, it shall be deemed to be,

an application on behalf of all persons who might apply.

61.(1) **Limitation period**—Subject to subsection (2), no application for an order under section 58 may be made after six months from the grant of letters probate of the will or of letters of administration.

(2) **Exception**—The court, if it considers it proper, may allow an application to be made at any time as to any portion of the estate remaining undistributed at the date of the application.

62.(1) **Determination of amount**—In determining the amount and duration, if any, of support, the court shall consider all the circumstances of the application, including,

(a) the dependant's current assets and means;

(b) the assets and means that the dependant is likely to have in the future;

(c) the dependant's capacity to contribute to his or her own support;

(d) the dependant's age and physical and mental health;

(e) the dependant's needs, in determining which the court shall have regard to the dependant's accustomed standard of living;

(f) the measures available for the dependant to become able to provide for his or her own support and the length of time and cost involved to enable the dependant to take those measures;

(g) the proximity and duration of the dependant's relationship with the deceased;

(h) the contributions made by the dependant to the deceased's welfare, including indirect and non-financial contributions;

(i) the contributions made by the dependant to the acquisition, maintenance and improvement of the deceased's property or business;

(j) a contribution by the dependant to the realization of the deceased's career potential;

(k) whether the dependant has a legal obligation to provide support for another person;

(l) the circumstances of the deceased at the time of death;

(m) any agreement between the deceased and the dependant;

(n) any previous distribution or division of property made by the deceased in favour of the dependant by gift or agreement or under court order;

(o) the claims that any other person may have as a dependant;

(p) if the dependant is a child,

(i) the child's aptitude for and reasonable prospects of obtaining an education, and

(ii) the child's need for a stable environment;

(q) if the dependant is a child of the age of sixteen years or more, whether the child has withdrawn from parental control;

(r) if the dependant is a spouse,

(i) a course of conduct by the spouse during the deceased's lifetime that is so unconscionable as to constitute an obvious and gross repudiation of the relationship,

(ii) the length of time the spouses cohabited,

(iii) the effect on the spouse's earning capacity of the responsibilities assumed during cohabitation,

(iv) whether the spouse has undertaken the care of a child who is of the age of eighteen years or over and unable by reason of illness, disability or other cause to withdraw from the charge of his or her parents,

(v) whether the spouse has undertaken to assist in the continuation of a program of education for a child eighteen years of age or over who is unable for that reason to withdraw from the charge of his or her parents,

(vi) any housekeeping, child care or other domestic service performed by the spouse for the family, as if the spouse had devoted the time spent in performing that service in remunerative employment and had contributed the earnings to the family's support,

(vii) the effect on the spouse's earnings and career development of the responsibility of caring for a child,

(viii) the desirability of the spouse remaining at home to care for a child; and

(s) any other legal right of the dependant to support, other than out of public money.

(2) **Evidence**—In addition to the evidence presented by the parties, the court may direct other evidence to be given as the court considers necessary or proper.

(3) **Idem**—The court may accept such evidence as it considers proper of the deceased's reasons, so far as ascertainable, for making the dispositions in his or her will, or for not making adequate provision for a dependant, as the case may be, including any statement in writing signed by the deceased.

(4) **Idem**—In estimating the weight to be given to a statement referred to in subsection (3), the court shall have regard to all the circumstances from which an inference can reasonably be drawn as to the accuracy of the statement.

63.(1) **Conditions and restrictions**—In any order making provision for support of a dependant, the court may impose such conditions and restrictions as the court considers appropriate.

(2) **Contents of order**—Provision may be made out of income or capital or both and an order may provide for one or more of the following, as the court considers appropriate,

(a) an amount payable annually or otherwise whether for an indefinite or limited period or until the happening of a specified event;

(b) a lump sum to be paid or held in trust;

(c) any specified property to be transferred or assigned to or in trust for the benefit of the dependant, whether absolutely, for life or for a term of years;

(d) the possession or use of any specified property by the dependant for life or such period as the court considers appropriate;

(e) a lump sum payment to supplement or replace periodic payments;

(f) the securing of payment under an order by a charge on property or otherwise;

(g) the payment of a lump sum or of increased periodic payments to enable a dependant spouse or child to meet debts reasonably incurred for his or her own support prior to an application under this Part;

(h) that all or any of the money payable under the order be paid to an appropriate person or agency for the benefit of the dependant;

(i) the payment to an agency referred to in subsection 58(3) of any amount in reimbursement for an allowance or benefit granted in respect of the support of the dependant, including an amount in reimbursement for an allowance paid or benefit provided before the date of the order.

(3) **Idem**—Where a transfer or assignment of property is ordered, the court may,

(a) give all necessary directions for the execution of the transfer or assignment by the executor or administrator or such other person as the court may direct; or

(b) grant a vesting order.

(4) **Agreement of waiver**—An order under this section may be made despite any agreement or waiver to the contrary.

(5) **Notice to parties before order**—The court shall not make any order under this section until it is satisfied upon oath that all persons who are or may be interested in or affected by the order have been served with notice of the application as provided by the rules of court, and every such person is entitled to be present and to be heard in person or by counsel at the hearing.

(6) **Exception**—Despite subsection (5), where, in the opinion of the court,

(a) every reasonable effort has been made to serve those entitled to notice; or

(b) after every reasonable effort has been made, it is not possible to identify one or more of the persons entitled to notice,

the court may dispense with the requirement of notice in respect of any person who has not been served.

1. Prepare a draft memo of law.

    a. What are the questions being asked?

b. What are the legal issues that you have identified? (Hint: Look at the note on page 254.)

c. What are the sections in the statute that are relevant to the issues?

d. What are the facts that are relevant to the law?

e. Discuss the law as it relates to the facts in this case.

f.   What is your conclusion? What action can be taken for your client?

2. Prepare a formal memo of law.

II. Prepare a memo of law from the information and materials provided below.

Memo

To: You

From: Lawyer

Re: *Brown v. Litoff*

Date: December 23, Year Zero

As you know, this action for arrears of rent under a commercial lease has been dragging on for years, partly because of the client's unreasonable behaviour.

Mr. Brown came in to see me yesterday to instruct me to add a tort claim—an action for assault and false imprisonment—to the claim for arrears. He says he's been thinking about the last time he talked to the defendant, Litoff, in Year Minus Two, when he demanded that Litoff pay the rent. He says that Litoff threatened him with violence and prevented him from leaving a room. He says that since Litoff is making him go all the way to trial on this action, he wants to put some heat on Litoff.

See if you can find out whether we can amend or not.

Further information: The law of Ontario applies.

A. The pleadings in the *Brown v. Litoff* action:

Assault and false imprisonment were not specifically pleaded. One paragraph of the pleadings states:

8. On or about the 14th day of March, Year Minus Two, the plaintiff attended at the defendant's office to discuss with him the payment of outstanding rent. The plaintiff states that the defendant refused to discuss payment or settlement. The plaintiff further states that the defendant shook his fist at him and told him not to come asking for the outstanding rent again.

B. Discoveries in the *Brown v. Litoff* action:

Discoveries were held in Year Minus One. The following appears in the transcript of the discovery of the defendant:

197. Q. Did the plaintiff come to your office on March 14, Year Minus Two to ask you about paying the outstanding rent?
     A. Maybe. I think so.

198. Q. Can you tell me what happened at that meeting?
     A. I told him I had no money to pay the rent.

199. Q. Did the two of you argue?
     A. Yeah. He called me an S.O.B. and said he'd put me out of business.

200. Q. Did you say anything in reply?
     A. Yeah, I think I told him if he didn't leave me alone I'd give him a good punch in the nose. Or maybe I took a swing at him. I don't remember.

201. Q. Did you hit him?

    A. Nah, the pipsqueak. He took off as fast as he could.

202. Q. Did you try to prevent him from leaving?

    A. Why would I? I was glad to see the back of him.

C. Ontario *Rules of Civil Procedure*, R. 26.01

26.01 On motion at any stage of an action the court shall grant leave to amend a pleading on such terms as are just, unless prejudice would result that could not be compensated for by costs or an adjournment.

D. *Limitations Act, 2002*, S.O. 2002, c. 24, Sched. B, s. 4

4. **Basic limitation period**—Unless this Act provides otherwise, a proceeding shall not be commenced in respect of a claim after the second anniversary of the day on which the claim was discovered.

E. *Denton v. Jones et al. (No. 2)* (1976), 14 O.R. (2d) 382 (H.C.J.)

APPEAL from an order of the Senior Master refusing plaintiff's application to amend the statement of claim.

R.E. Anka, for defendant, R.W. Marshall.

J.S. McNeil, for plaintiff.

GRANGE, J.:—This is an appeal from the order of the Senior Master refusing the plaintiff's application to amend her statement of claim. The appeal has a sad history. When it originally came on before me a preliminary objection was taken that the order appealed from was a final order and the appeal therefore lay to the Divisional Court. I reserved judgment on the objection and heard the appeal on its merits. I then decided that the preliminary objection was well taken and adjourned the motion to the Divisional Court under Rule 225(3) [rep. and sub. O. Reg. 115/72, s. 5].

Unfortunately at the time of making the latter order I did not appreciate that the writ in the action had been issued prior to April 17, 1972, when the *Judicature Amendment Act, 1970 (No. 4)*, 1970 (Ont.), c. 97, which gave the Divisional Court jurisdiction, was proclaimed. Accordingly, *A.J. Freiman Ltd. v. M.W. Kosub Ltd. et al.*, [1973] 2 O.R. 608, applied and this appeal lay to a Judge in Chambers regardless of whether the order was final or interlocutory. It has therefore been referred back to me for disposition.

The action is one for dental malpractice and in the claim as originally delivered the plaintiff alleged negligence on the part of the defendant Marshall in that he was instructed to extract certain upper teeth and had, in fact, extracted not only those upper teeth but all of the lower teeth as well.

Upon the publication of *Schweizer v. Central Hospital et al.* (1974), 6 O.R. (2d) 606, 53 D.L.R. (3d) 494, the plaintiff brought application to amend the statement of claim to allege trespass to the person based upon the same facts. The application came on before the Senior Master in December, 1975, and was dismissed. From that decision this appeal, after its many vicissitudes comes on for determination.

The main reason advanced in opposition to the amendment is, of course, that the dental operation took place on October 7, 1969, and that in the interval the limitation period, be it for dental malpractice (six months under the *Dentistry Act*, R.S.O. 1970, c. 108, s. 28, or one year under the *Health Disciplines Act*, 1974 (Ont.), c. 47, s. 17), for assault (four years under the *Limitations Act*, R.S.O. 1970, c. 246, s. 45(1)(j)), or upon the case (six years, *Limitations Act*, s. 45(1)(g)), had expired.

The defendant relies upon the principle stemming from the dicta of Lord Esher, M.R., in *Weldon v. Neal* (1887), 19 Q.B.D. 394 at p. 395, as follows:

> We must act on the settled rule of practice, which is that amendments are not admissible when they prejudice the right of the opposite party as existing at the date of such amendments. If an amendment were allowed setting up a cause of action, which, if the writ were issued in respect thereof at the date of the amendment, would be barred by the Statute of Limitations, it would be allowing the plaintiff to take advantage of her former writ to defeat the statute and taking away an existing right from the defendant, a proceeding which, as a general rule, would be, in my opinion, improper and unjust. Under very peculiar circumstances the Court might perhaps have power to allow such an amendment, but certainly as a general rule it will not do so.

This principle was acknowledged in *Radigan v. Canadian Indemnity Co. et al.*, [1953] O.W.N. 788, [1953] 3 D.L.R. 653, [1951-55] I.L.R. 488; where the Court of Appeal held it inapplicable to a situation where the insured sought to add an alternative claim under the same policy and was applied in *Pitt v. Bank of Nova Scotia et al.*, [1956] O.W.N. 872, where the Senior Master refused an amendment to claim recovery in nuisance against a municipality where the original claim was in negligence. Many other instances are given in Professor Garry Watson's learned discussion on the matter to be found in "Amendment of Proceedings After Limitation Periods." 53 *Can. Bar Rev.* 237 (1975), particularly at pp. 242-3.

I am not sure that the mere pleading of an alternative ground for relief arising out of the same facts constitutes the raising of a new cause of action—see *Canadian Industries Ltd. v. Canadian National R. Co.*, [1940] O.W.N. 452, [1940] 4 D.L.R. 629, 52 C.R.T.C. 31 [affirmed [1941] S.C.R. 591, [1941] 4 D.L.R. 561, 53 C.R.T.C. 162], where an amendment in a contract action was permitted to claim relief in negligence based upon the same facts upon the ground that such new claim did not create a new cause of action, but merely an alternative claim with respect to the same cause. We must always bear in mind the distinction between "forms of action" and "causes of action." ...

But even if the amendment here asked does constitute a new cause of action, I consider that there are circumstances justifying a departure from the general rule. In *Basarsky v. Quinlan et al.*, [1972] S.C.R. 380,

24 D.L.R. (3d) 720, [1972] 1 W.W.R. 303, Hall, J., equated the word "peculiar" in Lord Esher, M.R.'s exception with "special" in current usage and found that circumstances existed to justify an amendment, after the expiration of the limitation period, setting up a claim under the *Fatal Accidents Act* of Alberta where the original claim had been under the *Trustee Act* of that province. Among those circumstances were many that apply equally here. There as here, all the facts upon which the later claim could be based were already pleaded. There as here, there was no need to reopen discoveries and most important there as here, there was no possibility of prejudice to the defendants other than the inevitable prejudice of what might turn out to be the successful plea. To me this amendment comes within the spirit and intent of our Rules, particularly Rule 185 which is as follows:

> 185. A proceeding shall not be defeated by any formal objection, but all necessary amendments shall be made, upon proper terms as to costs and otherwise, to secure the advancement of justice, the determining of the real matter in dispute, and the giving of judgment according to the very right and justice of the case.

Moreover, the amendment seems to me to be precisely in line with the decision of Reid, J., in *Royal v. Municipality of Metropolitan Toronto et al.* (1975), 9 O.R. (2d) 522, which is almost the converse of the case at bar. There an amendment to include a claim for negligence was permitted after the limitation period had expired when the original claim was one for assault.

I would therefore allow the appeal and permit the amendment sought. Costs of the appeal should be in the cause.

Appeal allowed.

1. Prepare a draft memo of law.

   a. What are the questions being asked?

b. What are the legal issues that you have identified?

c. i.   What are the sections in the statute that are relevant to the issues?

    ii. What are the passages in the case law that are relevant to the issues?

    d. What are the facts that are relevant to the law?

e.   Discuss the law as it relates to the facts in this case.

f.   What is your conclusion? What action can be taken for your client?

2. Prepare a formal memo of law.

Standard Abbreviations for Commonly Used Report Series and Statutes

A.C. . . . . Law Reports, Appeal Cases (England)

A.C.W.S. . . . . All Canada Weekly Summaries

A.R. . . . . Alberta Reports

Admin. L.R. . . . . Administrative Law Reports

All E.R. . . . . All England Reports

Alta. L.R. . . . . Alberta Law Reports

App. Cas. . . . . Law Reports, Appeal Cases (England)

B.C.L.R. . . . . British Columbia Law Reports

B.L.R. . . . . Business Law Reports

C.B.R. . . . . Canadian Bankruptcy Reports

C.B.R. (N.S.) . . . . Canadian Bankruptcy Reports (New Series)

C.C.C. . . . . Canadian Criminal Cases

C.C.E.L. . . . . Canadian Cases on Employment Law

C.C.L.I. . . . . Canadian Cases on the Law of Insurance

C.C.L.T. . . . . Canadian Cases on the Law of Torts

C.C.S.M. . . . . Continuing Consolidation of the Statutes of Manitoba

C.E.D. (Ont. 3rd) . . . . . . Canadian Encyclopedic Digest (Ontario Third Edition)

C.E.L.R. . . . . Canadian Environmental Law Reports

C.L.R. . . . . Construction Law Reports

C.P.R. . . . . Canadian Patent Reporter

C.P.R. (N.S.) . . . . Canadian Patent Reporter (New Series)

C.R. . . . . Criminal Reports

C.R.R. . . . . Canadian Rights Reporter

C.T.C. . . . . Canada Tax Cases

C.T.R. . . . . Canada Tax Reports

Can. Abr. (2d) . . . . Canadian Abridgment (Second Edition)

D.L.R. . . . . Dominion Law Reports

E.R. . . . . English Reports

E.T.R. . . . . Estates and Trust Reports

F.T.R. . . . . Federal Trial Reports

Imm. L.R. . . . . Immigration Law Reporter

K.B. . . . . Law Reports, King's Bench (England)

L.A.C. (3d) . . . . Labour Arbitration Cases (Third Series)

L.R. . . . . Law Reports (England)

L.R. Ch. . . . . Law Reports Chancery Cases (England)

L.R.C.P. . . . . Law Reports Common Pleas (England)

L.R. Eq. . . . . Law Reports Equity (England)

L.R. Ex. . . . . Law Reports Exchequer (England)

L.R.H.L. . . . . Law Reports House of Lords (England)

L.T.R. . . . . Law Times Reports (England)

M.P.L.R. . . . . Municipal and Planning Law Reports

M.V.R. . . . . Motor Vehicle Reports

Man. L.R. . . . . Manitoba Law Reports

Man. R.	Manitoba Reports
N.B.R.	New Brunswick Reports
N.R.	National Reporter
N.S.R.	Nova Scotia Reports
Nfld. & P.E.I.R.	Newfoundland and Prince Edward Island Reports
O.A.C.	Ontario Appeal Cases
O.M.B.R.	Ontario Municipal Board Reports
O.R.	Ontario Reports
O.W.N.	Ontario Weekly Notes
Q.A.C.	Quebec Appeal Cases
R.F.L.	Reports of Family Law
R.P.R.	Real Property Reports
R.S.A.	Revised Statutes of Alberta
R.S.B.C.	Revised Statutes of British Columbia
R.S.C.	Revised Statutes of Canada
R.S.M.	Revised Statutes of Manitoba
R.S.N.	Revised Statutes of Newfoundland
R.S.N.B.	Revised Statutes of New Brunswick
R.S.N.W.T.	Revised Statutes of Northwest Territories
R.S.O.	Revised Statutes of Ontario
R.S.P.E.I.	Revised Statutes of Prince Edward Island
R.S.Q.	Revised Statutes of Quebec
R.S.S.	Revised Statutes of Saskatchewan
R.S.Y.T.	Revised Statutes of Yukon Territory
S.A.	Statutes of Alberta
S.C.R.	Supreme Court Reports
S.B.C.	Statutes of British Columbia
S.C.	Statutes of Canada
S.M.	Statutes of Manitoba
S.N.	Statutes of Newfoundland
S.N.B.	Statutes of New Brunswick
S.N.W.T.	Statutes of Northwest Territories
S.O.	Statutes of Ontario

S.P.E.I. . . . . Statutes of Prince Edward Island

S.Q. . . . . Statutes of Quebec

S.S. . . . . Statutes of Saskatchewan

S.Y.T. . . . . Statutes of Yukon Territory

Sask. L.R. . . . . Saskatchewan Law Reports

T.L.R. . . . . Times Law Reports (England)

U.C.C.P. . . . . Upper Canada Common Pleas Reports

U.C.Q.B. . . . . Upper Canada Queen's Bench Reports

W.C.B. . . . . Weekly Criminal Bulletin

W.D.C.P. . . . . Weekly Digest of Civil Procedure

W.L.R. . . . . Weekly Law Reports (England)

W.W.R. . . . . Western Weekly Reports

W.W.R. (N.S.) . . . . Western Weekly Reports (New Series)

Y.R. . . . . Yukon Reports

For abbreviations not found here, consult the front pages of any volume of *Canadian Case Citations* or *Canadian Statute Citations*.

Glossary

advanced query   function accessible through the search menu on the toolbar that allows you to search the full database using a Boolean search

appeal history   history of a case—for example, whether the case has been confirmed or overturned on appeal and the name of the highest court that reviewed the decision

bills   proposed statutes that are before Parliament or a provincial legislature but have not yet been passed

binding decision   existing decision that a judge must follow if the facts in that case and in the case before the court are sufficiently similar

binding law   law that must be followed by a court

Boolean search   method by which the computer hunts through thousands of documents to locate requested combinations of words or phrases; in a keyword search, used when you don't want to restrict your search by case name, court, judge, or counsel

case citation query template   allows you to search by case name or citation

case digest   summary of how a legal issue was decided in a particular case

concordance   a tool for finding corresponding sections in either an earlier or a later version of a statute

Contents Key   alphabetical list of all the subject titles in the CED

disposition   judge's orders set out at the end of a case

dissent   different decision by a minority of appeal judges

framework legislation   legislation for which the details are worked out in the regulations

general index   one of two finding tools to locate digested cases

headnote   editor's explanation of the case before the body

housekeeping provisions   sections that cover the details of statutes, such as the date of coming into force

index   alphabetical, detailed list of names, places, and subjects discussed in a source and the pages on which each entry appears

Index Key   separate binder combining the individual indexes from all titles and containing an alphabetical list of keywords, together with extensive cross-references within and among subject titles

issues   specific problems that the judge must solve to reach a decision

key and research guide   one of two finding tools to locate digested cases that uses the key classification system

key classification system   multi-level classification system

keyword and field query template   allows you to limit your keyword search to specific jurisdictions, specific years, and/or specific subject areas and/or classification phrases

keywords   words by which researchers search computerized sources for information stored randomly in databases

law of evidence   sets out the manner in which facts are proved in a trial or a proceeding

legislative history   given at the end of each provision in a statute

lines of authority   statement of existing law found in statutes, cases, and texts

long title   full, unabbreviated title of a statute

master   judge-like officer who decides certain procedural matters in the superior courts of some provinces

natural language search   allows you to search for information by asking your question using plain language

obiter dicta   Latin for "words by the way"

persuasive law   law that a court is not required to follow, but may follow if it wishes (usually case law)

preamble   part of a statute that outlines its purpose and main principles

primary sources   the actual statutes, regulations, and case decisions that create the law

private law   governs the relationship between persons, and includes such areas as contracts, family law, property law, real estate, torts, and wills and estates

procedural law sets out the procedure that a party must follow to enforce his or her rights in a court proceeding or to defend a proceeding

provision section or subsection

public law governs the relationship between persons (individuals and corporations) and the state, and includes such areas of law as municipal law, immigration and refugee law, environmental law, constitutional law, criminal law, and tax law

purpose the nature of the proceedings

query box small box located on the toolbar that works like the advanced query, but with less space in which to craft your query and without access to the word wheel

query templates accessible through the search menu on the toolbar; allow you to narrow your search to specific parts of the database

ratio decidendi Latin for "reasons for deciding"—the pre-exising principle of law on which the judge based the decision on an issue applied to the facts of the particular case

reasons for decision term for a case before it is included in a report series or legal database

regulations rules made under the authority of a statute

reported case judge's decision and reasons about a case published in a law report series

root expanders in a keyword search, used for both template and Boolean searching, to instruct Quicklaw to search for different endings or spellings of words

Rules and Regulations Key alphabetical list of the rules of court and regulations referred to in the CED's subject titles

search engine website with a computer program that searches a database of Web documents or websites to match supplied keywords

search operators keywords and Boolean connectors and expanders

secondary sources sources that summarize, discuss, or explain primary sources, and include legal encyclopedias, digests of cases, indexes to statutes, textbooks, and articles

short title abbreviated title of a statute

standard search allows you to search for information using keywords and a connector that is selected from the drop-down menu

stare decisis Latin for "to stand by those things that have been decided"

statute law created by Parliament or a provincial legislature

Statutes Key alphabetical list of all current federal and provincial statutes referred to in the various subject titles in the CED

statutory instrument　general term that includes federal regulations

style of cause　names of the parties in an action

subject index　also called a subject tree, a website that categorizes or indexes Web documents or websites using subject clssifications

substantive law　defines legal rights and obligations; legal rights may be enforced by way of legal proceedings, to which substantive law sets out the defences

substitution symbol　symbol used in a computerized search that replaces a single letter to find keywords spelled in more than one way

table of contents　chronological listing of chapters or article titles in a source together with the page numbers where each chapter or article starts

template search　in a keyword search, used when you have some information about a case you are looking for—for example, case name, court, judge, or counsel

terms and connectors search　not as limiting as the standard search template; allows you to construct a Boolean search using keywords and your own Boolean connectors and expanders

theory of the case　the cause of action or the defence, and the evidence that supports that cause of action or defence—also known as "the theory"

truncation symbol　symbol used in a computerized search to find all possible endings of a root word

unreported case　case not published in a law report series

user's guide　information in a research source about how to use that source

Index